A SPECIAL

2 BOOKS-IN-ONE SELECTION

for the Members of

THE LADIES' HOME JOURNAL
COOK BOOK CLUB

641 Lexington Ave., New York, N.Y. 10022

THE ART OF SCANDINAVIAN COOKING
AND
THE ART OF DUTCH COOKING
or HOW THE DUTCH TREAT

EACH VOLUME HAS ITS OWN SET OF PAGE NUMBERS AS IN THE ORIGINAL VOLUMES.

NIKA STANDEN HAZELTON

THE ART OF Scandinavian Cooking

Second Printing, 1965

The Macmillan Company, New York
Collier-Macmillan Canada, Ltd., Toronto, Ontario

Library of Congress catalog number: 65-12150

Printed in the United States of America

This Edition Published by
The Ladies' Home Journal Cook Book Club
by Arrangement with
The MacMillan Company, New York
Collier MacMillan Limited, London

Acknowledgments and Thanks

I would like to express my heartfelt thanks to all the people here and in Scandinavia who made this book possible by introducing me to new foods, by giving me old and new recipes, by researching food lore, by cooking dishes that I could not have sampled otherwise, and by helping me in more ways than I can mention.

Among the people I am especially grateful to are Mr. E. Storrusten, Mr. P. Prag, Mrs. M. Bernard and Mr. R. Norgrenn of the Norway Travel Association in New York and Oslo; Mr. Kai Johannsen, Head of the Press and Information Department of the Danish Ministry for Foreign Affairs, Mr. A. Christiansen, Counselor of Embassy, Mr. J. Laursen of the Danish Information Office in New York, Mr. J. Ranten of Copenhagen and Mrs. R. Holmes of the Federation of Danish Dairy Associations; Mr. B. Nordholm of the Swedish Information Office in New York, Mr. M. Lindahl of the *Swedish-American Monthly* as well as Mr. I. Ingvarsson of the Embassy of Iceland and the Staff of the Finnish Consulate in New York.

My very special thanks for their great help go to the Countess Madeleine Hamilton of Malmö, Mr. P. Debry of Corn Products Inc., Mr. G. Wennergren, Mr. L. Hegdahl and Mr. and Mrs. P. Innset, all of Trondheim, Mr. and Mrs. G. Björnson of Tromsö, and to Mr. and Mrs. C. Pedersen of Copenhagen and Mr. Derek Blix of Oslo. Both Mr. Pedersen and Mr. Blix manage Pan-American World Airways in Copenhagen and Oslo, and they both helped me far beyond the call of duty to go to distant and difficult places in pursuit of recipes. I couldn't have done it without their assistance.

Contents

Introduction

In the minds of most Americans, the Scandinavians, that is, the Danes, Norwegians, Swedes, Finns and Icelanders, are one great big uniform group with few, if any, differences in their ways of living and eating. Compared to other European groups, such as the Latin nations, the Scandinavians surely have an enormous amount in common. Yet they are very different from each other—different enough so that even a tourist can see that being in Denmark is very different from being in Sweden.

The same goes for their foods. Though similar dishes (under the same or other names) are found again and again in the Scandinavian countries because of their geographical, racial and social bonds, each of the five countries has very typical dishes of its own. The origins of these dishes are lost in history. Many of them, such as the porridges and preserved fish and meats, may no longer be common fare, but they have left their imprint on the country's taste.

Scandinavian cooking is quite different from American cooking. It is richer, because the cold climate of the North demands that more fats be eaten. But all the opulent sauces and clouds of whipped cream do not seem to affect the Scandinavian figure much; this does seem most unfair to the visitor limited to the low-calorie lettuce leaf. Scandinavian cooking is basically meat and potato cooking, which makes it irresistible to most American men. The desserts are lovely, another point in favor from the male point of view, for in every man there lurks a dessert lover craving to be satisfied.

This book is, of necessity, not an all-inclusive collection of Scandinavian recipes. From the wealth of existing recipes I have made a choice of those that I and my friends, both here and in Scandinavia, have thought of as being representative of the country of origin, as having special appeal to Americans, and as introducing that delightful element of discovery that makes cooking fun. Thus this book is an introduction and a guide to a very good way of eating for people inclined to believe that Scandinavian food is more than smorgasbord and Swedish meatballs.

To those of my readers who might look for a favorite recipe and not find it, I offer my apologies, hopeful of their understanding of the purpose of this book.

Since food has to be related to daily living, I have tried to tell as much about that as I could in a cookbook. For the readers who want more information about Denmark, Norway, Sweden, Finland and Iceland, I suggest that they contact the Tourist Offices of these countries, where they will find the staff always most helpful.

All the recipes in this book have been tested with standard kitchen equipment; I have deliberately left out recipes that call for special pots and pans which are hard to get. I have also omitted recipes too alien to our tastes, such as the many ways of serving herring and other fish, of making blood and other sausages, fruit soups and gruels, and of baking breads that we are more likely to buy rather than make ourselves. However, if any reader is looking for such a specialty recipe, he should contact me in care of the publishers of this book, and I will do my best to oblige.

The recipes in this book are authentic; that is, they are presented as they are prepared in the countries of their origin. They are not the American adaptations of foreign dishes, because I wanted to present the real thing to my readers. Needless to say, I have gathered these recipes and checked their authenticity to the best of my knowledge on trips to the Scandinavian countries undertaken for this purpose.

All the measurements in the recipes are even, and unless otherwise specified, they make 4 to 6 servings. All the recipes were tested by me, with the help of Helen Feingold, a home economist, to whom I here express my thanks for her invaluable help.

I hope that Scandinavian food will give as much pleasure to

my readers as it has given to me and my friends. I also hope that it will acquaint Americans with the ways of people who rank first in the world of kindness, honesty, cleanliness, and good food.

NIKA STANDEN HAZELTON

How Is Scandinavia Different from America?

The four Scandinavian countries—Denmark, Norway, Sweden and Finland—are like a family, where the members share a basic style of living, but do things their own way. More of the differences later; what I would like to do here is to give a bird's-eye view of the things that strike the American tourist most when he first comes to Scandinavia.

First comes the Scandinavians' love for appetizer and delicatessen foods. The groaning table, heaped with every kind of goodie, is called *Smørrebrød,* or butter and bread, in Denmark; *kold bord* in Norway; and *smörgåsbord,* or sandwich table, in Sweden. The Finnish name is *voileipäpöytä,* or sandwich table, which sounds so different from the other words because Finnish belongs to a completely different family of languages, whereas Danish, Norwegian and Swedish are similar enough so that if you know one, you can understand the others. The Scandinavians never seem to tire of these appetizers. They eat plain and simple ones at home and fancy ones when they eat out, but appetizers are a staple part of the diet.

The next thing that surprises the visitor is the care with which the Scandinavians cook fish. They buy fish alive, if at all possible, and choose it as carefully as an American woman would choose a mink coat. The results are superb: the fish you eat is firm, delicate and not at all "fishy." And you don't tire of eating it every day. Unless you've been in Scandinavia, you'll never know that plain boiled cod or pike can be the best of all fish.

The next surprise is the relative unimportance of vegetables, although this is changing, thanks to modern transportation and food processing. The Scandinavians are potato people, and they eat potatoes at every meal, sometimes twice. (Naturally, these of necessity are generalizations and I bow my head to escape the brickbats.) Boiled potatoes, or rather potatoes boiled and steamed dry, are the rule. Very good they are, too, because the Scandinavians raise potatoes as we raise other vegetables, in many varieties. So are the sugar-browned potatoes which are the usual alternative to boiled potatoes. Sometimes, both are served, the first with the fish, the second with the meat. And sometimes you will even see potato chips placed alongside the browned potatoes. Occasionally, mashed potatoes will be eaten, but it is not often. The Scandinavians love their potatoes boiled, and who is to blame them if they aren't interested in other ways of cooking them?

Equally surprising to the visiting American is the lavish use Scandinavians make of sauces, both hot and cold. Most of them are excellent; all of them are devastatingly rich, since they are thickened with eggs and sweet or sour cream, rather than with much flour. Melted butter is much used as a sauce for boiled fish. Mayonnaise seasoned with mustards, anchovies, or capers and whipped sweet or sour cream flavored with horseradish are used for the appetizer salads. The great French sauces, such as Hollandaise and béarnaise, are favorites. Compound (that is, flavored) butters are served for sandwiches, fish and meats. Each dish comes with its own sauce in Scandinavia; if it didn't, it would probably be considered undressed. Thus, at one good meal, you may eat some kind of mayonnaise with your appetizers, melted butter with your fish, cream sauce with your meat, and whipped cream with your dessert. I hasten to say, however, that Scandinavians at home eat a very simple everyday diet, with, most likely, either one fish dish or meat dish and perhaps a dessert. It's the visitor eating in the superb Scandinavian restaurants who meets up with so many sauces at one meal. However, the Scandinavians love sauces, and cream sauces (with cream, and I mean the good rich and untrifled-with cream of the North) and gravies reign supreme.

As a next surprise to the American visitor comes the casual way of dealing with vegetables and salads, and their scarcity, compared to American plenty. The salads especially are treated like colorful accessories for the cold table. A plain tossed green salad is rare; most of the salads are wonderful combinations of different ingredients, bound with some kind of mayonnaise or cold cream sauce. The exceptions are pickled cucumbers and pickled beets, the kings of the daily table. There are historical and geographical reasons for this paucity of vegetables, which is changing, thanks to the modern canning and freezing industries.

As for Scandinavian desserts, they are irresistible and utter ruin for the figure-conscious visitor. These noble creations go from the fresh fruit jellies to soufflés, large tiered cream cakes, almond paste cakes, chocolate rolls, napoleons, jam cakes, cakes filled with vanilla cream, meringue tortes filled with jam, all decorated with baroque swirls of the most delicious whipped cream. Almonds in every shape—extract, paste, whole, sliced, chopped—and whipped cream are the leitmotivs of Scandinavian desserts. Then there are the wonderful berries of the far North, unmatched in flavor, especially the arctic strawberries and the cloudberries, which look like big yellow blackberries—all served with whipped cream, what else?

Apart from being prepared to taste good, there are sound dietary reasons for the richness of Scandinavian food. The fat is warming in a climate that is cold, or at least cool, the greater part of the year. We must also remember that before the use of modern heating people had to struggle much more on their own to keep warm; fat in the diet was essential for this. The proof of this is that, rich as the Scandinavian food may be, the Scandinavians are not nearly as portly, if they are portly at all, as Americans would be, living on the same kind of diet in America. But to the visitor, it does not seem fair that all this delicious food agrees so well with the natives.

Also very different from what one finds in America are the Scandinavian restaurants, the Scandinavian ways of drinking, and Scandinavian home entertaining. More about this later.

Scandinavia is the place to see how modern transportation and modern food processing have revolutionized daily life. Though a number of the things that we now take for granted in America, such as a supply of vegetables and fruits unlimited the year around, are still a novelty there, many foods are packaged in far more advanced ways than in the United States. Mayonnaise and mustard, for example, are packaged in tubes, to be squeezed out like toothpaste, and the modern supermarkets of these Northern lands, some far above the Arctic Circle, compare favorably with ours both as to supplies and convenience.

All this has happened within our lifetime. The isolation that prevailed in the not very distant past is almost impossible for a modern American to imagine. The immense forests of Sweden, the wilderness of lakes in Finland, the high mountain ranges of Norway, the remoteness of Iceland before the air age, coupled with a long snowbound winter, kept the people of the North away from each other and from the outside world. Even though in all of Scandinavia road construction is progressing at a great rate, in Norway, for instance, the coastal waterways are still the nation's main highways, because, thanks to the warm waters of the Gulf Stream which winds its way around those Northern parts, they are free of ice all year round.

The isolation, the northern latitudes, and the short growing season, forced the people to make do with what they had. The staples of life were the grains, such as wheat, barley, oats and much rye, made into the many plain and sweet breads and pancakes of Scandinavia, and, in the old days, into porridges and gruels. Other staples were the fish and seafood, especially plentiful in the sea, lakes and streams, and meat, such as pork, lamb, mutton and beef. But meat was never extravagantly used as in England and in the United States; to this day, Scandinavian meat cookery is thrifty, making much of stretching dishes such as meatballs, and utilizing every scrap of the animal in sausages, blood puddings, heart stews and liver dishes. The vegetables included first and foremost potatoes, beets, cucumbers, cabbage, and the various roots which kept through the winter, as well as the seasonal peas, beans and lettuces, and mushrooms, found wild in the greatest variety and profusion.

Game and wild birds are still a part of the diet of Scandinavia; in some parts, such as in the forests of Sweden and Finland, they abound. As for fruit, there are the unmatched berries of the North, blueberries, cranberries, currants, strawberries, raspberries, and the yellow arctic cloudberries which are the best of all; there are tree fruits such as apples, pears, cherries and plums, and, in some of the more sheltered parts of the region, even tree-ripened peaches and apricots.

The widespread use of dairy products also harks back to the past; cheese still ranks very high in the diet. The fats of Scandinavia are butter, cream, salt pork, and much margarine. In Norway, the liver of the national fish, the cod, is much prized.

But if you had to describe the basic and general diet of Scandinavia in a few words, these would be bread, fish, meat and potatoes, cooked in a substantial manner. In the old days, and that is not so very long ago, foods were preserved at home in the oldest way known to man—drying—and to this day, many of the native dishes have an aura and feeling of history about them. As we see on the smorgasbord, the taste for pickled and cured foods persists, especially for fish, particularly for the ubiquitous herring, although today the job of preparing these foods has mainly been taken over by the professional canner.

Also, the commercial baker is taking over the making of the many wonderful breads, and even cakes and cookies. The knäckebröd, the hardtack of Sweden and Finland, used to be baked in great flat rings, to be strung over poles for keeping, because the old-time baking ovens on the farms were not placed inside the house, but outside, and were snowed under during the long winter. The housewife had to bake for the months ahead, and store her bread so that it would dry out and thus keep. Now, these breads come from the store, and very good they are too. But vestiges of the great old baking days, when, as we read in the old books, baking was one of the housewife's main occupations, are found in the infinite variety of baked foods of all kinds that are still made at home for festive occasions, such as Christmas. "I baked you a little something," a Danish woman will tell you when you come to see her, but more and more she and her Scandinavian sisters might say, "I went and bought you a little something."

The old-time diet used to be starchy in the extreme, and even the modern Scandinavian diet is very starchy, compared to American standards. Had it not been for the fish, consumed with the livers, the milk products and, above all, for the potatoes, eaten with every meal, there would have been serious vitamin deficiencies. We, in our American economy of abundance and fear of fattening foods, do not realize the lifesaving quality of the potato; as formerly in starving Ireland, their vitamin content saved the race in Scandinavia.

Isolation and the limited number of foods produced the conservative food habits of Scandinavia, just as economic and historical factors produce the food habits of any country. Even in the upper classes the conservatism was extreme. A friend of mine, the Countess Madeleine Hamilton, who grew up in the castles of Southern Sweden, remembers the fixed order of the weekly menu of her childhood, as unmovable as the planets. On Sunday there would be a roast, to be finished at Monday lunch as *Pytt i panna,* a hash served with pickled beets, and at supper. On Tuesdays and Fridays the fisherman would come around with his wagon filled with fresh herring, cod, halibut and other fish. On Thursday, a big food day, the meal would be the thick Swedish yellow pea soup that is still eaten throughout Sweden on that day, sometimes accompanied by Swedish *Punsch.* Once a week there would be lamb with dill sauce, or pork with turnips.

This conservatism still lingers in the food habits of the modern Scandinavians. To us, it is incomprehensible that potatoes, which are eaten at almost every meal, are almost always boiled or at best browned, to mention the most popular way after boiling, and seldom prepared in the many other possible ways. The past also explains the importance of traditional foods on special days, especially in Sweden.

The daily diet of the majority of the Scandinavian people is still very monotonous, compared to the ordinary American diet. It is also on the bland side, and perhaps the combination of monotony and blandness explains the delight in the piquant foods of the smorgasbord, and the richness and extravagance of food for entertainment and in restaurants. Where we, after a party, will ask "Did you have a good time?", the Scandinavians, especially the Danes, will say instead, "What have you eaten?"

Yet the established eating habits are disappearing, thanks to modern communications and modern food processing. The pioneer work of the press, especially in the magazines, which the Scandinavians devour, the excellent home economics schools for teachers, the classes in home economics taught in schools to boys as well as girls, are working a profound change in Scandinavia's food habits. And when the Scandinavians modernize their ways, they make our American ones look old-fashioned. Their practical, imaginative and beautiful buildings (and not luxury buildings) to house people at a low cost hit the American visitor between the eyes. The architecture of Helsinki, the home furnishings of Denmark, the schools and churches of Norway, the outstanding apartment houses of Sweden, are taken for granted by the people of these countries, and are miles ahead of what we know at home.

Today, we in America are apt to look at commercially canned foods with a blasé air. Yet the excellent and inexpensive products of modern canning have made a world of difference to the diet of the North. For instance, we Americans consider canned peaches as the most common of foods. In Scandinavia few peaches will grow because of the cold; until they could be canned and marketed within the reach of everybody, peaches were a rarity. They still are a delight, as are apricots and pineapple, and are featured in many desserts of the luxury restaurants. Whereas in the past the only fruits available were the delicious but seasonal berries, apples, pears, plums, and the dried fruits, especially prunes (hence the prevalence of prunes in so much of Scandinavian cooking), now modern canning has literally brought a world of wonderful new foods to Scandinavia. The same goes for vegetables; many, such as broccoli, had never been heard of before modern processing.

If we are to judge by American food trends, frozen foods will change Scandinavian eating habits as much as canned foods have —perhaps even more radically. Scandinavia is almost universally electrified, and this, combined with the acceptance of the co-operative system, has made communal freezing lockers commonplace. It was not hard for frozen foods to gain universal acceptance, both for processing and home consumption. In Sweden the remarkable genius of the Findus organization has made Sweden the model for the production of frozen foods in all of

Europe. This achievement was helped by the fact that Southern Sweden, with a climate similar to our Northwest, produces some outstanding peas, spinach, and other vegetables. The coast of Norway is dotted with hundreds of fish-freezing plants, many of which produce the frozen fish that we pick up in our own supermarkets. In Denmark extremely good trout is frozen—some of it reaches America. Everywhere there is much experimenting with new frozen products and supermodern, locally made machinery.

As for the wonders of modern transportation, they are never so apparent as when you see salad from Italy and artichokes from France in wintry Copenhagen, or Israeli bananas, grapes, and oranges and American apples near the North Cape of Norway. These are no longer luxuries; yet during the Northern Swedish childhood of Bittan Valberg (a beautiful blonde who is also a great artist in rug designing) Santa Claus presented the children, to their delight, with such then rare treats as oranges and almonds.

The old is going and the new coming in. Today it is difficult for a visitor to find the old-fashioned traditional Scandinavian foods, such as the porridges, unless a friend will prepare them. During the tourist season such foods will be featured by a few restaurants such as the Frascati Restaurant in Oslo and the restaurants attached to the great open-air museums. The tourist would do well to ask for them and taste them, if only in the spirit of seeking historical information. Some of them, such as the air-dried mutton of Norway, are delicacies of the first order.

The new is coming in, but it has not yet destroyed the pleasure in the first fresh foods of the season. The first rhubarb, the first berries, the first peas and lettuce of the season, are greeted by Scandinavians with a pleasure lost to us Americans who take fresh all-year-round foods for granted. This same pleasure is echoed in the frequent description of foods as "pure" and "fresh-tasting," no doubt an unconscious harking back to centuries of preserved foods, when fresh foods were as longed for as the spring sun after the long dark winter.

How the Scandinavians Live

The American visitor to Scandinavia who stays long enough and gets to know the people of these countries cannot help being struck with the contrast between home and restaurant eating, (see page 17) and with the way the Scandinavians entertain guests.

Home eating, when there are no visitors (and visitors are cooked and baked for with a bang) is very simple compared to our American home eating. That is, generally speaking; and here, I cannot help speaking in general. In Denmark and Norway lunch is an open sandwich or two—not one of the luscious concoctions of the restaurants, but bread covered with a little herring or other fish, or with a meat leftover, or with a bit of cheese. In Sweden lunch is more like an American one, with an omelet or a hot course. In Finland lunch, though often a hot meal, is very simple and might be just pork gravy and boiled potatoes. Dinner, too, is far simpler for the ordinary citizen than in America: a dish of fish and potatoes, or some kind of minced meat and potatoes, or a thick soup. Several vegetables, a salad, relishes and dessert at one meal are by no means taken for granted as they are in America.

The farmers, too, live very simply compared to our American farmers. A Danish farmer—and Danish farmers enjoy a very high standard of living—will eat a simple breakfast of porridge, with some cheese, or an egg, and coffee. His dinner will be a substantial meat or fish dish with boiled potatoes, or a thick soup, and the third meal of the day—taken either at noon or at night, depending on the circumstances—will be open-faced sandwiches with cold cuts and pickled fish. Coffee is the universal drink, and there might be a snack of coffee with cake or cookies, but there are none of the accoutrements of the American farm table, such as pancakes, hot breads, fried potatoes and bacon or ham and eggs at breakfast, with jams and fruits and the groaning table of dinner and supper. Yet the Danish farmer works very hard, and

I may say, is as advanced, and sometimes even more advanced, in the methods of scientific farming as his American counterpart.

But when it comes to entertaining the Scandinavians go all out. Hospitality is one of the supreme Scandinavian virtues, but it is not as casually extended as it is in the United States, where you are asked to drop in for a cup of coffee or to take potluck. Neither is it extended as here at home, as a gesture of noncommitting, easy-come, easy-go friendship. Generally speaking, the Scandinavians have to like you before they invite you to their homes. Fortunately, they usually like Americans and then they can't do enough for you.

Hospitality, in Scandinavia, means food, and plenty of it. Guests must eat, even if it is only coffee, cake and cookies. And preferably, these must be home-baked, in several varieties. Therefore, unless the hostess is a provident one and keeps such goodies at hand, guests come only when invited, so that the hostess has had enough time to prepare the food that she expects to serve and that her guests expect her to serve. This makes for gracious and face-saving entertaining, but not for casual social life. I may say, however, that the approach to hospitality is more casual in Norway, and much more like our own, than it is in Denmark and Sweden.

Compared to Americans, the Scandinavians care a great deal about what others think of them, and our American insouciance and "so-what" attitudes sincerely pain them. Their best face is turned towards the world; it is the living room and not the bedroom that is really fixed up, and the luxury of bathroom and closet furnishings, for instance, which here can be gratified in an American dime store, is there rather a prerogative of the sophisticated. The Scandinavian hostess greatly cares to put out a real spread for a guest, and she feels genuinely mortified when she thinks she has not done enough. No American visitor can tell her, unless she is used to our casual ways, that one would as soon just visit and not eat; and if eat we must, we would rather eat very little.

Neither is it simple to be a guest in Scandinavia. The utmost punctuality is demanded, and that means that you must appear on the dot at the time you are invited, or else you are considered discourteous. It is customary to bring flowers, or to send them beforehand, or, at a pinch, the day after the party. You shake hands with your hostess and say, as you leave the table, "*Takk for maten*" (if you are in Norway, or its Swedish, Finnish, Danish or Icelandic equivalent) which means, roughly, thank you for the food. You thank your hostess profusely as you leave her home and telephone or write your thanks the next day. And when you see your hostess again, you thank her for the last time. If you don't do all these things because you did not know them, your hostess will forgive you. But she won't forgive you for being late.

Sitting down to a meal, even if it is only coffee and cake, is a very great pleasure in Scandinavia, because the tables are so beautifully set and the food so prettily arranged. Imagine a table covered with a brightly colored cloth or with a damask when the dinner is formal. Tall candles in low candlesticks and, above all, the most imaginative flower arrangements are part of the setting. Candles are always burning when the guests are being entertained. In Denmark a candle is lit when the guest enters the house, and there are candlesticks everywhere—on the coffee table, the mantel, the sideboard. The flowers of Scandinavia are most luxuriant—more beautiful, and used more abundantly than elsewhere. Flowers are a necessity in daily life rather than a luxury as in America, and they are found in the most humble homes. The flower arrangements on the tables are delicious, often echoing the colors and designs of the table settings, and of the figurines with which the Scandinavians are fond of adorning their tables. I remember an arrangement of red, white and blue flowers in several vases which greet the American guest in a distant town in Northern Norway, the delicious sprays of wild flowers in a castle of Southern Sweden, the table decorated in the red and white of the Danish flag at a coffee party in a Danish farmhouse. The national flag is another decoration much found in Scandinavia, displayed, as we do not display ours, on the festive table, decorating cakes and foods and the Christmas tree.

Food is dished up with similar loving care, so the food forms a picture on the dish. The dishes are large and shapely, to allow plenty of room for decorating. Titian could not have lavished more care on a decorative detail than a Scandinavian, especially a Danish, housewife. The pink salmon slices curl on tender green lettuce, radish roses peer out behind the parsley sprigs, feathery dill floats over the gravy. Game birds are arranged in a star pattern on a big dish, separated by fat stalks of succulent, snowy asparagus bound together with red pimiento rings. The meats come to the table carved, surrounded by formal gardens of baby carrots and tiny peas, wee potatoes and infant heads of cauliflower. Carving at the table is unknown, and the vegetables are part of the meat platter. The art of arranging foods is taught in every household course. Every Scandinavian cookbook has illustration upon illustration of beautifully presented foods to guide the housewife, not to mention the pictures that show her how to fold napkins in any number of shapes.

Americans are apt to think that electrical appliances are a privilege of their country. This is no longer so; in electrified Scandinavia more and more appliances are found in the home of the ordinary citizen. Especially in Sweden and Norway washing machines are common, but electric frying pans, rotisseries and dishwashers are not. The Nordic housewife's manner of life is a contradictory one; she may be extremely conservative in many ways, but she is also extremely receptive to what is practical and modern. The imaginative use of plastics is an example; I have never seen more beautifully designed every-day plastic objects than in Sweden and Norway. And the modern Scandinavian home furnishings—furniture, silver, glass, ceramics and textiles—both in beauty and quality go far beyond our American ones. For quality and honest presentation of merchandise still count in Scandinavia.

The Way the Scandinavians Drink

Americans and Scandinavians differ in their toping not only as to the kind of spirits, but also in the way they are consumed. The Americans favor mixed drinks of hard liquor, or plain hard liquor in an off-hand, casual manner. The Scandinavians do not drink mixed drinks, but plain ones accompanied with a ritual.

Before we get to beer and akvavit, the native spirits of Scandinavia, let me say that good wine is drunk when it can be afforded. Bordeaux and Burgundies, fine German wines, but especially vintage reds, are imported into all of the Scandinavian countries, and a dinner party without wine is impossible. And the wines are excellent. In Norway all wine is bought by a state monopoly, which also sells it, and it is bought with the utmost care. The Scandinavians know and care for vintages, and they don't stop at the table wines, but also enjoy excellent port and sherries. I'll never forget the outstanding port a Danish pig- and cow-farmer served me casually at 11 in the morning, with a home-baked cookie.

Since grapes won't grow in those Northern latitudes, the native wines of Scandinavia consist of a few pleasant fruit wines and cordials. Cherry Heering, a Danish liqueur, is the best known, and is an agreeable potion that can be bought in America. Denmark seems to have the edge on making the cup that cheers; though all of the countries make good beers and akvavits. The Danish brands of Tuborg and Carlsberg, Pilsner-type beers both, like most Scandinavian beers are household words over there and available everywhere in America. Danish akvavit, which comes from the jolly and picturesque city of Aalborg, is also famous and readily available here.

Akvavit, whose name derives from the Latin and winningly means the water of life, is a fiery, clear spirit with a more or less faint taste of caraway. It is made in almost the same way as gin, but usually from the mild potato, though more recently from barley. Akvavit is a drink about as old and as fierce as the Vikings, for red-blooded men and women. It is drunk ice cold from thimble-sized glasses, and at the beginning, or smorgasbord stage, of the meal, or occasionally with the first course. Akvavit is invariably followed by a beer chaser, which makes Scandinavian countries the home of the boilermaker. The boilermaker is accepted by kings, poets and peasants alike, both male and female, for the women of Scandinavia, unless they are teetotalers, are right in there pitching.

Home brewing is an old Scandinavian practice, but it is, unfortunately, on the way out. But these mild "house beers" have their counterparts in commercially brewed beers of varying mildness. One such, almost without any alcohol, but looking like any beer, has saved the face of many a lad not old enough to be served regular beer.

The Scandinavians love to drink, and they would drink much more liquor if it were not (with the exception of beer), so terribly expensive. The liquor laws are stringent too. Though not in Denmark, in the other countries strong temperance and religious movements have laid down the laws. In some, such as Norway and Sweden, you can't drink without eating, and there are bars only in some specially privileged tourist hotels. Or else you can't drink over the weekend. Whatever the regulations, drinking is not made easy, but it persists, because such is human nature, especially human nature in a cold climate. To make drinking even more difficult for the Norwegians, only towns over 4000 people can get their own state liquor stores, and then only when a local referendum results in agreement to have one.

But in Denmark you can drink the clock around, which is not the least of the reasons why the parched citizens of the Scandinavian countries take themselves there for vacations, and why tourists rejoice when they touch Danish soil.

In all of the Nordic countries the official attitude to liquor is most stringent. Motorists, who think nothing of zipping along at a cool eighty or more, say a positive "no" when you offer them a second drink before dinner. If you tell them that they can't possibly get drunk on so little, they explain with a wan smile that if there should be an accident, however slight, and patently through no fault of your own, you are automatically punished if the alcohol test administered by a mistrusting police shows that there is more than a minimum of alcohol in your system. In Denmark, to boot, insult follows injury, because the Danish papers are apt to publish the names of people convicted for drunken driving, which does them no good at all in their own most respectable countries. Needless to say, there is very, very little drunken driving in Scandinavia.

A glass of akvavit is called a *snaps* in Denmark, Sweden and Finland, but the Norwegians call it a *dram*. The magic word of the drinking ritual is *skål* or *skol,* in English "skoal," though the Finns say "*tervevdeksenne*."

There is no native cocktail hour in the lands of the North, unless the natives are living like Americans. At the best, you may get a predinner glass of sherry or an apéritif before settling down at the table to serious eating and drinking. Here the drinking ritual begins, and it is a lot of fun, especially for the female visitor, who likes to gaze long and deeply into handsome, reciprocating Nordic eyes.

This ritual has some slight variations, but here is the basic procedure which will see you through. Never lift your glass to your lips, or, worse, drink first. Listen closely to the word *skål* or *skol,* which comes after your host has spoken his *velkommen til bords* which means "welcome to the table." When you hear the magic word, grasp your glass and bring it up slightly north of the region of the heart. But do not let your lips touch it yet. As a guest, your host will look straight at you with a purposeful, magnetic stare, glass raised (in Sweden, they used to say at the level of the third button of the uniform). Then you drink simultaneously, and if you are either very experienced or very inexperienced, you toss it down with a gulp. Then you return your glass south of your chin, from where it came, glance again into your skoaler's eyes, nod your head around the table in a rather stately manner, deposit your glass and reach for your beer to quench the fires of the akvavit. The same procedure applies to wine, but not to beer.

When the urge for another drink seizes you, take the initiative in a bold manner—don't forget the word *skål* but repeat the ritual procedure. You yourself can *skål* anybody as often as you want or as long as the going is good, and earn the gratitude of your fellow diners. But you can't *skål* your hostess as often as you want, presumably because somebody has to keep her wits about her, though she can *skål* you to her heart's content.

Now this ritual, described in cold blood, sounds complicated, just as the process of breathing sounds complicated if you try to describe it in detail. In reality, Scandinavian drinking is as easy as breathing, and takes practically no practice at all. A couple of drinks, and you're there, skoaling as naturally as you put food in your mouth. It's a very pleasant practice, in more ways than one, as many a lad or lass gazing his way through Scandinavia will tell you.

Scandinavian Restaurants

Generally speaking, the Scandinavians don't eat out the way we so often do—to avoid cooking, or because it is quicker. When they eat out, they do so for a treat, and they expect their restaurants to be tops. Consequently there are few plain eating places, compared to the many in America, but there are a good number of superb restaurants that rank along with the finest of Europe.

For an American visitor, Scandinavian restaurants are a revelation as to what restaurant dining can be. Not since the days of Diamond Jim Brady has the public been catered to with such opulence, including a profusion of fresh flowers of the very best quality and the soothing music of real live musicians. The menus are enormous, the waiters attentive, the prices reasonable for such superb food and service—no wonder the American visitor overeats constantly. The food of the top restaurants of Copenhagen, Oslo, Trondheim, Stockholm and Helsinki, as well as that of the larger cities in these countries, is elegant and international in a French manner; even the menu cards are usually translated into French and English for the convenience of the visitor. But the food, on its way North, has assumed local characteristics, just as a French ballerina would swathe herself in furs on her Northern tournées. Scandinavian–French–international food is richer in butter and cream and mushrooms than its fountainhead. It is also vastly more exquisite in the way of decorative flourishes—aspics, half-moons of puff pastry, lobster claws, artfully arranged vegetables, swirls of butter cream and whipped cream—than any food that I've seen outside of a chefs' exhibition. The food is always presented with charm; the plates are hot, the dishes from which warm-hearted waiters serve you with verve and elegance are kept hot on hotplates for your second and third servings. It is with apologies that a few restaurants have introduced a "plate service" for a few dishes, in which your food comes to you already served. The shortage of help has been the cause for this, but plate service is considered barbarous since it deprives the chef and the diner from creating and admiring the visual composition of a dish. Mercifully, there are still enough chefs and apprentice chefs around in Scandinavia, properly trained in trade schools with high standards and no nonsense, whereas in America, the few good chefs left flee into industry.

The wine lists of Scandinavian restaurants, even of the provincial ones, are excellent. Red wines, especially the Bordeaux and Burgundies, are favorites, and the ports and brandies match the vintage wines in quality.

Scandinavian restaurants customarily provide music. A trio, or a small orchestra, are as much a part of Scandinavian dining as a table set with fresh flowers. Usually there is dancing also, for the Scandinavians of all ages are great dancers and will dance away the night, especially in the towns away from the capitals, where dancing in the restaurants might be the one amusement in town, aside from the movies.

All this makes for a gaiety and elegant charm that in America can be found only in a very few luxury spots, and even then it is not so lighthearted and pleasing.

Excellent service is not limited to top restaurants in Scandinavia. When you order a cup of coffee, a soda, or a beer, the waitress will pour your beverage for you with the invitation of "*Var så god!*" which means "if you please." With "*tack,*" the word for thanks, "*var så god*" must be the most used words in any of the Scandinavian countries.

How to find out about a good restaurant when you are in a Scandinavian town? The best source of information is the local Tourist Office or Tourist Association, which keeps strict tabs on local establishments, without any commercial tie-ups, so that the information is straight. In every town there is such an organization, since the Scandinavian countries are set up to help tourists and visitors. From my long experience with the tourist offices, I can only report that they are overwhelmingly willing, helpful and resourceful.

Another good source of information is the head porter in a

hotel. Scandinavian service is different from ours, and from that of continental Europe, inasmuch as there is much politeness but no servility and very little mercenariness or help given only in expectance of a tip. And this attitude goes all the way through, from the head porter in a big hotel in one of the capitals to the chambermaid in a small country inn.

Almost all good Scandinavian hotels have good restaurants. But in the capitals, and in the big cities, many of the outstanding restaurants are not connected with hotels. In the smaller and smallest towns, however, the best restaurant, and often the only real restaurant, is the one in the town's best hotel, where the local people go to dine and to dance. To an American visitor, used to the dreariness of provincial American hotels, the small-town hotels of Scandinavia will come as a revelation. They're new, they're modern, they're gracefully furnished with the best of their country's modern furnishings, whether they are in Southern Denmark or Northern Norway, and they operate on that old-fashioned idea, now almost lost in the United States, of being personally agreeable to the guests.

Unfortunately, it is not easy in Scandinavia to find the interesting, old-time regional dishes in the restaurants. The simpler eating places will have local, family food, not very interestingly cooked, but not the ancient dishes of Scandinavian folklore. If you are at all interested in them, again, ask your local Tourist Office. Some of the restaurants connected with the folk museums feature old dishes, and some big restaurants, such as the Frascati in Oslo, will offer these dishes during the tourist season.

Generally speaking, when dining in a restaurant it is worthwhile to ask the waiter about the local specialties. The salmon or cod might be outstanding, or there might be some other dish that cannot be found anywhere else, such as the smoked reindeer tongues of Finland, or ptarmigan and local venison or other meats, or a special dessert like cloudberries. These are foods not known in America, and it would be a great shame to pass them up because of ignorance.

No visitor should miss a visit to a Scandinavian *konditori,* or coffee and cake shop. It is an experience that destroys what little moral fiber there might be left when one is faced with the temptation to try all the delicious, beautiful, rich and completely irresistible pastries. But then, after all, why not, why not?

To sum up: the small, unknown bistro with superlative food, so dear a tourist myth, though sometimes (but rarely) a reality, does not exist in Scandinavia. What exists are splendid palaces of good living, and handsome living at that, at prices that, according to American standards for such food and service, are ridiculously low.

Danish Fare

The Danish breakfast consists of several kinds of dark and white breads, served with generous slabs of the marvelous Danish butter, jam, and perhaps an egg and a bit of cheese. For lunch, most Danes take their open-faced sandwiches with them to work and eat them with a glass of milk. If you are curious, as I was, to know how open-faced sandwiches are transported without being squashed, let me tell you that there are special flat metal sandwich boxes in which to put them.

The Danes have their dinner around 6 o'clock and then they go out, especially in Copenhagen, which is the city par excellence for going out. Everybody goes out to the cafés to drink coffee and eat cake, to the wine shops, to Tivoli, the amusement park in the middle of the city which is straight out of the 18th century and even more enchanting than described, and to dance. Later in the evening the Danes strengthen themselves with more sandwiches and beer. By moving from one place to the other you can amuse yourself in Copenhagen all night long, which is one of the reasons why all the other Scandinavians look upon Copenhagen the way we look upon Paris.

Denmark is rich in good foods. First there is the Danish butter, higher in fat content and lower in salt and water content than our American butter, firm, yet smooth to spread, and simply delicious. Equally excellent is the Danish cheese, especially the Blue cheese (and Mycella is best among Blues), the mild, rich and golden Samsoe, the delicate Havarti, all of which can be readily found in the United States. There are many more delicious cheeses in Denmark, among them the Crema Danica, a cream cheese better than most Bries, which can be found in specialty and cheese stores here in America.

The reason that the Danish butter and the Danish cheeses are so outstanding is that the beginning of the product, milk, is of such excellence. Danish milk production, like all farm production, is strictly controlled by the government which maintains many experimental stations, agricultural schools, and an army of inspectors to advise, help and control the farmers. The butter and cheeses are made in small factories, and the butter or cheese master knows every cow that gives the milk he uses. In fact, the cows of Denmark are registered, like so many voters, for the control of their production, a state of affairs that must seem enviable to an American politician, since nonproducing cows are eliminated. One of the most charming bucolic sights in Denmark, a bucolic enough country, is the reddish-brown and the black-and-white Danish cows, grazing in their immaculate, orderly fields or standing in their immaculate, orderly barns, serene in the knowledge that they are most scientifically bred by experts, that they give the best of all possible milk, and that their rich milk is made into first-class cheese or butter under the most hygienic circumstances. I, for one, think that it would be delightful to be a cherished Danish cow.

The same scientific approach goes for the Danish pig. Before I sing the praise of this noble animal, I would like to say that the reason for Denmark's scientific agriculture is one of necessity. The country is tiny, with no natural resources, and in order to maintain her high, humane and advanced standard of living, Denmark must export. Half her exports are agricultural products, and with waste of any kind, this would not be possible. Hence the registered Danish cow, hence the standardized Danish pig, shaped and made lean by eighty years of selective breeding, which gives, no matter where in Denmark, bacon or ham of the identical quality.

Pigs is not pigs in Denmark. Seven million of these cosseted creatures live in handsome, spotless styes and feed on a balanced diet of buttermilk and the most scientific pig feed to grow to a certain size and to become as lean as possible, because that is what is wanted by the buyers to whom the Danes sell their pork. Danish pork is also extremely flavorful, and Danish ham and bacon, beginning with a superb raw product and processed with skill, are probably among the tastiest in the world. Danish canned pork products are widely distributed in the United States, at very reasonable prices, and I recommend that my readers investigate them.

Pork is the staple meat of the Danish, veal and beef come next, and lamb is a luxury. Most often meats appear ground and minced. The most popular of all minced meat dishes, whatever the animal, is *Frikadeller*. The Danes have an inordinate passion for *Frikadeller,* which they eat all the time, hot or cold, with fried onions on top and/or a fried egg, and in other combinations which have other names, but are still ground meat. As for birds, the Danes like duck and goose, stuffed with apples and prunes, and roasted. The goose is the traditional Christmas bird.

Danish fish and seafood are outstanding, plentiful and wonderfully fresh, as in all of Scandinavia. The salmon from Randers in Jutland, a jolly little town, is said to be the best, but the most famous of all the creatures of the deep is the tiny sweet Danish shrimp, no larger than the end of a thumbnail. These shrimp make the king of all sandwiches, piled high on a slice of buttered dark bread, and washed down with akvavit and beer. With the exception of caviar (and there is quite a passable kind of Danish caviar), the shrimp have no equal as appetizers. It takes an experienced sheller about an hour to shell enough of these tiny shrimp for a couple of sandwiches; I used to watch with fascination the shrimp sheller lady at the Hotel d'Angleterre in Copenhagen, who operated with both hands, without looking.

Mention must also be made of eel, which the Danish eat in large quantities, either smoked, jellied or stewed. Americans squirm when they hear the word eel, but once they get to smoked or stewed eel, especially smoked eel, they will admit it is very good indeed.

Except for potatoes (which turn up at every meal, and sometimes twice at a meal, boiled and browned and almost never in any other form), the Danes don't think much of vegetables except as decorative items. The salads, too, are very different from ours. With the exception of pickled beets or cucumbers, they are a mixture of cooked meats or fish or vegetables, sauced with a bland, rich dressing, and an accessory rather than part of the menu. The lettuce leaf has the function of setting off a handsome sandwich topping, as a lipstick sets off a pretty face.

As for desserts and cakes, the Danes love them. There is *Fromage,* not a cheese, but a cream stiffened with gelatin and whipped cream. There are the fruit porridges thickened with potato flour (cornstarch substitutes for it without any change in the recipe) and served with whipped cream. There is an array of delicious cakes and tortes, with much almond paste and more whipped cream. But these confections are for festive occasions, not for every day. Then, strong men are seen to weep because they can eat no more.

Danish family food is thrifty and substantial, but the party food is great. It seems amazing that such elaborate meals can be cooked on the separate gas rings and the free-standing little ovens which are still found in a great many homes. To an American it also seems astonishing that Danish housewives and farm women do not seem overly eager for laborsaving appliances. On a Danish farm, the college-trained farmer will use the latest farm machinery, but his wife, unlike her American counterpart, does not feel the need for the appliances taken for granted in any American farm kitchen. On the other hand, the co-operative system functions in ways unknown to us; in Denmark, it is often cheaper to send out the laundry to a co-operative laundry than to acquire a washing machine. And in the place of home freezers, community freezing lockers are common—and accessible, since (in small Denmark) there are none of the distances Americans are used to.

Danish food is becoming much lighter and better balanced than it was. The home economics schools are excellent, and the government agencies, such as the Danish Dairy Board, do enlightening work among the homemakers, much as the home economists of our extension services do. The old-time porridges and other heavy foods are on the way out; more vegetables and fruits for all-year consumption are in. But light or heavy, modern or old-fashioned, one thing must be said for all Danish food: it is tasty.

Norwegian Fare

The Norwegians have a most practical way of living. They eat a substantial breakfast, a quick sandwich at a twenty-minute lunch and dinner around 4 or 5 o'clock. After that, they are free to enjoy the day which ends with a cup of coffee or tea and another sandwich. The Norwegians like to get out into the open, which is understandable enough considering the shortness of the springs and summers, and they arrange their lives accordingly.

From tip to bottom, Norway's scenery is spectacular. The sea is in the mountains, the mountains are in the sea. There are orchards, enormous forests, waterfalls and glaciers, and from May to September there is practically no darkness, to compensate for the darkness of the other months.

Norwegian food rather resembles Danish food, or vice versa, since once upon a time, the two countries were under one flag. To this day the Norwegians and Danes feel more akin to each other than to the other Scandinavians.

The great Norwegian breakfast (which in hotels is a complete smorgasbord) includes a glass of milk, for the Norwegians are great milk drinkers, a boiled egg, some kind of herring or other fish, oatmeal during the cold season, and a bit of one or two of the excellent Norwegian cheeses, as well as several breads, butter, jam, and coffee. For lunch, Norwegians will have a quick cup of coffee and an open sandwich.

Middag, or dinner, which is eaten around five in the afternoon, can be a hot soup, a simple meat or fish dish with boiled potatoes and a vegetable, and if there is no first course such as soup, there might be a dessert, a pudding or fruit concoction. The soups include fruit soups, as in all of Scandinavia, sometimes they are eaten hot and sometimes cold, sometimes at the beginning of a meal, and sometimes at the end. They are good soups, and beginning a meal with a fruit soup isn't really so very different from beginning it with a fruit cup topped with sherbet.

In the evening, around 9 or so, coffee and sandwiches or a bit of cake will be served.

Old-time Norwegian food used to be heavy and rather monotonous because of the climate, the short growing season, and the lack of communications. This is no longer so. Modern Norwegians eat a considerable amount of fruits and vegetables, fresh, frozen, or canned. In the towns way above the Arctic Circle, civilized modern towns that could be in our own Northwest, the shops abound in inexpensive American apples, Israeli oranges and West Indian bananas, which the children buy as our children buy candy.

Again, owing to the conditions described above, the Norwegians excel at the art of home pickling and home curing of fish and meats. Much less of this is done today, which is a pity, because some of these old-time dishes are excellent.

The most popular meats in Norway are lamb and mutton. Game, such as elk and reindeer, and game birds, such as grouse, ptarmigan and others, are plentiful in the endless Norwegian forests, and great favorites, though by no means cheap. In fact, they are in the luxury class. Usually, they are cooked larded, and in sweet or sour cream—a method used in much of Norway's cooking.

Norway is primarily a fish-eating country, and it is impossible to sing sufficient praise of the excellence of Norwegian fish and fish cookery. The cold water of her seas and the utter freshness of the fish sold produce fish with an unforgettable firm texture, with no trace of fishiness in the taste. I shall forever remember the fish market in Narvik, above the Arctic Circle—a large enclosed hall chock full of fish, but without odors.

Cod and salmon are the fish held in highest esteem; cod is eaten for Christmas, and treated with much reverence. So is salmon, but salmon is in the luxury class. A food that is new to us Americans is whale meat, which is inexpensive and popular. The Norwegians are the world's greatest whalers, and whale meat is found in all of the markets. It is dark red in color, and tastes like beef. It is on the tough side, like some cuts of beef, and can be cooked like these. There isn't a trace of fishiness in the flavor.

The national cake of Norway is the *kransekake,* a rich almond-paste confection baked in decreasing rounds to form a tower. The Norwegian women also bake many cakes and cookies, but not nearly as many as the Swedes. Generally speaking, their cookies resemble each other's, being made with lots of butter and almonds in some form or other.

Norwegian fruit is very good, especially the berries. The Arctic cloudberries, called *multer* in Norwegian (they also grow in Finland and Sweden and are just as much appreciated there as in Norway), have an unforgettable flavor. The strawberries of the Arctic, which grow large and sweet under the midnight sun, are among the best I've ever tasted.

Another surprise in Norway is the chocolate, which is excellent. In general, Norwegian food is bland, but this too, is changing. In the ultramodern and extremely well-taught household schools and home-economics classes of the public schools (I am thinking of one, high on a hill in Trondheim, which must be the perfect modern school), not only modern cooking is taught, but also a delightful international geography of flavorings. And in Tromsø, the capital of the Arctic, there is a brand new Cooking School for seamen apprentices, where the lads that will go to sea, as most Norwegians do, learn rather fancy cooking as well as housekeeping. As the director explained to me, this is necessary in order to staff Norway's merchant marine with good cooks, or else there is trouble with the crews.

In a fairly short time Norway has recently become food conscious and, more than that, gourmet conscious. This has had an endearing effect on the Norwegian male, a creature not known for domesticity. Eminent gentlemen of the steadier professions have banded together in gourmet cooking clubs, and well-known writers, like Leif Borthen, write about food in magazines and newspapers with a skill and attention to detail worthy of a Frenchman. The most amusing manifestation of this masculine interest in fancy cooking is a Cooking School for Men in Oslo, run by a lovely ex-model called Lillebil. This lady, who has winning ways, teaches her gentlemen French gourmet cooking, with all the spicing, flambéing and other tricks that anybody could wish for. The gentlemen clean the vegetables, she demonstrates cooking the food, they eat it together, and the gentlemen wash up. The school is a roaring success, needless to say, and Oslo husbands now teach their wives to make *coq au vin, quiche lorraine* and *pêches flambées,* as good a pasttime as any during the long Norwegian winter.

Swedish Fare

The thing that strikes the American visitor when he first sets foot on Swedish soil is the look of solid prosperity. Here are outstandingly imaginative, colorful and practical apartment buildings, with low rents, large modern industrial plants, roads full of Swedish-made cars, excellent home furnishings—here is indeed the wealth of which the other Scandinavians speak with a twinge of envy. The second thing that hits the American visitor between the eyes is the good looks of the population. The Swedes, male and female, are indeed beautiful people, with much natural elegance, and, also, excellent clothing. And the third is the universal complaint of the people that food is so terribly expensive that it makes entertaining prohibitive.

Sweden's riches and high standard of living are reflected in her food. Her cuisine is by far the richest and most varied of all of the Scandinavian countries. The Swedes are hearty eaters, and though their food is on the bland side, as is all Scandinavian food, it is not nearly as bland as that of the other countries. The Swedes like flavorings; anchovies are much admired, dill is the national food plant, cardamom and spices are used in baking. The Swedes are also fond of sweetened foods. In all of Scandinavia sugar is used far more in nonsweet cooking than it is in America, but the Swedes use much more sugar than the other people.

The American visitor who expects to find an enormous *smörgäsbord* in Swedish homes and Swedish restaurants is in for a disappointment. Except for great occasions, four or five appetizers at the most are passed around. Usually, there will be herring in some form or other, smoked salmon, a homemade liver paté, and a cheese. Of course the selection may be a different one from that mentioned here, but it is nothing like the spectacular overabundance of the American smorgasbord.

The Swedes eat a good many nourishing soups, including fruit soups, and much excellent fish and seafood. The salmon is excellent, and so is the fresh-water fish such as pike. Lobsters are highly thought of, and boiled crayfish (which look like miniature lobsters and are not shrimp) are the national passion. Their season is August to September, and they are the reason for most congenial parties, open-air ones preferably, held under a shiny moon, with much akvavit, beer and all-round merriment. Anybody who's been to a good crayfish party, and I can't believe there are any bad ones, is not apt to forget the experience, for the Swedes are outstanding party givers.

Far more meat is eaten at everyday family meals in Sweden than in the other Scandinavian countries. Pork, lamb and veal are boiled, pot-roasted, or minced in the ubiquitous meatballs. Oven roasts, such as we and the English like, are not common, and beef is not as good as in the United States. The meats, of course, come with rich, delicious cream gravies. Chicken, as in all of Scandinavia, is a party dish and a treat, though it is becoming less expensive. Goose, on the other hand, is a national bird, roasted with a stuffing of apples and prunes. Game and game birds, from the enormous Swedish forests, are common, and they are usually pot-roasted with bacon and cream.

The variety and excellence of baked foods is staggering. The American visitor in a Swedish home, especially in the country districts, finds it almost impossible to believe that Swedish women can bake so much, so well, and so often. Swedish home baking, to be consumed with coffee, which can be called the national drink, is about the best in the world.

Sweden's present food habits are in an interesting state of transition between the old and the new. On one hand we have a national cuisine of traditional foods, to be eaten in a ritual manner especially on holidays. Among them are the sausages, the Shrove Tuesday buns, the Christmas *lutfisk,* to mention a few—all of them dishes which for the conservative Swedes have an almost mystical significance. On the other hand, these same Swedes—very prosperous, very traveled, and well versed in foreign affairs—are the producers and consumers of the most modern canned and frozen foods. They are also thoroughly sophisticated in their restaurant food, which is French influenced, as is the restaurant food in all of Scandinavia. Somehow, though, in the clear air of the North, the cuisine of the European continent seems infinitely richer than at home, with combinations of meats and vegetables, or fish and vegetables, that are typically Scandinavian.

Though much is made of picturesque Swedish country customs such as gaily costumed maidens dancing around maypoles, a visitor would gain, to my mind, a much clearer view of what the Swedes really admire if he looked at the incredibly lovely and numerous Swedish castles and manor houses. In spite of democracy, Sweden is a formal country, with formal manners, which were set by the aristocracy. Today there are few, if any, servants in these great houses, filled with treasures of furniture and *objets d'art,* but the art of elegant living has not been lost. In comparison, what passes for gracious living in our country, or at least most of it, looks pretentious and shabby. One meal that lingers in my memory was a luncheon given by the Countess Charlotte Gyllenkrok, at her castle, Svenstorps, near Malmö. This lady, a great sportswoman and gardener, with one maid, produced a luncheon of exquisite filled puff tarts, a brace of wild ducks cooked with bacon and sour cream, accompanied by a salad and some superb wisps of pancakes. Few American restaurants would have cooked a meal as well, and fewer hostesses served it with greater ease.

Naturally, castle living is not the living of a whole nation. But at least for the middle classes, it has set a pattern of grace, a grace that is to be found on the farmer's table as well.

Finnish Fare

What strikes you first about Finland is the lyrical beauty of the country's green forests and the sparkling waters of the blue lakes, and the realization of how beautiful a truly modern city can be, that city being the capital, Helsinki. This city is full of light; the streets are broad and straight, the buildings are light in color, and everything is so fresh and clean and cheerful that it is a joy to behold. Helsinki is the living proof that well-planned functionalism is the best way to build and furnish a city's home and office buildings and that there is a great deal of beauty in really modern architectural planning. Much as I admire the old, I found it exhilarating to be in a city and among people who are not haunted by the ghosts of the past, and it is not surprising to find that some of the world's greatest modern architects, such as the late Eero Saarinen, have come from Finland.

The war took a dreadful toll of Finland. She lost a large part of her lands to Russia, the Germans ravaged the north, and she had to resettle her homeless people—all in a country that is anything but rich. Modern Finland is indeed a monument to faith, courage and resilience. The Finns wasted no time being sorry for themselves, though, heaven knows, they had ample reasons to be. After the war, they drew their belts awfully tight and rebuilt, and, to their greater glory, even paid their war debts to us, which is more than more prosperous countries ever did. If a people was ever to be respected and admired, it is the Finns.

Yet Finland is anything but a grim, self-conscious country. It has unrivaled yachting, fishing, hiking, skiing and other sports facilities, the Finns being natural athletes. For visitors, there is plenty of sightseeing: old castles and forts that date back to a time when Finland was part of Sweden, Lapland with its nomad reindeer herds, and, to my mind the most fascinating, the beautiful, advanced architecture of the new towns.

The Finnish food visitors see in the comfortable, modern hotels and restaurants resembles the usual Scandinavian food, with a tendency to the Swedish way of cooking, though the Finns, for instance, like their food less sweet than the Swedes. But there is an extremely interesting native cuisine that relates to the national folklore, which is still practiced in rural districts, though there, too, modern ways with foods are replacing the old ones.

Finland is not a rich country. The staples of her people's diet were the cereals, such as barley and rye, potatoes, fish and meat, especially pork. This is a country with many wonderful and diverse home-baked breads, coffee breads and cakes, but she excels at rye loaves. Dumplings, heavy soups and cereal porridges of barley, rye and rice are still much used in the country districts as one-dish meals, and they are often eaten with berry preserves and milk. The superb fish, both from the sea and from the lakes and streams, are carefully cooked and a cornerstone of daily eating. Fish, meats and vegetables are much used in stews and casseroles, of which the Finns seem to be fonder than the other Scandinavians. Clabbered milk, homemade cheeses (one is baked in the oven) and other cheeses are also much eaten. Many of the native Finnish dishes, such as the Karelian pasties, are historic ones, and very different from anything I've seen.

Pancakes, both nonsweet and sweet, are another staple. There are interesting variations, such as the blood pancakes made after a slaughtering, one of the many dishes of a frugal people who had to make the most of their yearly home slaughtering. Unfortunately, it is very hard for visitors to find any of these unusual dishes except in homes.

The Finns eat a good many simple puddings, and they eat a good deal of rice. Essentially, all of their food is meant to sustain life in a country where the winters are long and hard, and where people have to work hard to survive. On the whole, Finnish food is simpler, though more varied, than other Scandinavian food.

Special mention ought to be made of the excellence of the Finnish mushrooms which abound in the forests, and which are picked by the whole population. The same goes for Finnish berries; like all of the berries of a cold climate, they are superlatively delicious. The Finns eat them fresh and preserved, and they make some pleasant fruit wines and cordials from them.

Another interesting element in Finnish food are the dishes of Russian origin, such as the pastries filled with fish or meat and the soups. Finland was part of Russia; she was incorporated in that country in 1809 as an autonomous duchy and remained under Russian domination, at least technically, until she declared her independence in 1917. But it is Swedish culture that has left its strongest marks upon Finland, and that includes Swedish influence on Finnish food.

Needless to say, as everywhere in Scandinavia, the Finnish housewife takes great pride in serving her food attractively.

Icelandic Fare

Iceland is a country that should be much better known by American nature lovers. The scenery is unusual and outstandingly beautiful; there are fjords, volcanos, lava landscapes that look like the moon, waterfalls, lakes, spouting geysers, hot springs, light nights and the aurora borealis. The trout and salmon fishing are superb, waterfowl is abundant, and you can ride on the sure-footed, tough Icelandic ponies into the uninhabited parts of the country.

Iceland is only a short distance by Pan American plane from America and the best time to go there is from mid-June to September. The Gulf Stream keeps temperatures mild. The winter is warmer than in New York; I remember the consternation caused by a heavy January snowfall, the kind of snowfall that anybody living in the northern parts of the United States thinks nothing of winter after winter. The hotels in the capital are not luxurious, but most comfortable, and in the smaller cities, they are perfectly adequate. And they're always incredibly clean. A friendly tourist office will advise travelers how to achieve their hearts' desires.

But Iceland is not all nature. The small towns look like small Norwegian towns. Reykjavik, the capital, is a charming city of some 70,000 souls, with an old-world Scandinavian center that is small and houses, schools, hospitals and other institutions that are as modern as they come, and built of cement, for wood is scarce in Iceland. Most buildings are kept warm with heat generated by the hot springs which are nearby. This same source also heats acres of hothouses where vegetables and fruits (even bananas) are grown. Reykjavik has all the amenities of civilization anyone can wish for, from an excellent university, other institutions of higher learning, and vocational schools, to a very good national theater (amusing even when you don't understand a word of Icelandic—I myself do not), an opera, symphony and concerts. There is also an unusually interesting national museum of which I remember especially the old carved wooden church and home furnishings and some century-old portraits of clergymen with exceptionally forbidding faces.

The history of Iceland is an agitated one. The Norse settled it; before the 10th century it had been under the Norwegian and Danish crowns, and the Black Death, famines and starvations due to volcanic eruptions which blanketed the country under volcanic ashes, scourged the little island. But the country came out of all this as a triumph of human sturdiness and enterprise.

Iceland is famous for its ancient sagas, for having kept her language virtually unchanged for a thousand years (this is as if we still spoke the English of *Beowulf*), and for having had a National Parliament since 930 A.D. Iceland became independent in 1918, though it was still in union with the Danish crown. When the Germans invaded Denmark in 1940, first the British and then the Americans occupied Iceland to prevent it from falling into the hands of the Axis, who wanted it very badly because of its strategic location. In 1944, Iceland cut its remaining ties with Denmark and became an independent republic once more.

All this information does not strictly belong in a cookbook, except as background information to explain why this so very independent country, with its many national ways, eats and drinks like the other Scandinavian countries.

Fish is not only the main food in Iceland, fresh, frozen or canned, it is also its main industry. The country formerly used to be a predominantly agricultural country, and the remoteness of the farms, like that of the farms of Norway, taught people to preserve their foods. They dried, they salted and they smoked their meats and fish. The meat, that is, mutton, was preserved by pickling, and *hangikjöt,* smoked mutton, is still served with green peas and boiled potatoes in a white sauce as a typical Christmas dinner. Other specialties were sour whale blubber—I cannot imagine what this can taste like—fresh fish hung like game, salted skate and blood puddings. Most of these dishes are now obsolete, except for one, which dates back to the first settlers.

This is *skyr,* a clabbered milk, which is easy to make if you have access to unpasteurized milk.

But food in Iceland is pretty much the same as in the other Scandinavian countries. There are supermarkets in Reykjavik, full of imported foods, many of which bear the standard American labels. The women of Iceland are very skilled homemakers, thanks to the truly admirable Icelandic Household Schools. A visit to these schools is very worthwhile (and is easily arranged), particularly since some of them own fine collections of old and new woven and sewn tapestries.

The enormous American airbase in Iceland is a self-contained world and few of the personnel or their families take part in the ordinary life of the country. Nevertheless, most people understand English, and there is no difficulty in getting about anywhere; you couldn't wish for a friendlier people.

If there are not many recipes in this book under the Icelandic label, it is because the dishes are the same as those of Norway and Denmark.

Smorgasbord and Other Cold Tables

The smorgasbord, or more accurately, the cold table, that has come to be the symbol of Scandinavian cooking to most Americans, is quite a different proposition in Denmark from what it is in Sweden and Norway. (In Finland, the smorgasbord resembles that of Sweden.) The ingredients are the same, but they are arranged and eaten differently. The one common denominator is the icecold akvavit, with a beer chaser, that belongs to the cold table as love belongs to marriage. This drink is regarded by all Scandinavians as a promoter of digestibility, not to say conviviality, which indeed it is.

The groaning table piled high with some sixty appetizers, as featured in some Scandinavian restaurants in America, such as the Scandia in New York, does not exist in the Northern countries. The tables groan most in the Danish restaurants, with their endless variety of alluring open-faced sandwiches, of which more later. In Sweden the smorgasbord in its full glory started to disappear after the war. In Norway it is more ample at breakfast (that is, in hotels) than at lunch, which the Norwegians serve rather as on the European continent, with no great emphasis on what precedes the first course.

And we might remember that the smorgasbord in Scandinavia is a first course, and not the meal itself, as it has become in America.

In a good Danish restaurant, and I hasten to say that in this chapter, I am concerned with restaurants only, there is a special open-faced sandwich menu. An open-faced sandwich in Denmark is a slice of firm bread, white or different shades of brown, amply spread with butter, and covered with anything edible, from herring to eggs, caviar to eel, shrimp to cold pork roast, goose liver paste to hamburger and sausages in many varieties. Sometimes the sandwich is flat and covered with one kind of filling. Other times it is still flat, but there are several fillings arranged on it side by side. And again, it can be a many-storied structure of delectable combinations that prove irresistible even to the foreigner who approaches them with a dim view. *Smørrebrød* should be topped with a garnish that can range from meat aspic, chopped, to artistic mayonnaise pipings, pickles and pickled cabbage. As you can see, the sky is the limit. With two considerations, however—the first, that the food combinations must be complementary, and the second, that the whole affair must look as pretty as a picture. It goes without saying that Danish open-faced sandwiches are eaten with a fork and a knife, and that one, two or three, depending on the eater, are a complete meal, to be followed by the good strong Danish coffee.

When the sandwich menu is handed to you in a restaurant, you tick off the sandwiches you want, and the kind of bread you want them on. Space on the menu is provided for this. As I write this, I have in front of me the sandwich menu of the Hotel d'Angleterre in Copenhagen, an establishment of venerable and spacious luxury that makes it one of Europe's most distinguished hotels, and with service that is superlative. This menu is quite typical, which is why I am quoting it, though lesser restaurants have fewer varieties, of course. There is a choice of 5 breads and 156 different sandwiches, ranging from a modest slice of bread and butter to a *luxus snitter,* a luxury snack, according to the menu's thoughtful translation of what's what into English. You can have 22 fresh meat combinations, 12 possibilities along the salted and smoked meat line, 5 of smoked fish, 8 of fresh fish, 6 of salt fish, 10 of salads and so on. Prices for these elegant creations start at 30 cents and end around $1.50 apiece.

In other restaurants in Denmark the waiter will bring around several beautifully arranged trays of sandwich fixings, from which you choose. Fish, cold cuts, hot meats and cheeses are kept separately, and you have a different plate for each. The garnishes are not forgotten; they include potato salad, pickled beets and pickled cucumbers, mayonnaise salads, tomatoes, hard-boiled eggs, sliced oranges and prunes. In other restaurants, smaller ones, the fixings are on display on a buffet table, the so-called "cold table" to which you march up for your choice.

In Norway you will also find open-faced sandwiches, and very good ones, but in a far smaller variety and, generally speaking, presented with less opulence. That is, at lunch or in the afternoons or after dinner, when the need for a snack is felt, whereas breakfast in a first class Norwegian hotel such as the Prinsen in Trondheim is a smorgasbord of monumental proportions with the customary glass of milk and boiled eggs added to it since that is what the Norwegians like in the morning.

The Swedish *smörgåsbord* is a display of separate dishes, from which each guest helps himself before sitting down to the proper meal. A proper *smörgåsbord* should include several varieties of bread, butter, a few different kinds of herring, smoked or pickled salmon, a fish or seafood salad or aspic, with a mayonnaise, mustard or horseradish sauce, ham and other cold cuts, sausages, pressed meats, a few "little warm dishes" such as meatballs, creamed potatoes, or a potato and anchovy dish, and cheese. The cheese is never served sliced, but is left whole for the guest to cut to his individual choice.

The basic facts about smorgasbord are two, to simplify matters. The first is that there should be herring, and the second is that the dishes should be eaten as separate courses, each on a clean plate and with clean silver. The thought of piling up a plate with miscellaneous, unrelated foods is not a pleasant one to contemplate, and seeing it done is horrid.

When smorgasbord is a meal in itself, as it has become in America, sweet gelatin salads and even cookies and cakes are found on the table. Or tiny Swedish pancakes, with lingonberries, may serve as dessert, followed by the coffee which is Sweden's national drink.

The following chapter will give an indication on how to set up a smorgasbord for an American buffet party.

How to Set Up a Smorgasbord for a Buffet Party

A smorgasbord is an excellent way of entertaining a group of people since it is easily planned and prepared in advance.

The first thing a hostess contemplating a smorgasbord should do is to take a trip to a good Scandinavian or food specialty store. Specialty food stores can be found in department stores, and many supermarkets and dime stores have gourmet corners with foods suited to a smorgasbord. At the store the hostess should pick up as many varieties of canned herring and other imported canned fish as she thinks she will need. These are an integral part of the smorgasbord, and besides, she would be doing what her Scandinavian counterpart would do. Nobody expects a housewife to produce the almost endless variety of canned fish at home.

Then, since the sky is the limit at a smorgasbord, the hostess should choose as many tidbits as she fancies. If she feels she has to be authentic in her foods, she might choose the goodies imported from Scandinavia. The idea of a smorgasbord is to have variety, as well as foods that are not usually eaten at home, and the more of these the merrier.

The next step is to give some careful thought to the arrangement. This is extremely important, because a good smorgasbord is also to be looked at. Apart from the decorative aspects, the foods must be arranged in a neat, orderly manner, so that they can be eaten in their proper order, that is, in courses, beginning with fish. The best way to arrange a smorgasbord is on a long table, where the different kinds of dishes can be laid out in rows and in a related order.

The table, to look authentic, should be laid with a white cloth. Color is provided by flowers and accessories, such as candles, set at either side of the table towards the back, and the figurines so often found on Swedish tables. At one end of the table the plates, silverware and napkins are placed. There must be enough plates so that each guest can have a clean one for each course—the fish course, the meat and salad course, and the warm course. The plates need not be as large as dinner plates, but if the hostess does not have enough of them to last through the smorgasbord, they will have to be washed in-between. It is absolutely essential to have clean plates for each course. The same goes for the silver, and if paper napkins are being used, there should also be several changes of these.

At the opposite end of the table, on hot trays and candle warmers, are the hot dishes, such as the meatballs, the egg-and-anchovy dishes, the creamed potatoes, etc.

The foods can be arranged either in rows or in related groups. If the smorgasbord is to be an American one, that is, a complete meal, it should include coffee, cake and cookies. These are best arranged on a separate table, such as a card table laid with a white cloth.

Every smorgasbord must include several kinds of bread, such as white, light and dark rye, pumpernickel, Swedish rye crisp and Norwegian flat bread. There should be plenty of butter, shaped into rolls or curls, and each little butter dish should be garnished with a sprig of fresh parsley. And don't forget several kinds of cheeses, served in large chunks.

Making the food look attractive is as important as making it taste good. The canned fish need not be removed from the containers; the cans should be opened and the lids rolled back neatly to show the contents. Each can is set on its own little plate, and the plate is garnished with a lettuce leaf, or with a few dill sprigs, or with radish rosettes or lemon slices—anything that will make a can look pretty. The ham slices, the roast beef and the other cold cuts should be arranged in overlapping slices on platters; the sliced salmon rolled up and topped with twisted lemon slices; the patés topped or surrounded with chopped meat aspic; the caviar set on ice, with little plates of chopped onion, chopped hard-cooked egg yolk and egg white around it; and the salads should be bedded on lettuce. All the foods must be presented decoratively, so that the smorgasbord looks like a colorful painting.

Among the dishes suited to a smorgasbord found elsewhere in this book are *Gravad Lax,* Smoked Salmon and Scrambled Eggs, Pickled Herring, Salmon Aspic, Crab Meat Aspic, Lobster, Herring Salad (this is an essential), Jellied Vegetable Salad and Jellied Fruit Salad, all the various vegetable salads such as Knob Celery Salad, Cold Cauliflower with Shrimp, Pickled Beets, Pickled Cucumbers, Liver Paté, Jellied Veal; and among the warm dishes, Janson's Temptation, Baked Anchovies and Eggs, Ham, Creamed Potatoes, and Finnish Baked Mushrooms.

Danish Open-Faced Sandwiches

Danish open-faced sandwiches are a way of life in Denmark, but they'll never be one in America, land of the covered sandwich that can be firmly grasped and eaten on the run. I would therefore suggest that the American housewife reduce the big Danish open-faced sandwich in size, and use it as an appetizer or a canapé or as a *Snitte,* a slicelet which is nothing but a whole sandwich cut in two, either kitty-cornered or straight across, or in fancy shapes.

Danish open-faced sandwiches require a firm bread, and they also require a variety of breads. Dark breads are most commonly used, ranging from a really dark whole-grain bread to a light blond rye. Any American supermarket features a range of breads eminently suited for the purpose. The reason a firm bread should be chosen is that a soft one will get soggy or break down under the filling.

The butter needed for these sandwiches should be firm, but spreadable, so that the bread can be buttered evenly. Sweet butter is better than salted butter, and whipped butter has excellent spreading qualities. The butter can be made more interesting by adding a little mustard for meat sandwiches, anchovy paste for fish sandwiches, or chopped chives. For suggestions, see Compound Butters, page 154. The butter should not be spread too thickly, or its own taste might kill the taste of the filling.

Garnishes are an important part of the Danish open-faced sandwich, and here the sky is the limit. Among the most common garnishes are pickles, onion rings, lemon sliced extremely thin, capers, shredded horseradish, watercress, Boston lettuce leaves, sliced tomatoes, hard-cooked eggs, either sliced, or the yolks and whites finely chopped, radishes, parsley, chives, dill and paprika, as well as firm meat aspic, chopped or diced. Though a good Danish open-faced sandwich should be prepared just before eating, this is not always possible. When time must be saved, the bread may be buttered in advance, and the basic topping arranged on it, provided it is dry, and not soggy—for a soggy sandwich is the greatest of crimes. The garnish is then applied at the last minute. Thus readied, the sandwiches should be placed in orderly rows on greaseproof paper and without touching, so that they won't taste of each other. Needless to say, they should be kept in a cool place or refrigerated.

The general idea behind an open-faced Danish sandwich is to blend complementary flavors, and to make it look as attractive as possible. In order to do this beauty treatment, meats are folded over or rolled or arranged in overlapping slices, fish fillets arranged kitty-cornered fashion, fillings and garnishes arranged in rows or geometrical patterns, with lettuce leaves peering out from underneath, parsley or dill sprigs and radishes disposed in a fanciful design, and lemon slices twisted elegantly and perhaps half-dusted with paprika.

The following suggestions for open-faced sandwiches are but a few from the endless Danish variety, chosen for their universal appeal.

Shrimp Sandwich

The infinitesimally small Danish shrimp rank high among Danish sandwich toppings. In this country they can be bought canned. They should not be iced, or their delicate flavor will be lost. Top a piece of buttered bread with a leaf of Boston lettuce. Arrange shrimps on it in several overlapping rows, or pile high in the shape of a pyramid. Fifty to sixty small Danish shrimp are needed for one sandwich.

Herring Sandwich

Place slices of hard-cooked egg on buttered bread. Place one or more boned herrings lengthwise over the eggs. Decorate with watercress.

NOTE: Replace herring with anchovy fillets for Anchovy Sandwich.

Smoked Salmon and Scrambled Egg Sandwich

Smoked salmon, in Scandinavia, is usually served topped with scrambled eggs or with a plain baked egg custard. (However, scrambled eggs taste better.) Place a piece of smoked salmon on buttered bread topped with lettuce. Top the salmon with a diagonal strip of cold scrambled egg. Decorate with chopped dill.

Tomato and Raw Onion Sandwich

Top buttered bread with sliced tomato. In the center, arrange a small pile of chopped onion.

Roast Beef and Fried Egg Sandwich

Place slices of cold roast beef on buttered bread. Top with deep-fried onion rings and one fried egg for each sandwich. Serve hot. (Danish fried eggs are always sunnyside up.)

Ham, Chicken and Mushroom Sandwich

Top buttered dark rye bread with a large slice of ham. Place white chicken meat on ham. Arrange sautéed mushrooms on chicken and cover mushrooms with a thin slice of home made liver pate.

Pork, Spinach, Mushroom and Tomato Sandwich

Top a slice of buttered dark rye bread with a large slice of cold pork. Arrange a mound of cooked buttered chopped spinach in the middle of the meat. Place a sautéed mushroom cap at each corner of the sandwich. Top spinach with a fried tomato half.

Lobster Salad Sandwich

Top a slice of firm white bread, spread with anchovy butter, with slices of hard-cooked eggs. Arrange lobster salad over egg. Garnish with strips of meat aspic and little mounds of black Danish caviar.

Tartare Sandwich

A Danish favorite, made with raw meat and egg yolk. The meat should preferably be scraped, rather than ground. Scrape a piece of first-quality steak with a sharp knife in sufficient quantity to make a ½-inch layer on a slice of buttered bread. Make a hollow in the center of the meat. Circle the hollow with a ring of raw finely minced onion. Place a raw egg yolk in center of the hollow. Garnish with small mounds of raw minced onion, shredded fresh horseradish, capers and pickles at each corner of the bread. Blend before eating.

Blue Cheese and Egg Yolk Sandwich

Spread a piece of buttered white bread with Danish Blue cheese, forming a ring. Place an egg yolk in the center of the ring. Decorate with red radish slices. Break the yolk and spread it across the cheese before eating.

How to Freeze a Bottle of Akvavit in Ice

Akvavit must be served ice cold, but no ice must ever touch the actual drink. The simplest way of chilling a bottle of akvavit is to stand it in the refrigerator for a day or two, or until it is thoroughly chilled. In restaurants the akvavit bottle is often encased in a block of ice, which seems a complicated magic trick and impossible to achieve at home. Not so at all; all that is needed is a freezer and a large tin can. A can about 8 inches tall and about 3 inches larger in diameter than the akvavit bottle is needed, or a number 10 institutional size can.

First, freeze about ½ to 1 inch of water in the bottom of the can. Then place the akvavit bottle in the center of the ice at the bottom of the can. Add cold water almost to the top. Place the can in the freezer and make sure that the bottle remains dead center.

When the water surrounding the akvavit bottle is thoroughly frozen, dip the can quickly into hot water. The bottle in its coating of ice is easily removed. Serve by holding the bottle with a napkin and pouring the akvavit into thimble-sized glasses.

Appetizers, Salads

SCANDINAVIAN PICKLED BEETS

They are served everywhere, constantly.

24 medium beets
1 cup sugar
3 cups white vinegar
2 bay leaves
1 piece fresh horseradish (optional)

Scrub beets thoroughly and cook in boiling salt water until tender. Meanwhile, boil together sugar, vinegar and bay leaves. Peel cooked beets by slipping skins off while still warm. Slice—this is optional. Place beets in boiling vinegar mixture. Bring to a boil. boil 1 minute. Place in sterilized jars. A small piece of fresh horseradish in each jar will help preserve and flavor beets.

PICKLED CUCUMBERS

As common throughout Scandinavia as coleslaw in America.

½ cup white vinegar
2 tablespoons water
¼ teaspoon salt
⅛ teaspoon white pepper
3 tablespoons sugar
3 tablespoons minced dill or parsley
2 medium cucumbers

Combine all ingredients except cucumbers. Wash and dry cucumbers. Do not peel. Slice as thinly as possible—the cucumbers should be almost transparent. Place in serving dish. Pour dressing over cucumbers and refrigerate 3 hours or more before serving.

NOTE: Although it is not the Scandinavian way, I find it better to drain the cucumbers before serving.

MIXED HERRING SALAD

A must on all Scandinavian cold tables and a very good dish for all buffets.

2 salt herring (from specialty or fish shops)
1½ cups diced cooked beets
½ cup diced cooked potatoes
2 cups diced cold cooked meat (beef, pork, or veal)
2 apples, cored but not peeled, diced
1 dill pickle, diced
2 tablespoons capers, drained
2 hard-cooked eggs, chopped
1 teaspoon pepper
1 cup heavy cream, whipped
3 tablespoons white vinegar
1 teaspoon prepared mustard
½ teaspoon salt
1½ tablespoons sugar
3 hard-cooked eggs
1 cup chopped parsley

Wash herring and soak overnight in equal parts of milk and water to cover. Drain, dry, and cut off tail and head. Remove all bones and cut into small pieces. In deep bowl combine herring with beets, potatoes, meat, apples, dill pickle, capers and chopped eggs. Season with pepper and mix thoroughly. Stir into whipped cream the vinegar, mustard, salt and sugar. Add dressing to salad and toss lightly until blended. On serving platter pile salad into pyramid shape. Separate yolks and whites of 2 of the hard-cooked eggs and cut the other into 8 lengthwise slices. Chop yolks and whites fine; keep separate. Surround salad with alternate mounds of chopped egg yolks, chopped parsley and chopped egg whites. Arrange egg slices on top of salad in the shape of a blossom.

SWEDISH HORSERADISH BEET SALAD

I had this on a Swedish train, where it was very suitably served with fried fish.

3 to 4 cups cooked beets, cut in julienne strips
½ cup sour cream
3 tablespoons freshly grated horseradish
1 teaspoon sugar
½ teaspoon salt
⅛ teaspoon white pepper

Blend together first five ingredients and combine with beets. Chill; serve on lettuce. Decorate with sprigs of parsley.

DANISH KNOB CELERY SALAD

Knob celery is a biggish dark brown root which must be peeled. Is tastes like celery, but much more so, and is a great favorite throughout Europe. Knob celery can be bought at most good vegetable markets and it is not expensive.

3 medium celery knobs
½ cup heavy cream, whipped
½ cup mayonnaise
1 teaspoon prepared mustard

Peel celery knobs until only white part shows. Cut into slices about 1/16 inch thick or as thin as you can make them. Cut slices into slivers the size of toothpicks. Combine whipped cream, mayonnaise and mustard. Fold in celery slivers. Chill for 2 hours or longer. Serve on a bed of lettuce.

NOTE: This Knob Celery Salad is a standard item in Denmark, where it goes not only to the cold table and sandwiches, but is also served as a relish with meats and fish.

FINNISH SOUR CREAM CUCUMBER SALAD

4 cucumbers
1 tablespoon salt
1 cup sour cream
1½ tablespoons white vinegar
¼ cup salad oil
½ teaspoon sugar
3 tablespoons chopped dill
salt
pepper

Scrub cucumbers but do not peel. Cut off ends. Score with tines of a fork. Slice thinly. Sprinkle with salt and let stand at room temperature for 1 hour. Drain and rinse to remove salt. Squeeze dry. Combine sour cream, vinegar, salad oil, sugar and dill. Pour over cucumbers. Add salt and pepper to taste. Chill before serving.

NOTE: To be authentic, these cucumbers should be served in a glass dish and decorated with dill sprigs.

JELLIED PINEAPPLE AND WHITE CHERRY SALAD

For the smorgasbord or as a dessert.

2 3-ounce packages lemon-flavored gelatin
1 teaspoon salt
2 cups boiling water
2 cups cold water
2 tablespoons lemon juice
1 cup drained canned pineapple tidbits
2 cups (2 8-ounce cans) drained Royal Anne cherries, pitted and halved

Dissolve gelatin and salt in boiling water. Add cold water and lemon juice. Chill until slightly thickened. Fold in remaining ingredients. Pour into 2-quart mold rinsed with cold water. Chill until firm. Unmold on crisp salad greens.

JELLIED VEGETABLE SALAD WITH SOUR CREAM

The Swedish smörgåsbord always includes a jellied salad or two. This one is more interesting than most, thanks to the sour cream.

1 large size package (6 ounces) lemon-flavored gelatin
3 chicken bouillon cubes
2 cups boiling water
2 cups sour cream
⅓ cup tarragon vinegar
1½ cups celery, diced
1 cup unpeeled and thinly sliced radishes
1 cup diced cucumber
½ cup green pepper strips
¼ cup thinly sliced scallions
1 teaspoon salt
⅛ teaspoon pepper
lettuce
watercress
tomato slices

Dissolve gelatin and bouillon cubes in boiling water. Chill until slightly thickened. Combine remaining ingredients and fold into gelatin, blending thoroughly. Pour into a 2-quart mold rinsed with cold water. Chill until firm. Unmold on a bed of crisp lettuce and garnish with watercress and tomato slices. Serve with an herbed mayonnaise. Makes 12 servings.

SALMON ASPARAGUS LUNCHEON SALAD

Danish asparagus is thick, tender and snow white. Similar asparagus is imported in this country from France in glass jars, and can be bought in specialty stores. But any good asparagus will do for this colorful, attractive salad.

1 head Boston lettuce
½ lb. sliced smoked salmon
1½ to 2 lbs. asparagus (tender part only), cooked
⅔ cup stiff mayonnaise, made with lemon juice
½ cup heavy cream, whipped

Wash lettuce and pat dry with kitchen towel. Separate into leaves. Line serving dish with leaves so that leaves form a scalloped border. Shape salmon slices into rolls. Place in alternate rows with asparagus (in bundles of 4 to 5 stalks) on serving dish. Leave space in center of dish to hold small bowl with dressing. Combine mayonnaise and whipped cream and place in small bowl. Put bowl in center of serving dish. Serve chilled.

Soups

DANISH COLD BUTTERMILK SOUP

(*Kaernemaelkskoldskål*)

In Denmark this dish is served either as a soup or as dessert. It is surprisingly delicious, and well worth serving as a dessert on hot days.

3 eggs, well beaten
juice and rind of 1 lemon
5 tablespoons sugar
1 teaspoon vanilla
1 quart buttermilk
1 cup heavy cream, whipped (optional)

Beat eggs with lemon juice and rind, sugar and vanilla. Whip buttermilk until frothy. Beat buttermilk into the egg mixture, a little at a time. Chill until frosty. Top with swirls of whipped cream. Serve with stewed fruit, preserves or oatcakes.

DANISH APPLE SOUP

(*Aeblesuppe*)

A soup to the Danes, a dessert to Americans; very good after a cold lunch.

1½ lbs. tart apples, preferably greenings
2½ quarts water
1 stick cinnamon
rind of 1 lemon, cut into strips
¼ cup cornstarch
½ cup water
¼ cup sugar
½ cup white wine
6 pieces zwieback or rusk
whipped cream

Core and quarter apples. Do not peel. Combine with 1½ quarts of the water, cinnamon stick and lemon peel. Cook over low heat until apples are very soft. Do not drain apples, but press through a sieve or purée in a blender. Add remaining water. Blend cornstarch with the ½ cup water to a smooth paste. Add to apple mixture. Cook over low heat until soup is thickened and smooth, stirring frequently. Stir in sugar and white wine. (Soup should be tart, but if desired, more sugar should be added.) The soup should be the consistency of heavy cream. Crush zwieback and place crumbs in the bottom of each soup plate. Ladle soup over crumbs. Serve hot, topped with whipped cream.

OAT CAKES

Children love them.

½ cup butter
½ cup sugar
2 cups instant oatmeal

Melt butter; stir in sugar; stir in oatmeal. Fry over medium heat until oatmeal is golden brown. Pack mixture firmly into moistened egg cups or into tea-muffin-sized moistened muffin pans. Chill. Unmold and serve with the Buttermilk Soup.

SCANDINAVIAN BROWN CABBAGE SOUP

This soup is served in all of Scandinavia. In Sweden, more sugar is used, because the Swedes use far more sugar in their food than the other Nordics.

1 large head cabbage, cored and shredded
¼ cup butter
2 tablespoons brown sugar
1 quart bouillon or more, depending on thickness of soup desired
1 teaspoon salt
½ teaspoon pepper
¼ teaspoon allspice

In a deep kettle brown cabbage in hot butter on all sides. The color should be a light brown. Stir occasionally. Add sugar and cook until sugar is completely dissolved, stirring constantly. Add bouillon, salt, pepper and allspice and simmer covered, about 1 hour. Serve with dumplings.

NORWEGIAN CAULIFLOWER SOUP

(*Blomkålsuppe*)

One of Norway's national soups. Unlike most cream soups, it is not very thick.

1 large or 2 medium cauliflowers
1½ to 1¾ quarts boiling water
1 tablespoon salt
1½ tablespoons butter
2 tablespoons flour
2 egg yolks
2 tablespoons heavy cream
⅛ teaspoon nutmeg (optional)

Trim cauliflower and break into buds, but keep stalks and trimmings. Place entire cauliflower into boiling water and add salt. Simmer until buds are just tender. Remove buds and keep hot. Continue simmering until stalks and trimmings are very soft and mushy. Strain and reserve stock. Melt butter and stir in flour. When blended and smooth add hot stock, a little at a time, stirring constantly. Cover and simmer 10 to 15 minutes, stirring occasionally. Beat egg yolks with heavy cream and nutmeg. Remove soup from heat. Beat one cupful of hot soup into the egg–cream mixture, one tablespoon at one time. Gradually stir in remaining soup. Return soup to lowest possible heat and heat through. Do not boil, or even simmer, or soup will curdle. Add hot cauliflower buds and serve immediately.

NORWEGIAN SPINACH SOUP

(*Spinatsuppe*)

Another favorite Norwegian soup.

2 lbs. spinach, chopped, or 2 packages frozen chopped spinach
1½ quarts hot beef bouillon
3 tablespoons butter
2 tablespoons flour
salt
pepper
2 hard-cooked eggs, sliced

Cook spinach in hot bouillon for 10 minutes. Drain, reserving liquid. Keep spinach hot. Melt butter and stir in flour. When blended and smooth add hot stock, a little at a time, stirring constantly. Cover and simmer 5 minutes, stirring occasionally. Add spinach, salt and pepper, blending thoroughly. Cover and simmer 5 minutes longer, stirring occasionally. Serve with hard-cooked egg slices floating on top.

FINNISH SUMMER VEGETABLE SOUP

(*Kesäkeitto*)

Good for a summer luncheon, followed by pie or cake. The flavor of this soup depends on the freshness of the vegetables.

1 quart water
1 tablespoon salt
1 cup Frenched green beans
1 cup sliced carrots
1 cup cubed peeled potatoes
1 cup fresh peas
1 cup cauliflower buds
½ cup chopped spinach

2 to 3 tablespoons flour (depending on thickness of soup desired)
1 quart milk
3 tablespoons butter
¼ cup chopped parsley

Bring water and salt to a boil in deep kettle. Add string beans, carrots and potatoes. When these are half cooked, add peas, cauliflower and spinach. Cook until vegetables are just tender; do not overcook. Mix flour with a little of the cold milk to a smooth paste. Stir into hot soup. Add remaining milk and simmer soup for 10 minutes. Remove from heat and stir in butter and parsley. Serves 6 to 8.

SWEDISH POTATO DUMPLINGS

The Swedes like dumplings, and eat them not only in soup but by themselves, served with butter or a sauce.

¼ cup butter
2 egg yolks
½ cup fine dry breadcrumbs
½ cup firmly packed cooked mashed potatoes
¼ teaspoon salt
1 cup ham or luncheon meat, diced into ½-inch cubes

Cream butter and beat in egg yolks. Stir in breadcrumbs, potatoes and salt. Mix thoroughly. Knead and shape into a long roll. Cut off pieces about the size of a walnut. Flatten each piece in the hand and place a cube of ham in middle. Shape into a round dumpling enclosing ham completely. Cook, uncovered, in simmering soup or simmering water 10 minutes. Cover and cook 5 minutes longer.

DANISH YELLOW PEA SOUP

(*Gule Aerter*)

The Danish version of Scandinavia's most popular soup and a meal in itself.

1½ cups yellow split peas
1 quart water
1 teaspoon salt
1 lb. bacon or salt pork in one piece
1 diced celery root or 1 cup chopped celery
3 sliced leeks or 1 cup sliced scallions
6 cups water
3 carrots, sliced
3 medium potatoes, peeled and diced
1 large onion, chopped
1 lb. Danish (or Canadian) bacon, cut in ¼-inch slices
1 4-ounce can imported Danish cocktail sausages, or Vienna sausages, drained

Combine split peas, water and salt. Bring to a boil and simmer 1½ to 2 hours, or until tender and very soft. Strain through a sieve. Place bacon or salt pork into a large saucepan. Add celery and the green tops of the leeks. Add water. Simmer covered for 1½ to 2 hours or until meat is tender. Add carrots, potatoes, onion and the white part of the leeks. Simmer covered until vegetables are tender. Remove bacon or salt pork. Cut into slices and keep hot. Skim fat from broth. Stir in pea purée. If necessary, add some hot water, a little at a time, until the soup is the consistency of heavy cream. Add sliced Danish bacon and cocktail sausages. Heat soup to boiling point; simmer 5 minutes. Remove sliced Danish bacon and serve together with sliced bacon or salt pork and mustard. Serve soup as the first course, the meats as the second course. Cucumber salad and pickled beets are good with the meats.

SWEDISH MEAT DUMPLINGS FOR SOUP

¼ cup ground beef
¼ cup ground pork
1 small onion, ground
½ teaspoon salt
¼ teaspoon pepper
⅛ teaspoon allspice
2 tablespoons flour

Combine all ingredients except flour and blend thoroughly. Shape into small balls the size of a large marble. Roll in flour. Drop into simmering soup and simmer 20 minutes.

Fish and Seafood, Eggs

SCANDINAVIAN BASIC FISH STOCK FOR POACHING OR BOILING FISH

Though many Scandinavians boil fish in plain salted water, far superior results are achieved with the use of this fish stock. When you're buying fish fillets, ask your market to give you the heads and bones of the fish for the stock.

2 quarts water
½ cup vinegar
1 stalk celery
3 large sprigs parsley or 5 sprigs fresh dill
bones and heads of any white fish
12 peppercorns
1 small onion, quartered
1 teaspoon salt

Combine all ingredients and simmer, uncovered, 15 minutes. Strain liquid several times so that it will be clear. Cool stock before using it again. Makes about 2 quarts.

NORWEGIAN AND ICELANDIC COD
(*Torsk*)

Norwegian and Icelandic fish has no equal, thanks to the cold clean waters where it is fished and the care with which it is cooked. This applies especially to cod, a great delicacy in both countries and part of the Christmas dinner. Interestingly, like our oysters, cod is eaten freshly caught only in the months with an "R" in their spelling.

All this Northern fish has a firm, fine flesh that is a revelation to foreigners. The best cod for boiling and baking is the big Lofoten cod. The smaller cod caught around the coast of Norway is preferred for pickling and smoking. The Nor-

wegians consider it essential to have absolutely fresh fish—just caught.

Boiled cod is served with boiled potatoes, melted parsley butter, or a mustard sauce. In Norway, *red* wine is served with cod, preferably a claret.

A memorable dinner given by Mr. L. Hegdahl of Trondheim consisted of boiled cod with potatoes and melted butter and an excellent Medoc. It was followed by cloudberries with whipped cream. The dinner was unforgettably good because of the unparalleled quality of the ingredients, and the care with which the fish was cooked. Each slice was boiled individually, and second helpings came on fresh, hot plates.

The following directions may seem to make quite a production of boiling a piece of fish. However, the excellence of a cook is shown when it comes to preparing simple food simply, without any sauces or furbelows to mask a less perfect basic preparation.

To Prepare Cod

Clean fish. Rinse inside thoroughly to remove any trace of the blood. For sliced fish, cut off head and reserve; also reserve roes and liver. Place fish, either whole or in slices, in a large bowl. Cover with ice cubes. Set under running water for 30 minutes to firm flesh. Drain and dry thoroughly with kitchen towel or kitchen paper before cooking.

To Boil a Whole Cod

This is not the usual Norwegian way; slices are used most frequently. (The Danes boil fish whole more often than do the Norwegians.) Place whole fish in cold water barely to cover. To each quart of water add 2 tablespoons salt. Bring to a quick boil. Simmer about 6 to 8 minutes to the pound, depending on size of fish. Do not overcook. The water must not boil—it must barely simmer. Lift out fish carefully and drain. Place on platter within folded napkin to keep hot; the cloth will also absorb excess moisture.

NOTE: To make handling of fish easier, wrap in a long piece of cheesecloth. Leave long ends at either side of cloth, to serve as handles. Keep the handles outside of the pot while the fish is cooking. Grasp them to lift out the fish.

To Boil Sliced Cod

With sharp knife cut prepared fish into 1-inch slices. Set under ice and running water; drain and dry before cooking. In a large kettle boil water; add 2 tablespoons salt for each quart. (The water should be salty like sea water.) Lower fish slices, including head, into boiling water. Let the water come to the boil once more. Simmer for 1 to 3 minutes, or until bone can be removed. Do not overcook. Remove fish carefully; drain. Place on folded napkin and remove skin. Garnish with sliced boiled roe.

To Cook Cod Roe

Boil in salted water about 15 minutes.

To Cook Cod Liver

Cut in small pieces and cook in as little water as possible for 15 to 20 minutes. Serve liver pieces in water; add 1 tablespoon of vinegar and some freshly ground pepper. (Eating the cod liver, which does not taste like the cod liver oil of our childhood, has kept Norwegians happy and healthy.)

FINAL NOTE: The top of the cod head, the jaw muscles and the thick part of the neck, are considered especially good.

NORWEGIAN PRESSED COD

(*Persetorsk*)

Another favorite Norwegian cod dish.

Cut off head of fish and cut fish down the back. Leave belly whole. Clean fish, wash thoroughly and dry. Rub with coarse salt—about 1½ teaspoons for each pound of fish. Cover with salt the bottom of a bowl long enough to accomodate fish. Place fish on it. Sprinkle top of fish with more salt. Place a board or platter on fish to weigh it down. Keep in cold place for 2 to 3 days. Take up fish, drain and wash. Place fish between two boards and put a stone or some heavy weight on top to flatten. Let stand another day. To cook, wash again and dry. Cut into 2-inch pieces. Cook in boiling unsalted water 2 to 3 minutes. Serve with cooked carrots, melted butter and chopped hard-cooked egg.

DANISH FRIED EELS WITH CREAMED POTATOES

(*Stegt Aal med stuvede Kartofler*)

A Danish classic. Eels, when properly cooked as they are in Denmark, are delicious, and Americans would do well to overcome their prejudice against them.

3 large eels
salt
1½ cups flour
2 eggs, beaten
1½ cups fine dry breadcrumbs
⅓ cup butter
6 medium potatoes, peeled and cubed
¼ cup butter
¼ cup flour
2 cups milk
1 teaspoon salt
1 teaspoon grated lemon rind
½ teaspoon white pepper
2 tablespoons parsley, minced

Skin eels by cutting the skin around the head and peeling it back very slowly. You may need a pair of pliers to get started. Remove intestines from skinned eels and cut into 3-inch pieces. (Cut off the head.) Wash fish thoroughly and dry. Sprinkle with salt and let stand for 1 hour. Rinse with cold water and dry thoroughly. Roll eels in flour, then in beaten egg, and last in breadcrumbs. Melt butter in a skillet. Fry eels in it about 20 minutes, or until golden brown and tender. Turn fish occasionally. Cook potatoes in boiling salt water until tender. Drain; keep hot. Melt butter and stir in flour. Gradually add milk, stirring constantly. Cook over low heat until sauce is thickened and smooth. Stir in salt, lemon rind and pepper. Pour sauce over potatoes. Surround potatoes with fried eel pieces. Sprinkle with parsley.

NOTE: The Danes say that you must eat sufficient eel to make a ring around the plate with the bones.

FINNAN HADDIE NORWEGIAN STYLE

From Kirkenes in North Norway, a town near the Russian border. Here, in 1962, the beginning of the Iron Curtain looked simple: a dirt road leading over a bridge with the border shed. On the Russian side, a green garden gate; on the Norwegian, a yellow bar.

2 lbs. filleted smoked finnan haddie
1½ quarts water
1 tablespoon salt
1 cup butter
2 hard-cooked eggs, finely chopped
hot boiled carrots, sliced
salt
white pepper
butter
chopped parsley

Skin fish and cut into serving pieces. Boil gently in water and salt for 10 minutes. Drain; keep hot. Cream butter until soft and fluffy. Fold in hard-cooked eggs. Season to taste with salt and pepper. Arrange fish in center of hot serving dish. Arrange carrot slices around fish. Dot with butter and sprinkle with parsley. Serve very hot.

PRINCE FISH

(Prinsefisk)

1½ to 2 lbs. cod fillets (if frozen, thaw first)
milk
16 stalks asparagus, cooked, or canned or frozen asparagus, cooked according to package directions
2 cups hot medium white sauce, made with half milk, half heavy cream
3 egg yolks

Place fish in buttered baking dish. Cover with milk. Bring to a boil; simmer until fish is cooked and flaky, about 5 to 7 minutes or less. Drain off milk. Arrange asparagus in lattice pattern over fish. Beat egg yolks into hot white sauce. Pour sauce over fish and asparagus. Place in broiler 2 to 3 minutes or until top is browned and bubbly.

SCANDINAVIAN PICKLED HERRING

A universal favorite, both on the cold table and as a meal, when it is served with boiled potatoes and a sauce, such as mustard or horseradish. Dark bread and sweet butter are natural companions for this herring.

3 to 4 salted herring (from fish and specialty markets. They come packed in salt brine).
milk
water
⅔ cups wine vinegar
1 cup water
⅓ cup sugar
2 teaspoons allspice (optional)
2 medium onions, sliced
¼ cup sherry (optional)

Wash herring thoroughly in running cold water. Place in deep bowl and cover with equal parts of milk and water. Let stand overnight. Drain herring and dry. Cut off heads and trim away darkened edge of neck. Fillet herring, but do not remove skin. Trim bottom and side of each fillet to remove fins; cut away top fin. Cut fillets cross wise into ½-inch strips and set aside small tail ends. Combine wine vinegar, water, sugar and allspice and bring to a boil. Cool. In wide-mouthed quart-size jar or bowl place a layer of the tail pieces. Cover with onions. Repeat process, making alternate layers of herring and onions. Pour marinade over fish. Cover tighty. Let stand 2 to 3 days before using. At serving time drain fish and sprinkle sherry over it.

NOTE: This is but one version of dozens of pickled herrings. Essentially there is not much difference between recipes and the results are about the same.

AENNY'S BOILED HERRING OR MACKEREL

This was part of a typical Norwegian family meal Aenny Rödseth cooked for me in her home in Narvik, well above the Arctic Circle. She chooses the fish as she bicycles to work and picks it up on her way home. With the herring we had steamed potatoes, a mustard sauce and a cucumber salad. Dessert was the first rhubarb from the garden, made into a *rabarbragraut* with whipped cream.

2 lbs. herring, filleted (or filleted mackerel)
iced water
1 quart boiling water
1 tablespoon salt
2 bay leaves
5 whole peppercorns
¼ cup mild vinegar

Place herring fillets in iced water for 30 minutes, to firm them. Combine all other ingredients and bring to a boil. Pour over drained herring and simmer, without boiling, 5 to 7 minutes. Do not overcook. Drain; cut into serving pieces. Strain stock and pour over herring. Serve hot or cold, with boiled potatoes and a mustard sauce.

SWEDISH FRIED HERRING OR SMELT FILLETS

(*Stekt strömming*)

Excellent also when made with filleted mackerel.

2 lbs. herring or smelt fillets
1 teaspoon salt
¼ teaspoon white pepper
½ cup butter
1 cup chopped parsley or ½ cup chopped dill
2 eggs, beaten
2 cups fine dry breadcrumbs

Wash fish fillets in iced water. Dry on absorbent paper. Sprinkle with salt and pepper. Blend together ¼ cup of the butter with the parsley or dill. Spread on fish fillets and put together like a sandwich. Dip fish sandwiches in beaten eggs and roll in breadcrumbs. Shake free of excessive crumbs. Chill for 15 to 30 minutes. (This is not strictly necessary, but fish fries more easily.) Melt remaining butter and fry fish sandwiches in it until golden on all sides. Serve with mashed potatoes and a salad.

Variation

PICKLED FRIED HERRING OR SMELTS

(*Inlagd stekt strömming*)

Fried herring or smelts (see above) made with dill, cold
¾ cup white vinegar
¼ cup water

2 tablespoons sugar
5 peppercorns
1 medium onion, sliced
5 large dill sprigs

Combine vinegar, water, sugar, peppercorns, onion and dill. Bring to a boil; simmer covered 5 to 10 minutes. Strain and chill. Pour over fried fish and chill in refrigerator for 3 hours or overnight. Drain before serving. Very good for a smorgasbord.

SCANDINAVIAN BAKED PERCH OR PIKE WITH PARSLEY AND DILL

8 medium perch or pike, dressed
1 teaspoon salt
½ teaspoon pepper
½ cup minced parsely
½ cup minced fresh dill or 1 tablespoon dill seed
¼ cup boiling water

Set oven at 350°.

Sprinkle fish with salt and pepper. Butter a shallow baking dish. Place half of the parsley and dill on bottom of baking dish. Top with fish laid in a row. Cover fish with remaining parsley and dill. Pour water around fish. Bake 20 minutes or more, depending on size of fish, or until fish flakes. Transfer fish to hot serving platter and garnish with sprigs of parsley and dill, cucumber and lemon slices. Serve with boiled potatoes and a sauce of melted butter.

STEWED PERCH THE FINNISH WAY

Fresh-water fish is one of the glories of Finland; small wonder since the country has some 60,000 lakes. Fish is a cornerstone of Finland's diet and there are innumerable recipes. Many of them resemble closely the fish recipes of the other Scandinavian countries. The following one is different. The dish depends for its flavor on the different herbs.

6 to 8 medium perch
1 tablespoon salt
¼ cup chopped parsley
¼ cup chopped dill
2 tablespoons chopped chives or top of spring onions
¼ cup butter
1½ cups water

Wash, clean fish and dry thoroughly. Sprinkle with salt, inside and out. Lay fish in buttered deep skillet or casserole. Combine herbs and sprinkle on top of fish. Dot with butter. Add water; cover tightly. Simmer over low heat 15 to 20 minutes, or until fish tests flaky. Transfer fish to hot serving dish and pour pan juices over it. Serve with boiled potatoes.

FINNISH BAKED STUFFED PIKE

An unusually good stuffing that works well for other fish too.

Stuffing

⅓ cup rice
½ lb. fresh spinach or 1 package frozen chopped spinach
1 teaspoon salt
½ teaspoon pepper
2 eggs, beaten

Cook rice. Cook spinach and chop fine, or cook frozen spinach according to directions. Combine rice and spinach; season with salt and pepper. Blend in beaten egg yolks.

1 3-lb. pike
1 tablespoon salt

¼ cup butter
⅔ cup fine dry breadcrumbs
about ⅔ cup hot water

Set oven at 350°.

Rub fish with salt inside and out. Stuff with stuffing and sew up or fasten with skewers in the usual manner. Melt butter in baking dish. Place fish in dish and spoon melted butter on all sides. Sprinkle with breadcrumbs. Bake for 5 minutes. Pour hot water into baking dish around fish. Cook about 30 to 35 minutes or until fish tests flaky. Start basting fish occasionally after it has browned.

SCANDINAVIAN POACHED SALMON

Scandinavian salmon is superlative. It is cooked and treated with the greatest reverence. Salmon can be cooked in boiled water, but for best results use a good court bouillon for poaching.

Court Bouillon for Salmon
(*or other fish*)

Combine 3 quarts water, 1 quart dry white wine, ½ cup white vinegar, 3 medium onions, cut in quarters, 2 diced carrots, ½ stalk celery, 1 bay leaf and 5 sprigs fresh dill (or 1½ tablespoons dill seeds) or parsley. (Dill is preferable to parsley.) Bring to a boil and simmer, covered, for 1 hour. Strain before using to poach fish.

Fresh salmon, from 1-lb. piece to whole fish
court bouillon

In order to keep fish intact, wrap in cheesecloth, leaving long ends at either side that will serve as handles. Pour sufficient court bouillon to cover salmon in deep, long kettle or fish boiler. Place rack in kettle. Bring court bouillon to a boil, reduce heat so that bouillon barely simmers. Lower fish on rack. Simmer, covered, about 7 to 8 minutes to the pound. If the fish is very large, allow an extra 5 to 10 minutes. Test for doneness by inserting knitting needle or thin skewer into center of fish. When fish is done, remove carefully from kettle. Unwrap; the skin should come off with the cheesecloth. Trim fish, or, if it is to be served whole, leave head and tail on. Transfer to hot platter, garnish with parsley or dill sprigs. Serve salmon with any standard béchamel or Hollandaise, or with Mustard or Horseradish Sauce, and with Butter-steamed New Potatoes.

NORWEGIAN FRIED SALMON OR TROUT

(Ristet Laks eller Ørret)

This is much better than the usual fried salmon or trout.

2 lbs. salmon steaks, or trout, prepared for cooking
1½ teaspoons salt
¼ teaspoon pepper
2 tablespoons olive oil
2 tablespoons white vinegar
1 tablespoon fish stock or dry white wine
1 egg, slightly beaten
dry breadcrumbs
butter

Place fish in shallow baking dish forming one layer. Combine salt, pepper, olive oil, vinegar and fish stock or wine. Sprinkle over fish. Let stand 2 hours. Baste occasionally with marinade. Drain fish and dry thoroughly. Coat with beaten egg and breadcrumbs. Melt butter in skillet to the depth of ¼ inch. Place fish in skillet, side by side. Do not crowd. Fry over low heat until browned at the bottom. Carefully turn over with broad spatula. Add more butter, if necessary; the pan should not be dry. Continue cooking until browned. Serve on hot dish, garnished with lemon. Serve melted parsley butter separately. Boiled potatoes are the best and usual accompaniment.

SWEDISH MARINATED SALMON
(*Gravad Lax*)

I wish to sing the praises of this wonderful dish which, though immensely popular in Scandinavia, is almost unknown in the United States. *Gravad lax* is used like smoked salmon (it looks like it too) but it is infinitely more delicate in flavor. In fact, it is salmon at its best. This dish is not cooked, which may surprise my readers. And the thought of eating uncooked fish may appall them. But I know that anybody who has once tried *gravad lax,* which is exceedingly easy to make, will want to make it again and again for the most elegant parties.

Important: You must have plenty of fresh dill for *gravad lax*. Nothing else will do. Also, you must use fresh salmon that has not been frozen, or the dish will be a failure. The action of the seasonings on the fresh fish is what gives it its fine texture and flavor.

7 to 8 lbs. fresh salmon in one piece, with bones in
⅔ cup salt
½ cup sugar
1 tablespoon whole white pepper, crushed
1 teaspoon whole allspice, crushed
6 tablespoons cognac
2 large bunches fresh dill

Buy middle cut from salmon. Clean fish, leaving skin on. Carefully remove bone so that two big fillets remain. Rinse in iced water and carefully dry with kitchen towel, taking care that fish does not break. Mix together salt, sugar, pepper and allspice. Rub seasonings carefully into all sides of the fish. Sprinkle with cognac. Wash dill and place ⅓ of it in bottom of deep bowl. Use an enamel, china, stone, or stainless steel bowl, but not an aluminum one. Place one piece of salmon, skin side down, on the dill. Place another third of the dill on the salmon and top with second piece of salmon, skin side up. Cover with remaining dill. Set heavy plate or board on salmon. Refrigerate no less than 24 hours, and preferably, 36 hours. Drain fish, scrape off dill and spices and slice thinly on the slant, away from the skin. Serve with lemon wedges, mustard sauce and plenty of freshly ground black pepper. Makes about 15 servings.

NOTE: *Gravad lax* will keep about 8 days in the refrigerator, wrapped in aluminum foil.

For an extra Scandinavian touch, cut skin of *gravad lax* into half-inch strips. Fry in hot butter until crisp and serve with salmon.

If *gravad lax* is not part of the smorgasbord but a course in itself, it is served with steamed potatoes with butter sauce and cucumber salad, and is accompanied as well by a mustard sauce.

NORWEGIAN FILLETS OF SOLE FREGATTEN

Fregatten is a very quietly elegant new fish restaurant overlooking Oslo harbor. The fish is cooked and served in a manner that is beautiful and reminiscent of the great Paris fish of yesteryear.

Many of Fregatten's fish dishes cannot be made at home since they require ingredients beyond the home cook's scope, such as lobster fumet, shrimp butter made from the shell (for shrimp sauce), and a number of sauces that are then combined with other sauces. Neither can the home cook hope to produce a fish platter decked out by chefs who might be painting a picture. But here is one dish that can be made at home.

6 fillets of sole
1/4 cup butter
1 teaspoon salt

- **¼ teaspoon white pepper**
- **1 tablespoon grated onion or 1 large shallot, grated**
- **¼ cup cognac**
- **¼ cup dry white wine**
- **24 small shrimp, cooked, shelled and deveined**
- **12 stalks white imported asparagus (from specialty shop)**
- **1 egg yolk, beaten**
- **⅔ cup heavy cream**

Cut fish fillets into halves lengthwise. Roll each half and fasten with toothpicks. Place in skillet. Combine 2 tablespoons of the butter, salt, pepper, onion, cognac and wine. Pour over fish. Bring to a boil and reduce heat. Simmer covered 10 minutes or until fish is white in center. Transfer fish to a hot platter and keep hot. Place one or several small shrimp in the center of each fillet roll. Arrange remaining shrimp and asparagus around fish in a decorative pattern. Keep in warm place. Reduce pan juices by boiling to about ⅓ of the original liquid. Beat egg yolk into cream. Remove pan juices from heat and stir in egg mixture. Stir in remaining 2 tablespoons butter. Pour sauce over fish.

FINNISH FRIED SALMON STEAKS

These are done the simplest possible way. But I learned in Finland the secret of really good pan-fried fish, that is, fish in thick slices or steaks, such as salmon, swordfish, tuna, etc. The fish must be pan-fried over heat that is barely medium. It should not be slow, but barely medium, I repeat, and it should not be cooked for too long. The medium temperature prevents the fish from becoming cooked too fast on the outside and remaining underdone inside. Since fish has a delicate texture, you have to be careful of the outside while you are cooking it, since it has a tendency to crumble if overdone. Thus, a barely medium heat will penetrate to the inside of the fish while keeping the outside intact.

And the shorter cooking time, together with the medium heat, will keep the fish moist and flavorful.

To pan-fry Finnish salmon steaks, simply wash and dry fish, rub with a little salt and coat with fine white breadcrumbs. Heat equal parts of butter and olive oil (the olive oil prevents the butter from overbrowning, to put a chemical process simply) and gently fry steaks in fat until golden on both sides. Serve fish on hot platter, with lemon slices and any fish sauce. In Finland the pan juices are poured over the hot fish on the platter before serving.

SWEDISH SALMON ASPIC

From Paul Debry who runs Corn Products, Inc., in Sweden and hobnobs with the best cooks, such as one of the chefs for the King of Sweden.

2 quarts water
1½ tablespoons white vinegar
1½ teaspoons salt
5 sprigs fresh dill or 1 tablespoon dill seed
8 peppercorns
8 whole allspice
2 bay leaves
1 lb. fresh or frozen salmon
¾ lb. shrimp, shelled and deveined
2 unbeaten egg whites
4 envelopes unflavored gelatin (about 4 tablespoons)
½ cup cold water
2 tablespoons lemon juice
½ teaspoon salt
¼ teaspoon pepper
2 hard-cooked eggs, cut in quarters
¼ cup mayonnaise
watercress
dill mayonnaise

Combine water, vinegar, salt, dill, peppercorns, allspice and bay leaves in large kettle. Bring to a boil and boil 5 minutes. Wrap salmon in cheesecloth and place in boiling water. Reduce heat and simmer 5 minutes. Add shrimp; simmer until shrimp are pink and fish flakes, about 5 minutes. Remove fish and shrimp; reserve. Strain stock into saucepan and add egg whites. Bring to a boil slowly, stirring constantly. Remove from heat; cover and let stand 15 minutes. Strain through double thickness of cheesecloth and measure 1½ quarts. Sprinkle gelatin on cold water; soften for 5 minutes. Add to hot stock and stir until gelatin is completely dissolved. Add lemon juice, salt and pepper. Pour enough mixture into a 9 by 9 by 1¾-inch pan to form a ⅛-inch layer. Chill until set. Arrange shrimp and hard-cooked eggs, cut side down, in a decorative pattern on the chilled gelatin. Blend mayonnaise with 1½ cups of the remaining gelatin. Pour over shrimps and egg; chill until set. Flake salmon into bite-size pieces. Arrange on mayonnaise–gelatin layer. Pour on remaining gelatin. Chill until set. Unmold on serving platter. Garnish with cucumber slices and watercress and decorate with dill. Serve with additional mayonnaise, diluted with lemon juice to taste, and mixed with dill.

NORWEGIAN TROUT

(Ørret)

Excellent fresh-water or sea trout abounds in Norway, land of innumerable streams and endless coastal waters. The Norwegian housewife, who likes to buy her trout live (as well as other fish), never washes it since washing softens the flesh, a suggestion worth adapting in America. To clean trout, remove the head and draw out the entrails. With a long, thin knife, loosen the tissue over the backbone and sides of the belly. Clean the fish with absorbent kitchen paper. Dry well with paper. Stuff a clean piece of paper into the fish until it is ready to be cooked. Boil, or pan-fry in butter, and serve with boiled potatoes, melted parsley butter and cucumber salad.

NORWEGIAN CORNED TROUT

(*Rakørret*)

This is a Norwegian national dish, beloved by the natives, though the foreigners take to it with caution. Personally, I learned to like it, like Scotch whisky. I have not made this dish, but since it belongs in a book with typical dishes, I take this recipe from Mrs. Sverdrup's cookbook *Norwegian Delight*. She tells me that it is a cinch.

Freshly caught trout
salt
sugar
water

A 1- to 2-lb. fish is a good size for corning. Clean, sprinkle head and body cavity with salt. Arrange fish in a wide-mouthed stone crock or small wooden barrel, belly side up. Sprinkle salt and 1 teaspoon sugar over each layer of fish. Weigh layers down with a plate with a weight on it to form juice. The juice should cover the fish completely. Keep in a cool place 3 months. Drain, and serve very cold with thin rye bread and butter. Beer and schnapps is a must with this lordly repast, says Mrs. Sverdrup.

NOTE: The canny Norwegians corn their trout at the end of August when the fish are fat.

ELISE SVERDRUP'S BAKED MACKEREL

Mrs. Sverdrup is a foremost Norwegian food expert and cookbook writer, and an excellent cook herself. She lives in a fairy-tale cottage with beautiful antiques.

2 lbs. mackerel, filleted
4 to 6 fresh tomatoes, sliced
salt
pepper
1 cup heavy cream

Place mackerel, skin side down, in buttered baking dish. Top with tomato slices. Season with salt and pepper. Pour heavy cream over fish. Bake about 30 minutes or until fish is flaky. Serve as is, with a tossed green salad on the side.

SCANDINAVIAN BOILED LOBSTER

(*Kokt Hummer*)

Lobster is a great favorite, especially in Sweden. To cook, plunge a live lobster into 4 quarts boiling water, combined with 5 tablespoons salt and 1 bunch of fresh dill, tied together. (If no dill is available, use parsley instead.) Serve lobster with mayonnaise or any cold sauce, including Sharp Sauce (page 165).

SWEDISH LOBSTER SOUFFLÉ

(*Hummersuffle*)

3 tablespoons butter
3 tablespoons flour
1 cup light cream, heated
6 eggs, separated
½ teaspoon salt
¼ teaspoon white pepper
1 cup chopped lobster meat
1 tablespoon chopped dill

Set oven at 350°.

Melt butter and blend in flour. Add cream gradually, stirring constantly, and cook until mixture is smooth and thick. Cool sauce. Beat in egg yolks, one at a time. Season with salt and pepper. Fold lobster and dill into mixture. Beat egg whites until stiff but not dry and fold into lobster mixture. Butter a 2-quart soufflé dish and coat it with fine dry breadcrumbs. (The breadcrumbs are optional, but they are used in Sweden.) Pour soufflé mixture into dish and bake about 30 to 40 minutes, or until puffed and golden. Serve immediately, with steamed potatoes and melted butter or hollandaise. Makes 3 servings.

NOTE: Though the quantities of the Lobster Soufflé can be doubled, it is far better to make 2 smaller soufflés rather than 1 large one. Smaller soufflés bake better.

SCANDINAVIAN CRAB MEAT ASPIC

Handsome for the smorgasbord table.

1 large size package (6 ounces) lemon-flavored gelatin
4 chicken bouillon cubes
1 teaspoon salt
2 cups boiling water
3 tablespoons lemon juice
2 tablespoons cognac or ⅓ cup lemon juice
¼ teaspoon white pepper
2 cups sour cream
2 teaspoons grated onion
2 cups flaked fresh or canned crab meat
1 cup chopped celery
3 tablespoons chopped dill or parsley
lettuce
tomato slices

Dissolve gelatin, bouillon cubes and salt in boiling water. Add lemon juice and cognac (or ⅓ cup lemon juice), pepper, sour cream, and grated onion. Blend thoroughly. Chill until slightly thickened. Then fold in crab meat, celery and dill. Pour into a rinsed 2-quart mold or individual molds. Chill until firm. Unmold on a bed of crisp lettuce and garnish with tomato slices. Serve with Cucumber Mayonnaise. Makes about 12 servings.

SWEDISH CRAYFISH

(*Kräftor*)

The beginning of the crayfish season in August is a national event in Sweden, celebrated with special parties and much akvavit and beer. There is nothing in America to compare to the Swedish crayfish season. It is a national ritual.

Crayfish are not shrimp; they resemble lobsters, but are much smaller. They are seldom found in eastern United States, but they are sold in Oregon and Washington, Louisiana, Wisconsin and Minnesota.

Crayfish are boiled in a simple court bouillon. As they are eaten, the heads should be laid side by side in a circle along the outer edges of the plate. The outermost tip of the bill, cut with a tiny knife, is considered a special delicacy.

Like lobster, crayfish should be alive before boiling.

40 to 50 crayfish (for 5 to 6 servings)
4 quarts water
5 tablespoons salt
1 bunch fresh dill, tied together

Wash crayfish thoroughly in fresh water. Pull off the tiny wing in the center of the tail. Combine water, salt and dill. Bring to a boil and boil 5 minutes. Place 10 crayfish into boiling water. Bring water again to a rapid boil and add next 10 shellfish. Repeat process with remaining crayfish. Simmer, covered, about 5 minutes. Remove from heat. Cool crayfish in stock and leave standing for 1 to 2 hours. Drain, arrange on platter and decorate with dill sprigs.

NOTE: Shrimp can be cooked in this manner, with excellent

results. Cook 3 to 5 minutes depending on size. Tiny shrimp should be plunged in boiling court bouillon, withdrawn from heat and cooled in bouillon. This will cook them through, but preserve their texture.

NORWEGIAN FISH PUDDING

(*Fiskepudding or Fiskefarse*)

Fish pudding is served in Norway at least once a week. Cold, it is either sliced and warmed in butter, or eaten as a sandwich topping. This pudding, which is one of the most typical of Norwegian dishes, should be snow white, light but firm, with a somewhat spongy consistency. It is always made with fresh fish, and it is usually served with a melted butter sauce, or a shrimp, lobster or tomato sauce. The pudding is very delicate and excellent in a rather bland way.

Making fish pudding in the traditional way is a very laborious job. It is much easier done in the electric blender. When steaming the fish pudding, the water in which it sits in its mold should be barely simmering. It must not boil, or the pudding will have holes.

butter
breadcrumbs
2 lbs. white fish, preferably cod or haddock (in Norway cod is usually used) without skin or bones
1 tablespoon salt
2 tablespoons cornstarch
1 cup light cream or milk
1 cup heavy cream

Butter a 1½-quart mold or casserole. Dust with breadcrumbs. Check fish to be sure that no bones remain. Sprinkle fish with salt; cut into pieces. Push fish once through the finest blade of a meat grinder. Slowly stir in cornstarch, and grind four times more. Mix together light cream and heavy cream. Stir in cream very slowly, beating well all the time. (The slow addition of the cream and its proper incorporation is the secret of a good fish pudding.) The mixture should be fluffy. Pour into buttered mold and smooth top.

Cover mold with its own cover, or butter some aluminum foil or nonwaxed paper, cover mold and tie paper. Set mold in pan of simmering water, which should come three quarters of the way to the top of the mold. The water must not boil. Steam about 1 hour or until a silver knife blade inserted into fish pudding comes out clean. Unmold on hot plate; drain. Serve with lobster or shrimp sauce or melted butter.

The pudding can also be set in a shallow pan with water and baked in a moderate oven (350°) for about 50 minutes or until it tests done.

NOTE: The prepared fish mixture can also be shaped with 2 spoons into small balls and poached for a few minutes in simmering water. Or it may be shaped into flat cakes and fried in butter.

Blender Method

Cut prepared fish into small pieces. Place a few pieces at a time into blender container and purée at high speed. Do not attempt to purée more than a few pieces at a time. Beat cornstarch into fish. Divide fish and cream into 4 portions each. Blend at high speed 1 portion fish and 1 portion cream at a time. Transfer blended portion to bowl and repeat until all fish and cream are used. Beat mixture vigorously with slotted spoon for ½ minute. Cook as above.

NOTE: Do not attempt to serve Fish Pudding to company if you've never made it before. It is a delicate dish and requires a little practice. Also, some recipes call for butter and eggs, not indigenous to traditional *Fiskepudding*. In this case it loses its snow-white beauty and becomes a soufflé.

FISH GRATIN

(*Fiskegratin*)

Popular throughout Scandinavia, made with either fresh or leftover fish. This particular version comes from Captain F. Kristjansen, an inspector of the Bergen Line, with whom I sailed around Northern Norway. This gentleman is a *bon vivant,* with winning ways.

2 lbs. fish fillets (cod, haddock, plaice, flounder, pike, etc.)
1 teaspoon salt
½ teaspoon white pepper
¼ cup lemon juice
2 tablespoons butter
6 tablespoons butter
6 tablespoons flour
¾ teaspoon salt
¼ teaspoon white pepper
3 cups light cream, heated
3 egg yolks
3 tablespoons butter
1 cup cooked, shelled and deveined shrimp, coarsely chopped
1 cup cooked lobster, chopped
¼ cup grated Parmesan cheese

Set oven at 350°.

Place fillets in buttered 2-quart baking dish. Sprinkle with salt, pepper and lemon juice. Dot with 2 tablespoons butter. Cover dish with aluminum foil or lid and bake about 20 minutes, or until fish flakes. While fish is baking, make sauce. Heat butter and stir in flour. Cook until smooth, but do not let brown. Gradually stir in hot cream, and cook over low heat until sauce is thick and smooth, stirring constantly. Remove from heat and beat in egg yolks, one at a time, and the 3 tablespoons butter. Sauce must be very smooth and hot. Remove foil or cover from fish and drain off excess liquid. Top fish with shrimp and lobster.

Pour hot sauce over fish and sprinkle with Parmesan cheese. Set dish on broiler rack 4 or 5 inches away from source of heat. Broil about 2 to 3 minutes until golden brown.

BOILED SWEDISH LUTFISK

A must for a Scandinavian, especially for a Swedish Christmas, but a dish that is beloved only by Scandinavians, as far as I can judge. Lutfisk is cod treated with lime, and in the old days this treatment took place at home. Now even the Swedish housewife buys her lutfisk prepared for cooking. In America, Scandinavian delicatessens will have lutfisk at Christmas time.

3 lbs. prepared lutfisk, cut in serving pieces
salt
boiling water, about ½ cup

Lutfisk is delicate to handle and it is best to place the pieces in a piece of cheesecloth, tying the ends.

Boil salt and water in large deep frying pan. Add lutfisk, either wrapped in a cheesecloth or in pieces, skin side down. Cover pan and bring to a simmering, not boiling point. Simmer about 10 to 15 minutes or until fish flakes easily. Lift out fish carefully and drain well. Place on hot platter and remove skin and fins. Serve with freshly ground black pepper, a dash of mustard and a dash of allspice; also serve boiled potatoes and cream sauce. (These are the classic Swedish Christmas foods to go with lutfisk.)

BAKED LUTFISK

Set oven at 300°. Place prepared lutfisk, skin side down, into large shallow baking dish. Sprinkle with about 2 tablespoons water. Bake about 30 minutes. Serve as above.

DANISH BACON AND EGG PANCAKE

(*Flaeskeaeggekage*)

A very pleasant luncheon or supper dish. The tastier the bacon, the better the pancake.

½ lb. sliced Danish or other bacon
6 eggs
½ cup milk or light cream
1 tablespoon flour
½ teaspoon salt
3 tablespoons chopped chives

Fry bacon in a skillet until golden brown. Remove bacon and drain. Keep fat in skillet. Crumble bacon into small pieces. Beat eggs with milk, flour, salt and chives. Reheat bacon fat, and pour egg mixture into it. When omelet begins to set, sprinkle the crumbled bacon on top. Lift cooked omelet edges with a fork so that the uncooked portion runs underneath. Cook until eggs are set and golden brown. Fold and serve hot. For a firm omelet, turn on a plate and replace omelet in skillet uncooked side down. Brown lightly and serve.

FINNISH SPINACH PANCAKES

Finland, like Sweden, is a pancake land. These spinach pancakes, which make a good entrée, should be made small and thin, since, thanks to the spinach, they take longer to cook through than plain pancakes.

1 cup milk
1 teaspoon salt
⅛ teaspoon nutmeg
1 cup flour
2 tablespoons melted butter
2 eggs
1 teaspoon sugar

½ lb. fresh spinach, blanched and chopped, or 1 package chopped frozen spinach, thawed and drained
butter

Season milk with salt and nutmeg. Sift in flour, a little at a time, beating constantly. Stir in melted butter. Let mixture stand for 30 minutes to 1 hour. Beat eggs with sugar and stir into batter. Add spinach. Prepare pancakes as usual. In Finland, these pancakes are served with lingonberries.

SWEDISH PANCAKES
(*Plättar*)

To be authentically small and very thin, Swedish pancakes ought to be baked in a Swedish pancake pan, which has depressions for each pancake. They can be bought in good housewares stores or in Scandinavian supply houses. But these pancakes may also be baked on a hot griddle, by the tablespoonfuls.

Incidentally, pancakes are a staple in all Scandinavian countries, and basically, there is not a great deal of difference among them. The Norwegians often eat theirs cold, folded over.

4 eggs, separated
1 cup flour
½ teaspoon salt
1 teaspoon sugar
1 cup milk
3 tablespoons sour cream
lingonberry preserves or applesauce

Beat egg yolks until thick. Sift together flour, salt and sugar. Add to egg yolks alternately with milk. Stir in sour cream. Beat egg whites until stiff but not dry. Fold into batter. Heat pancake pan and butter each depression. Pour about a tablespoon of batter into each depression and spread out evenly. Brown on one side, turn and brown on the other side. Serve at once with preserves or applesauce.

JANSON'S TEMPTATION

An immensely popular Swedish combination of anchovies and potatoes, two foods of which the Swedes are very fond indeed. As for the unknown Janson, who knows whether he fell?

6 medium potatoes, sliced wafer thin
12 anchovy fillets, drained, cut in pieces
1 onion, diced fine
¼ teaspoon pepper
2 cups light cream
2 tablespoons butter

Set oven at 350°.

Place a layer of half of the potatoes in a buttered baking dish. Top with anchovies and onion. Sprinkle with pepper and top with remaining potatoes. Pour cream over mixture and dot with butter. Bake about 30 minutes or until potatoes are tender and the top delicately browned. About 10 smorgasbord servings or 4 to 6 main course servings.

BAKED ANCHOVIES AND EGGS

A favorite hot smorgasbord combination. If you like a stronger anchovy flavor, increase the quantity of anchovies according to taste.

8 anchovy fillets, drained
3 eggs
2 cups light cream
2 tablespoons chopped parsley

Set oven at 350°.

Place anchovies in a buttered baking dish. Beat together eggs, cream and parsley. Pour over anchovies. Bake about 25 minutes or until set and golden brown. Serve hot on the smorgasbord table.

Chicken
and Other Birds,
Meats

SCANDINAVIAN ROAST CHICKEN

Scandinavians roast their chickens not in the oven, but in a heavy pan on top of the stove. Parsley is a favorite stuffing, and cream sauce is the standard chicken sauce.

1 3- to 4-lb. whole broiling chicken
2 teaspoons salt
½ teaspoon white pepper
6 tablespoons butter
1 to 1½ cups chopped parsley
1 cup chicken bouillon, boiling

Rub chicken inside and out with salt and pepper. Mix half of the butter with the parsley. Stuff chicken with mixture; truss. Heat remaining butter in heavy casserole or Dutch oven. Brown chicken in it on all sides. Cover with boiling bouillon. Simmer, covered tightly, for 40 to 50 minutes or until chicken is tender. Check occasionally for dryness; if necessary, add a little more boiling bouillon. Transfer chicken to hot serving platter and keep hot while making sauce.

Sauce

3 tablespoons pan drippings
3 tablespoons flour
1 cup broth from pan (if there is not sufficient broth, add boiling bouillon to make 1 cup)
⅔ cup heavy cream
salt and pepper to taste
dash of ground cardamom (optional)

Heat pan drippings and stir in flour. Cook until golden, stirring constantly. Gradually stir in boiling broth and cook until thickened and smooth, stirring all the time. Reduce heat to lowest possible level and add cream. Season to taste. Simmer, covered, for 5 minutes, stirring occasionally. Strain and reheat.

NOTE: For a richer sauce add 3 tablespoons softened butter to heated strained sauce, beating vigorously until butter is absorbed.

To serve, decorate chicken platter with leaves of Boston lettuce, slices of tomato, and parsley sprigs. Serve sauce separately. Browned potatoes and a tossed green salad would complement the roast chicken.

NORWEGIAN CHICKEN WITH SOUR CREAM

(Stekt kylling med sur fløte)

This comes from Leif Borthen, a hospitable Oslo journalist who has done much to promote the cause of sophisticated cooking, both in the word and deed.

1 3-lb. frying chicken (about), cut in serving pieces
1 teaspoon salt
½ teaspoon white pepper
¼ cup butter
¼ cup cognac
2 cups milk
¼ cup sherry
¼ cup chopped parsley
½ cup sour cream
mushroom caps sautéed in butter
broiled tomato halves
parsley sprigs

Skin chicken and rub with salt and pepper. Heat butter in large, heavy skillet. Brown chicken in it on all sides. Flame by pouring cognac over chicken and lighting the heated spirit. When the flame has died down, cover with milk. Simmer, covered, over lowest possible heat about 35 to 45 minutes or until chicken is tender. Baste occasionally with the milk, which will clot. Add sherry and parsley and cook 3 minutes longer. Transfer chicken pieces to hot platter and keep hot. Stir sour cream into pan juices and pour sauce over chicken. Garnish with mushroom caps, broiled tomato halves and sprigs of parsley. Serves 3 to 4.

DANISH CHICKEN BREASTS SOUBISE

6 whole chicken breasts, skinned and boned (the butcher will do this)
1 quart chicken bouillon, boiling
6 tablespoons butter
3 large onions, sliced as thinly as possible
4 tablespoons butter
¼ cup cognac
1 tablespoon flour
½ teaspoon salt
¼ teaspoon white pepper
⅓ cup heavy cream
2 medium truffles, peeled (optional)

Place chicken breasts in heavy casserole or Dutch oven and cover with boiling chicken bouillon. Add the first 6 tablespoons of butter. Cover tightly and simmer 30 minutes or until done. Drain; keep hot and reserve stock. Meanwhile, cook onions in heavy saucepan with 2 tablespoons of the butter for 15 minutes. Cook over lowest possible heat, stirring frequently. Onions must not become brown but should remain white. After 10 minutes of cooking time, stir in cognac. Sprinkle with flour, salt and pepper, and cook 3 minutes longer. Add ¾ cup of reserved chicken stock and simmer, covered, over lowest possible heat for 1 hour and 15 minutes. The onions must be simmered for this length of time and they must be kept as white as possible. Rub onion mixture through fine sieve or purée in blender. Place in top of double boiler and add cream. Taste and correct seasonings. Add remaining butter and stir until completely melted. Coat hot chicken breasts with part of the sauce and decorate with truffle cut-outs. To serve, place chicken breasts on heated platter. Surround with mounds of buttered baby peas and carrots, and small browned potatoes. Decorate with parsley sprigs. Serve remaining sauce separately.

NORWEGIAN PTARMIGAN OR SNOW BIRD
(*Ryper*)

A great delicacy from the Arctic, justly admired by all of Scandinavia. The birds are usually cooked in about the same way in all the countries. This version comes from the Prinsen Hotel in Trondheim, a very modern and handsome hotel which has several excellent restaurants with mile-long menu cards offering an international cuisine done up with a lavish hand, as well as a fine cellar.

Ptarmigan can be bought occasionally in American specialty stores. The following recipe is equally successful with other birds, such as grouse, quail and snipe.

Game birds must be well larded or covered with fat during cooking or they tend to become dry.

4 ptarmigan
4 large slices of bacon or salt pork
1 teaspoon salt
½ teaspoon white pepper
1 cup butter
1 cup boiling water
1 cup hot milk
1 to 1½ cups sour cream or sweet heavy cream
2 slices Norwegian goat cheese or ½ cup Blue cheese

Clean birds, wash and dry. Tie a slice of bacon around the breast of each bird and fasten with toothpick or skewer. Or else, lift skin of the breast and insert bacon under the skin. Tie legs to the body. Sprinkle with salt and pepper. Reserve 1 tablespoon of the butter. Heat remaining butter in deep skillet. Brown birds in it on all sides. Gradually add the boiling water. Simmer, covered, over low heat for 15 minutes and then add hot milk. Simmer for 1½ to 3 hours, depending on the age and size of the birds. Keep skillet covered except for a crack to allow steam to escape. When meat shrinks away from the bones and birds are nearly done, stir in sour cream. Birds should cook about 30 minutes in sour cream. Transfer cooked birds to hot serving dish and keep hot. Bring gravy to a boil and add cheese. Check for seasoning. If gravy is too thick, dilute with a little hot water; if too thin, add a little more sour cream. Stir remaining tablespoon of butter into gravy. Pour gravy over birds. Serve with green peas or other vegetables, boiled potatoes, and lingonberry or cranberry preserves.

NOTE: It is considered a sin to put even a speck of flour into a first class ptarmigan gravy.

SWEDISH ROYAL POT ROAST

(*Slottsstek*)

Excellent. The anchovies give it its subtle flavor, which is not at all fishy.

4 lbs. beef, chuck or round
2 teaspoons salt
1 teaspoon allspice
½ teaspoon pepper
3 tablespoons butter
3 tablespoons brandy or whisky
⅓ cup hot bouillon
2 medium onions, sliced
3 minced anchovy fillets, or 1 teaspoon anchovy paste
2 bay leaves
2 tablespoons white vinegar
2 tablespoons molasses or dark syrup

Rub meat with salt, allspice and pepper. Heat butter and brown meat in it on all sides. Pour brandy over hot meat and flame. Add all other ingredients and blend. Simmer covered over very low heat about 2 hours, or until meat is tender. Remove meat to hot serving platter and keep hot. Make gravy. Slice meat and surround with little mounds of buttered peas, carrots and cauliflower buds, and decorate with tomato and cucumber slices and parsley. Pour a little of the gravy over the meat and serve the rest of the gravy separately.

Gravy

Make gravy from pan drippings in usual manner. Flavor with ¼ teaspoon anchovy paste and fold in 1 cup heavy cream, whipped.

FINNISH SOUR POT ROAST

A kind of sauerbraten, but flavored more interestingly with beer, horseradish and juniper berries. In Finland, fresh horseradish and a juniper branch with berries are *de rigueur.*

1 4-lb. beef round
2 quarts beer
2 cups cider vinegar
1 cup sugar
1 teaspoon salt
1 teaspoon whole peppercorns
½ teaspoon ground or 1 teaspoon whole allspice
1 ½-inch piece ginger root or ½ teaspoon ground ginger
1 ½-inch piece fresh horseradish or 2 teaspoons bottled horseradish
12 juniper berries, crushed

Trim beef of excess fat. Combine all other ingredients. Place meat in deep bowl. (Do not use an aluminum bowl.) Pour marinade over meat. Let stand in refrigerator for 5 days. Rinse, dry and pot-roast in the usual manner.

SCANDINAVIAN SEAMAN'S BEEF
(Sjömansbiff)

This is the Swedish version, and a very good one, of a popular Scandinavian dish. This casserole lends itself to informal buffet entertaining when hearty food is needed. Though the preparation takes a little time, this can be done in the morning, or the night before the casserole is needed. Also, the Seaman's Beef does not suffer if kept waiting.

2 lbs. chuck or round, or other boneless beef
1½ teaspoons salt
1 tablespoon freshly ground pepper
6 bay leaves, crumbled
1 12-ounce can beer or ale
⅓ cup flour
⅔ to 1 cup butter
2 lbs. raw potatoes, peeled and sliced
3 large raw carrots, sliced
3 large onions, sliced

Cut meat into thin 1-inch squares about ¼ inch thick. Sprinkle with salt and pepper. Place in deep container and sprinkle with crumbled bay leaves. Pour beer over meat. Let stand 4 hours or overnight.

Set oven at 350°.

Drain meat and dry. Reserve beer marinade. Coat meat with flour. Heat one third of the butter and fry meat over high heat until golden on both sides. Reserve meat. Fry potatoes in the same skillet for 3 minutes and reserve. Add more butter and fry carrots for 3 minutes and reserve. Add remaining butter and fry onions until soft and golden. Arrange alternate layers of potatoes, meat, carrots and onions in buttered 2½-quart casserole. The first and last layers should be potatoes. Pour reserved beer marinade over meat mixture. Cover with lid or aluminum foil and bake about 1½ hours or until meat and vegetables are tender. Check occasionally for moisture; if too dry, add a little more beer, about ⅓ cup at a time. Serve with a tossed green salad or with sliced tomatoes and cucumbers.

SWEDISH BEEF LINDSTRÖM

A piquant hamburger which is extremely good. The patties should be large and flat.

2 lbs. ground steak
3 egg yolks
¾ cup mashed potatoes
2 teaspoons salt
½ teaspoon pepper
¼ cup heavy cream
¾ cup cooked beets, finely chopped (or pickled beets)
⅓ cup onion, finely chopped
⅓ cup capers, chopped
butter

Blend together meat, egg yolks, mashed potatoes, salt and pepper. Gradually beat in cream. Combine beets, onion and capers and blend into mixture. Shape into large flat patties and fry quickly in butter on both sides.

NOTE: In Sweden, Beef Lindström is often served with a fried egg on top.

DANISH BONELESS BIRDS

(Benløse Fugle)

This dish, with variations, is found in all Scandinavian countries. The Danish bacon is sold canned throughout the country and is very tasty.

Danish bacon or salt pork, cut in strips a little shorter than length of meat

Round steak cut in ½-inch-thick slices, 2 per person
salt
pepper
minced parsley
butter
boiling bouillon
flour, cream for gravy

If salt pork is used, soak in cold water if too salty. Dry before using. Pound meat thin with meat pounder or rolling pin. Season with salt and pepper. Use little salt, since bacon or pork are salty. Place a strip of bacon on each slice of beef, and top with a teaspoon of minced parsley. Roll up and fasten with toothpicks. Melt butter and fry birds on all sides until brown. Add boiling bouillon to cover. Simmer, covered, for 1 hour or until meat is tender. Transfer meat to heated platter and keep hot. Make cream gravy in the usual manner. Pour sauce over meat or serve separately. Serve with new potatoes sprinkled with parsley and cucumber salad.

NORWEGIAN BREADED BREAST OF VEAL

Inexpensive and very good family food.

3 to 4 lbs. breast of veal
boiling water
1 tablespoon salt
2 egg whites, slightly beaten
1 cup fine dry breadcrumbs
1 teaspoon salt
¼ teaspoon pepper
¼ cup butter
1 cup hot bouillon or veal stock

Cut meat into serving pieces. Place in heavy saucepan and cover with boiling water. Add salt. Bring to a boil; skim as often as needed. Reduce heat. Simmer covered 1 hour or until meat is tender. Drain; reserve stock. Dry meat with kitchen toweling and remove meat from bones. Trim pieces; brush with egg white. Combine breadcrumbs with salt and pepper. Coat meat pieces with breadcrumbs. Heat butter and fry meat until golden crisp. Transfer to hot serving dish and keep hot. Stir bouillon into pan and blend with drippings. Boil until the right consistency for sauce has been obtained. Serve meat with green peas, fried potatoes and serve gravy on the side.

SWEDISH VEAL CUTLET À LA OSCAR

This combination of the tenderest veal, lobster, asparagus and béarnaise sauce is a specialty of first-class Scandinavian restaurants. This particular version comes from the luxurious Kronprinsen Restaurant in Malmö, where the cuisine ranks with the finest in Europe, both as to preparation and service.

The asparagus used in Sweden is snow white and very tender. This kind of asparagus can be bought here in specialty stores imported in glass jars.

2½ lbs. boneless rump of veal, ¾ inch thick
1 teaspoon salt
¼ teaspoon white pepper
¼ cup butter
20 stalks hot cooked asparagus, tender part only
1½ cups hot cooked lobster meat, diced
Béarnaise Sauce

Cut meat into 5- or 6-pound serving pieces and trim away all fat and gristle. Rub meat with salt and pepper. Melt butter in large skillet. Over medium heat, cook meat until golden on both sides. Reduce heat, and simmer covered about 10 to 15 minutes or until meat is tender and cooked through. Arrange meat on hot serving platter. Place 2 asparagus spears on each side of each round. Fill center with lobster. Cover with Béarnaise Sauce and decorate with parsley sprigs. Serve with Browned Potatoes and a tossed green salad.

SWEDISH BRAISED BEEF ROLL

(*Oxrulader*)

The Swedish version of a dish that is universally popular in all of Scandinavia. The secret is to use lean, well-flavored bacon, such as imported Danish bacon or hickory-smoked bacon.

2 lbs. round steak, cut ¼ inch thick
¼ teaspoon pepper
2 teaspoons prepared mustard
½ cup minced parsley
8 slices bacon, about ¼ inch thick
flour
3 tablespoons butter
½ cup hot bouillon
¼ cup heavy cream

Pound meat as thin as possible without breaking it. Use meat mallet or rolling pin. Cut into 8 strips about 4 inches long and 2 inches wide. Season on one side with pepper and spread thinly with mustard and parsley. Place one slice of bacon on the mustard side of each strip of meat. Roll up and secure rolls with toothpicks or small skewers. Coat rolls with flour. Heat butter in heavy skillet. Brown beef rolls on all sides. Add hot bouillon. Simmer, covered, over low heat ¾ to 1 hour, or until meat is tender. Place beef rolls in hot serving dish and keep hot. Add cream to pan juices, scraping bottom of the pan and stirring constantly. Pour over beef rolls and serve with any kind of potatoes and a green vegetable.

BÉARNAISE SAUCE

Béarnaise is made like Hollandaise sauce. The difference between the two sauces is that béarnaise is flavored with wine, vinegar, shallots, pepper and tarragon whereas Hollandaise is flavored with lemon juice.

¼ cup wine vinegar
¼ cup dry white wine
1 tablespoon minced shallots or green onions
½ tablespoon dried tarragon
⅛ teaspoon white pepper
1/16 teaspoon salt
3 egg yolks
2 tablespoons cold butter
⅔ cup melted butter
1 tablespoon minced parsley

In small saucepan boil together vinegar, wine, shallots, tarragon, pepper and salt until the liquid has been reduced to 2 tablespoons. Strain; cool to lukewarm. Add egg yolks and beat briskly with a wire whip. Place saucepan over lowest possible heat. Add 1 tablespoon of the cold butter and beat into sauce. Beat in remaining tablespoon of cold butter. Then beat in melted butter, drop by drop, until sauce thickens. Stir in minced parsley. Makes 1½ cups sauce.

SCANDINAVIAN VEAL POT ROAST

(*Kalvestek*)

This is the standard way of making a veal roast in all of Scandinavia. Veal is a delicacy, and cooked this way, it will remain juicy.

4 to 5 lbs. veal roast (rump or leg)
2 teaspoons salt

½ teaspoon allspice
¼ teaspoon pepper
3 tablespoons butter
½ cup bouillon
2 carrots, sliced
2 onions, sliced

Make sure that the meat has not been larded by the butcher. If so, remove sheets of fat. Rub meat on all sides with salt, allspice and pepper. In heavy casserole or Dutch oven brown meat on all sides in hot butter. Lift meat with a fork, and pour bouillon, carrots and onions into casserole. Place meat on vegetables. Cover tightly. Simmer about 1½ to 2 hours, or until meat is tender. Remove meat to hot platter, slice, and keep hot. Make cream gravy in the usual manner, using heavy cream instead of milk. Or, for a different gravy, purée vegetables and pan drippings in blender. Dilute to proper consistency with heated heavy cream. Heat through but do not boil. Serve gravy separately. Serve meat with browned potatoes and vegetables, arranged decoratively around meat slices.

DANISH VEAL PATTIES

(*Kalve Frikadeller*)

In Denmark the meatball reigns supreme. And good and inexpensive food it is, too.

1½ lbs. ground veal
½ cup butter, melted
1 teaspoon grated lemon rind
1½ teaspoon salt
½ teaspoon white pepper
2 tablespoons plain soda water (this gives lightness)
1 egg, beaten
1 cup dry breadcrumbs
2 tablespoons butter
1 cup sweet or sour cream

Combine veal, melted butter, grated lemon rind, salt and pepper. Stir in soda water, Shape quickly into patties. Dip patties into beaten egg and breadcrumbs. Heat butter and cook patties in it about 10 to 15 minutes, depending on size of patties. Turn once. Transfer cooked patties to hot serving dish; keep hot. Stir cream into skillet and heat thoroughly. Pour over patties. Serve in the Danish manner with plain boiled potatoes and cucumber salad.

SWEDISH JELLIED VEAL LOAF

No smorgasbord is complete without jellied veal, and there are a great many recipes for it. Most of them would be too bland for our American tastes, since Scandinavians like bland foods. The following recipe makes a well-flavored loaf which holds together without gelatin and keeps in the refrigerator for 4 to 5 days.

1 meaty veal shank (about 2 lbs.)
2¼ lbs. veal shoulder
1¼ lbs. lean pork
2 quarts water
1 large onion, sliced
2 tablespoons salt
4 bay leaves
4 whole allspice or ½ teaspoon ground allspice
½ teaspoon pepper

Place veal shank and meats into deep kettle. Cover with water and add all other ingredients. Bring to boiling point. Skim and simmer, covered, over lowest possible heat until meat is very tender. This will take about 2 to 2½ hours. Drain meat and reserve. Strain broth. Simmer broth uncovered until reduced to 7 cups liquid. Cool and chill in refrigerator. Remove every trace of fat from top of chilled broth. While broth is chilling, cut meats into ¼-inch cubes or push through medium blade of meat grinder. Return meat to skimmed broth and bring to boiling point. Cook uncovered 3 minutes. Pour meat into 3-quart mold or loaf pans. Chill overnight until firm. Unmold on bed of lettuce. Serve with pickled beets. Makes about 16 servings.

SWEDISH ROAST LEG OF LAMB

(*Lammstek*)

The coffee, provided it is not overly strong, gives an excellent color to the meat and a subtle taste to the gravy.

1 5-lb. leg of lamb
1 tablespoon salt
1 tablespoon pepper
2 medium onions, sliced
2 medium carrots, sliced
1 cup hot bouillon
1½ cups hot coffee
½ cup heavy cream
2 teaspoons sugar

Set oven at 450°.

Trim lamb of all excess fat. Rub salt and pepper into the meat. Place meat on a rack in a roasting pan and roast 30 minutes. Pour off fat or remove with baster. Reduce oven heat to moderate (350°) and place onions and carrots into the pan. Combine bouillon, coffee, cream and sugar and pour over meat. Continue roasting for 1 to 1½ hours, depending on the degree of doneness desired. Baste very frequently. Transfer lamb to warm serving platter and keep hot. Strain gravy and press vegetables through a sieve or purée in a blender. Garnish lamb with parsley and broiled tomatoes. Serve with Browned Potatoes and a green vegetable. Serve sauce separately.

SWEDISH BOILED LAMB WITH DILL AND DILL SAUCE

(*Kokt lamm med dillsås*)

This very popular and excellent dish must be made with fresh dill, which can be bought all the year round in many American markets, and in all Scandinavian and Jewish vegetable stores.

3 lbs. breast or shoulder of lamb
boiling water
1 tablespoon salt to every quart of water
4 white peppercorns
1 bay leaf
5 dill sprigs

Trim meat of excess fat and scald quickly in boiling water. Drain, place in casserole or Dutch oven, and add boiling salt water to cover. Bring to a boil and skim. Add remaining ingredients. Simmer covered 1 to 1½ hours or until meat is tender. Drain and reserve stock. Cut meat in serving pieces. Place on hot platter and garnish with more dill sprigs. Serve with Dill Sauce and boiled potatoes.

Dill Sauce

2 tablespoons butter
2 tablespoons flour
1½ to 2 cups stock from lamb
2 tablespoons chopped dill
1½ tablespoons white vinegar
2 tablespoons sugar
salt to taste
1 egg yolk, beaten

Melt butter, add flour and stir until smooth. Add hot stock gradually, and cook until mixture is thickened and smooth.

Simmer, covered, 10 minutes, stirring frequently. Add dill, vinegar, sugar and salt to taste. Remove from heat and stir in beaten egg yolk. Serve hot.

ROAST LAMB À LA KRAMER

This was the *pièce de résistance* of a perfect Swedish spring dinner served to me at the Hotel Kramer in Malmö. Arthur Kristensson, the *maître,* composed it, beginning with salmon and toast, and continuing with roast lamb and new vegetables and strawberries and cream. We drank a 1955 Château Fonroque, sherry and Swedish punsch.

1 5-lb. leg of lamb, trimmed
1½ tablespoons salt
½ tablespoon white pepper
1 lemon, cut in half
¼ cup butter
½ cup fine white dry breadcrumbs
2 tablespoons minced parsley

Set oven at 300°.

Rub lamb with salt and pepper and the lemon halves. Place on rack in roasting pan, and roast, uncovered, 12 minutes per pound for rare or 18 minutes per pound for well done. Carve lamb in the usual manner, but do not cut the slices off the bone—they must remain attached. Keep hot. Melt butter and brown breadcrumbs in it. Stir in parsley. Spread mixture over lamb. Turn oven to hot (450°) and continue roasting for about 10 minutes, or until topping is crisp. Transfer to serving platter and garnish with rows of buttered baby carrots, small bundles of asparagus tips, small mounds of coarsely chopped buttered spinach, whole mushroom caps sautéed in butter, and small grilled tomatoes. Decorate with parsley.

NORWEGIAN LAMB AND CABBAGE
(*Får i Kål*)

The national meat dish of Norway. Norwegian lamb is excellent, since it grazes on the grass of salt marshes, like the prized *pré salé lamb* of France.

4 lbs. lamb (any cut, but inexpensive cuts will do)
1 firm medium cabbage
1 celery root or 1 cup diced celery
1½ tablespoons salt
⅓ cup flour
boiling bouillon or water
2 tablespoons black peppercorns tied in a cheesecloth bag

Trim lamb of excess fat and cut in 2- to 3-inch serving pieces. Core and cut cabbage into 1-inch wedges. Peel celery root and dice. In heavy saucepan or Dutch oven place a layer of meat, fatty side down. Top with cabbage and sprinkle with some of the celery, salt and flour. Repeat process; there should be at least 3 layers of meat and vegetables. Add bouillon to cover lamb and cabbage half way. Add bag with peppercorns. Cover tightly and bring to a slow boil. Check occasionally; if necessary, add a little more bouillon. Cook over low heat until meat is tender, about 1½ to 2½ hours. Remove bag with peppercorns before serving. Serve with boiled potatoes.

NOTE: For a richer dish, stir ½ cup sour cream into *Får i Kål* before serving.

NORWEGIAN SPICED RIBS OF MUTTON
(*Bergen Pinnekjøtt*)

This is another Norwegian national dish and a specialty of the west coast at Christmas time. Americans are not very likely to make it, but in case one of my readers should be seized with the desire, here is the recipe, both the original method and the modernized version.

Traditional Method

Salt a rack of mutton as described in Cured Leg of Mutton (*Fenalår*). Dry in a drafty place for about 3 weeks. To cook, cut through each rib bone for single pieces. Soak meat in cold water for 3 hours. In a large kettle, make a rack of birch twigs. Take twigs a little longer than the diameter of the kettle and press down to make a platform about 1 to 2 inches above the bottom of the kettle. Fill with cold water to the level of the twigs. Place strips of meat on twigs. Cover tightly. Steam about 2 hours. Check for drying out from time to time, and, if necessary, add more water to keep up level. Serve with mashed potatoes and mashed yellow turnips.

NOTE: The birch twigs give *Pinnekjøtt* its typical taste.

Modern Version

2 lbs. ribs of mutton
2 tablespoons salt
1 tablespoon sugar
1 to 2 teaspoons pepper
2 cups boiling water

Trim meat. Combine spices and rub into meat. Dry in drafty place for 3 days. Set oven at 450°. Cut meat into strips. Place in roasting pan and brown in hot oven for 15 minutes. Pour boiling water over ribs. Reduce oven heat to 350°. Cook ribs about 1¾ hours, basting every 10 minutes with pan drippings and more boiling water, if needed. If ribs are drying out, cover with buttered tin foil or nonwaxed paper.

NORWEGIAN CURED LEG OF MUTTON
(*Fenalår*)

This is one of the world's best cold cuts, and is really out of this world. No visitor to Norway should neglect to demand it. The mutton is first cured and then dried for months in the pure fresh

Norwegian air. The air is an essential ingredient to make *Fenalår*. If you live in one of our cooler states and have access to a leg of mutton (not lamb), try making *Fenalår*. The following recipe is a standard one.

In Norway *Fenalår* is prepared in September when the sheep are fat after their summer pasture. It is eaten in May, June or July. As you travel through the countryside, you see the legs of mutton hanging in drafty spots at the back of the barns.

1 8- to 9-lb. leg of mutton
¼ cup cognac
1 teaspoon saltpeter
2 lbs. salt
½ cup molasses
1 cup water

Trim meat and rub thoroughly with cognac. Combine all other ingredients and spread over meat. Place meat in deep stone container and leave in brine for 1 week. Turn several times. Drain and dry meat. Then make a new brine.

Brine

1 gallon water
4 lbs. coarse salt
1 lb. sugar
1 tablespoon saltpeter

Combine all ingredients and bring to a boil. Cool. Place meat in brine for 1 week. Drain, dry and smoke lightly. Hang in drafty place for curing—at least 4 months. The meat should shrink about half the original weight. To serve, cut in wafer-thin slices and remove the outer edge of the fat. Serve on sandwiches, with fried eggs or as a main dish with spring vegetables and potatoes and melted butter. *Fenalår* may also be cured for 2 months only; then it is cooked like a ham and eaten hot.

AUNE'S PORK CASSEROLE

Aune Merikallio is a Finnish home economist who works in this country but still eats in the Finnish way at home. This pork–sauerkraut–apple and potato combination makes an excellent main course for a cold day.

1 4- to 5-lb. fresh pork shoulder
2 teaspoons salt
½ teaspoon pepper
2 teaspoons prepared mustard
3 cups drained sauerkraut
3 medium apples, pared, cored and sliced
1 tablespoon sugar
4 medium potatoes, peeled and sliced

Set oven at 350°.

Trim meat of excess fat. Rub on all sides with salt, pepper and spread with mustard. Place meat on rack in roasting pan. Roast for 1 hour; drain off fat. Remove meat and rack from pan. In the roasting pan now make a layer of sauerkraut. Sprinkle apples with sugar and place on sauerkraut. Top with potatoes. Replace meat in pan on top of potatoes. Cover pan with lid or with baking foil. Return to oven and bake for 1½ to 2 hours longer or until meat is cooked. During cooking time baste meat several times with pan juices. Serve with pickled beets.

NOTE: This dish can also be made on top of the stove, in a deep kettle. The procedure is the same.

NORWEGIAN PORK ROAST PIQUANT

(Svinekam Piquant)

Norwegian men have taken up cooking as their hobby, a far more daring thing than it would be in America. This excellent roast comes from Derek

Blix, who manages the Pan American office in Oslo and helps writers in distress, like this one.

¼ cup prepared Dijon-type mustard
1 tablespoon prepared horseradish
1 teaspoon anchovy paste
1 tablespoon sugar
1 pork loin, about 3 to 4 lbs.
⅔ cup fine dry breadcrumbs
2 cups boiling dry white wine or water

Set oven at 325°.

Combine mustard, horseradish, anchovy paste and sugar, and blend to a smooth paste. Trim excess fat off meat. With a brush, spread meat on all sides with mixture. Place on rack in baking pan. Cover top and sides with breadcrumbs. Roast 35 to 40 minutes to the pound, or until meat thermometer registers 185°. After 1 hour of roasting time, pour 1 cup boiling wine or water into pan. Be careful that the wine or water does not touch the meat. When the liquid has evaporated completely, pour remaining wine or water into pan. Serve on a platter surrounded by alternating mounds of tiny buttered peas, carrots and small browned potatoes.

SCANDINAVIAN PORK TENDERLOIN WITH PRUNES

A favorite in the North. This looks well carved, the dark prunes showing against the lighter meat.

12 large prunes
1½ to 2 lbs. pork tenderloin, in one piece
1 teaspoon salt
½ teaspoon pepper
½ teaspoon ground ginger
3 tablespoons butter
1 cup hot bouillon or water

Soak prunes in hot water until plumped. Drain and dry prunes. With a sharp knife slit prunes and remove pits. Trim excess fat off meat. With a sharp knife cut tenderloin lengthwise about two thirds through. Arrange prunes in a neat row inside tenderloin. Fasten with skewers or tie with string. Rub meat with salt, pepper and ground ginger. Brown tenderloin on all sides in hot butter. Add hot bouillon or water. Simmer, covered, over low heat, about 1½ hours or until meat is tender. Baste occasionally; if necessary, add a little more hot bouillon. To serve, carefully remove skewers or string. Makes 4 servings. Make gravy by straining and skimming pan juices and pouring over meat. Or make cream gravy in the usual manner and serve separately.

FINNISH PORK SAUCE

(*Sianlihakastike*)

The standard daily lunch for most Finnish people. Served with boiled potatoes.

½ lb. salt or fresh pork, sliced
3 tablespoons flour
1 medium onion, chopped
3 cups hot water, about

In hot skillet, brown meat quickly on all sides. It should be crisp. Remove meat and keep hot. Stir flour into pan drippings. Cook until browned, stirring constantly. Add onions and continue cooking until onions are browned. Do not burn. Stir in hot water, a little at a time. Cook until sauce is thickened and smooth. Return meat to sauce. Check for seasoning; salt is needed when fresh pork is used. Cook over lowest possible heat about 30 minutes, stirring occasionally. Serve hot with boiled potatoes.

NOTE: Sometimes, the sauce is seasoned to taste with mustard, or paprika, or tomato purée. Or a little cream may be added to it.

DANISH PORK STEW WITH PRUNES

16 dried prunes
water
4 lbs. pork, with bone (any cut)
½ cup flour
1½ teaspoons salt
½ teaspoon pepper
¼ teaspoon ginger
3 tablespoons butter or margarine
½ cup sherry or Madeira
⅓ cup heavy cream

Plump prunes in water until soft. Drain and dry. Trim pork of excess fat and cut into serving pieces. Combine flour with salt, pepper and ginger. Dredge pork pieces with flour. Heat butter in heavy saucepan or casserole and brown pork in it on all sides. Pour off most of the fat. Add prunes and sherry or Madeira. Cook, covered, over low heat for 1½ hours or until pork is tender. If necessary, add a little hot water. Transfer meat to hot serving dish and keep hot. Stir cream into pan juices and simmer 1 minute. Pour over meat. Serve with boiled potatoes and a green salad.

NOTE: Instead of 4 lbs. of pork with bone, use 2 to 2½ lbs. of boneless pork.

DANISH PORK FRIKADELLER

All the Norse love meatballs, but the Danes' affection and use for them amounts to a national passion. *Frikadeller* are made from every kind of meat. They are eaten continually, either hot or cold. The club soda makes them light.

2 lbs. lean pork, ground fine
½ cup flour

1 egg
1 tablespoon grated onion
1 teaspoon grated lemon rind
1 teaspoon salt
½ teaspoon pepper
½ cup club soda or water
4 tablespoons butter
½ to ¾ cups light or heavy cream

Combine pork, flour, egg, onion, lemon rind, salt and pepper. Blend thoroughly. Stir in club soda gently. Shape meat into small balls, using hands. Heat butter in skillet. Brown pork balls on all sides. Lower heat and cook about 20 minutes or until done. Transfer pork balls to hot serving dish and keep hot. Add cream to pan juices. Bring to a quick boil, stirring constantly. Pour over pork balls. Serve with boiled or browned potatoes and pickled beets.

NOTE: If *Frikadeller* are to be served cold, omit gravy.

DANISH COOKED HAM IN MADEIRA SAUCE
(*Kogt Skinke med Madeira*)

From the Rødirg Kro, a charming old inn in South Zeeland.

1 2-lb. canned Danish ham
⅓ cup dark brown sugar
2 tablespoons Madeira

Set oven at 350°.

Remove ham from can and remove gelatin coating. Make a paste of brown sugar and Madeira. Spread paste over ham. Bake for 30 minutes. Slice and serve with Madeira Sauce.

Madeira Sauce

¼ cup butter
2 teaspoons grated onion or 1 teaspoon instant onion powder
¼ cup flour
2 cups brown stock or beef bouillon, hot
⅓ cup Madeira
½ teaspoon salt
¼ teaspoon pepper

Melt butter. Stir in onion and cook over low heat 2 minutes. Stir in flour. Gradually add hot brown stock or beef bouillon. Cook over low heat until sauce is thick and smooth, stirring constantly. Add Madeira and salt and pepper. Reheat, but do not boil. Serve hot over sliced ham.

Madeira Sauce for Tongue

Tongue, cooked in the usual manner, is a Danish favorite, both hot and cold. Sauce is often served with it.

Plump ¼ cup yellow raisins in hot water. Drain; add the hot raisins to Madeira Sauce (see above) before adding the wine and seasonings. Proceed as above.

SWEDISH CHRISTMAS HAM

Part of the traditional Christmas Eve supper in Sweden, but very good all the year round. The following recipe begins with the curing of the ham, but a cured one can also be used for baking, though not quite as satisfactorily. Allow about 3½ weeks for a home-cured ham.

Curing for Ham

1 10- to 12-lb. fresh ham
1 cup salt

¼ cup sugar
2 teaspoons saltpeter (from the drugstore)

To Cure Ham

Prepare a large stone crock or a deep enamel pan. Do not use aluminum. Combine 1 cup salt, ¼ cup sugar and 2 teaspoons saltpeter. Wipe fresh ham with a cloth. Rub salt mixture into the ham on all sides. Sprinkle any remaining salt mixture over ham. Place ham in crock. Let stand in a cool place or refrigerator for 3 days.

Brine

3 cups salt
½ cup brown sugar
1 tablespoon saltpeter
2 teaspoons whole cloves
4 to 5 quarts boiling water

To Make Brine

Add salt, sugar, saltpeter and cloves to boiling water. Boil for 2 minutes. Cool. Pour brine over ham in crock. (Do *not* remove the previous salt mixture from ham.) The ham should be completely covered by the brine. Place a plate weighted down with some canned goods or other heavy objects on ham to keep it down in the brine. Cover crock. Let ham stand for 3 weeks.

Seasonings for Cooking Ham

boiling water
3 bay leaves
12 whole peppercorns
12 whole allspice
1 medium onion

To Cook Ham

Remove ham from brine and drain thoroughly. Place ham in deep kettle and cover with boiling water, bay leaves, whole pepper, allspice and onion. Cover kettle. Simmer ham until tender, about 4 to 5 hours. Do not boil ham, but keep liquid just at simmering point, not more. Remove ham from heat and let cool in liquid. Drain cooled ham. Trim off skin and excess fat. Place ham on rack in roasting pan. Set oven at 350°.

Glaze

2 egg whites
2 tablespoons sugar
2 tablespoons dry mustard
⅓ cup fine dry breadcrumbs

To Glaze Ham

Beat egg whites until they stand in soft peaks. Beat in sugar and mustard. Brush mixture over ham, fat side up, and cover well on all sides. Cover thinly but evenly with breadcrumbs. Bake ham 35 to 45 minutes or until glaze is brown. Remove ham to platter.

Garnish

paper frills, parsley, soft butter

To Garnish Ham

Garnish bone of ham with a paper frill and surround with parsley sprigs.

NOTE: If the ham is to be served cold, fill smallest pastry tube with softened butter and pipe decorative swirls and loops on ham. You might also write on it: *God Jul,* that is, Merry Christmas!

HAM LEFTOVERS WITH MADEIRA SAUCE

6 slices Danish ham
1 tablespoon butter
1 tablespoon flour

1 teaspoon tomato paste
¾ cup Madeira
⅔ cup heavy cream
salt and pepper to taste

Set oven at 350°.

Remove ham from refrigerator while preparing sauce. Butter a shallow ovenproof dish and warm slightly. Arrange ham slices in it so that they overlap somewhat. Melt butter and stir in flour and tomato paste. Add Madeira and cook over low heat until mixture thickens, stirring constantly. Remove from heat, and slowly add the heavy cream. Season with salt and pepper. Pour sauce over ham and bake 10 minutes or until ham is heated through.

NOTE: If your ham leftovers do not make presentable slices, cut the ham into cubes or strips, and serve the dish over hot buttered toast, rice or noodles.

CANNED DANISH PORK LOIN WITH QUICK CURRANT SAUCE

Canned Danish pork loin, imported into this country, resembles Canadian bacon, though it is more full-flavored.

1 small canned Danish pork loin, thickly sliced (about 1 lb.)
¼ cup butter
3 tablespoons red currant jelly
1 to 2 teaspoons prepared mustard
1 teaspoon grated onion or ½ teaspoon instant onion

Brown pork loin slices in butter on all sides. Remove to hot platter; keep hot. Into the skillet in which the pork loin was browned stir red currant jelly, mustard and onion. Blend thoroughly and heat through, but do not boil. Pour over pork loin slices and serve with browned potatoes.

NORWEGIAN CURED HAM
(*Spekeskinke*)

Another Norwegian specialty cold cut which is extremely good. It can be prepared like *Fenalår* (Cured Leg of Mutton).

DANISH BACON AND POTATOES
(*Braendende Kaerlighed*)

A very simple and remarkably good Danish family dish. For best results, use the readily available (in U.S.A. supermarkets) canned smoked Danish pork loin, which is excellent, or Canadian-style bacon.

Cut as many slices of bacon as you'll need. Fry them and keep them hot. Pile very hot and very rich mashed potatoes on a flat serving dish in the shape of a pyramid. Surround with fried bacon slices. Garnish with parsley and serve with pickled beets on the side.

SWEDISH HASH
(*Pytt i panna*)

Simple, nourishing and good.

6 tablespoons butter
3 medium onions, diced
3 cups diced, boiled peeled potatoes
3 cups diced, leftover meat
salt
pepper
fried eggs
cucumber pickles, sliced

Heat 2 tablespoons of the butter and cook onions in it until soft and golden. Transfer to hot plate. Brown potatoes in 2 tablespoons butter and transfer to hot plate. Brown meat in remaining butter. Return onions and potatoes to skillet and mix thoroughly with meat. Season with salt and pepper and heat through. Arrange on hot platter and garnish with fried eggs (1 for each serving) and sliced cucumber pickles.

NORWEGIAN BROWN HASH
(Brun Lapskaus)

A standard Scandinavian way of using up leftovers. This particular version comes from Doris Løkke of Bodø in North Norway, well above the Arctic Circle. Doris, a Swiss girl, married a Norwegian in Brazil. After living on a farm in a remote Norwegian valley, where things had not changed for a hundred years, she now runs the Bodø Tourist Office with great efficiency and keeps house for her husband and three children as well.

3 cups chopped cold roast pork or ham or beef
3 cups chopped cold peeled boiled potatoes
⅓ cup butter or margarine
2 medium onions, sliced
1½ teaspoons salt
½ teaspoon pepper
1 cup boiling bouillon, about
¼ cup sherry (optional)

Brown meat and potatoes in hot butter. Add onions, salt and pepper. Add boiling bouillon to cover. Bring to a boil; reduce heat. Cover and simmer over low heat about 45 minutes, stirring occasionally. If necessary, add a little more boiling bouillon, one tablespoon at a time. All the bouillon must be absorbed in the finished dish. Stir in sherry. Serve very hot, with parsleyed steamed potatoes and cucumber salad.

DANISH HASH

(*Hachis*)

Meat is so much more expensive in Scandinavia than in the United States that the thrifty housewives of these countries have learned the art of good leftover dishes like this one.

2½ cups leftover roast or boiled beef or pork
2 medium onions, chopped
¼ cup butter
¼ cup flour
1½ cups beef bouillon
½ cup red wine
1 teaspoon Kitchen Bouquet
¼ cup pickle relish
½ teaspoon salt
6 fried eggs
12 small sugar-browned potatoes

Grind meat finely. Cook onion in hot butter until soft and golden. Stir in flour. Gradually stir in the beef bouillon and red wine. Cook over low heat until smooth and thick, stirring constantly. Stir in Kitchen Bouquet, pickle relish, salt and ground meat. Heat through thoroughly. Serve hot topped with fried eggs and sugar-browned potatoes.

SWEDISH MEATBALLS

(*Köttbullar*)

The dish that made Swedish cooking beloved to Americans. Small, they are for the smorgasbord; bigger for an entrée; when served as entrée, they must have their cream gravy in the Swedish manner.

There are probably as many ways of making Swedish meatballs as there are Swedish housewives.

They can be made from one kind of meat only, but I think that a combination gives a better flavor. Whatever the ingredients, the meatballs must be light and should not be handled too much.

2 tablespoons butter
¼ cup onion, finely chopped
½ to ⅔ cup fine dry breadcrumbs
¾ cup light cream
¾ lb. ground round steak
¼ lb. ground veal
¼ lb. ground lean pork
2 teaspoons salt
¼ teaspoon pepper
⅛ teaspoon cloves
⅓ cup butter
¼ cup boiling water

Heat butter and sauté onion in it until soft and golden. Soak breadcrumbs in cream. Combine onion, breadcrumbs, meats, salt, pepper and cloves and blend thoroughly, but with a light hand. Shape mixture with hands into small balls. Wet hands so that meat will not stick. Heat butter and fry meatballs until brown on all sides, shaking pan continuously to prevent sticking. Add boiling water and simmer over lowest possible heat for 5 minutes longer. For the smorgasbord serve on toothpicks. For an entrée make larger meatballs, and make cream gravy as usual with pan juices.

FINNISH KARELIAN "HOTPOT"

(*Karjalan Paisti*)

A typical Finnish meat dish, which must be made with the three different kinds of meat or it won't be right. The flavors combine very well, provided the dish is baked extremely slowly. In Finnish country homes the "hotpot" is often left overnight in the residual heat of the oven after the baking of bread.

1 lb. lean pork
1 lb. beef round
1 lb. boned lamb
2 teaspoons salt
½ teaspoon pepper
½ teaspoon allspice
6 medium onions, sliced
hot bouillon or water

Set oven at 350°.

Cut meats into 2-inch cubes. Sprinkle with salt, pepper and allspice. Arrange alternate layers of meats and onions in deep casserole or baking dish. Add just enough hot bouillon or water to cover meats. Cover and bake about 3 hours, or until meats are fork-tender. Check occasionally for moisture; if necessary, add a little more hot bouillon. The dish should have some, but not too much, pan juice. Serve with boiled or baked potatoes.

FINNISH LIVER CASSEROLE

Liver is a favorite in all Scandinavian countries, and it is cooked with far more imagination and taste than in America. This Finnish liver casserole is excellent, and even non-liver-eaters will like it.

½ cup butter, melted
1 medium onion, chopped
2 eggs
3 cups milk
1½ lbs. beef liver, ground raw
3 cups cooked rice
¾ cup dark corn syrup

½ cup raisins
1 tablespoon salt

Set oven at 400°.

Pour 2 tablespoons melted butter into skillet. Add onion and cook over low heat until soft and transparent. Beat eggs in large bowl until foamy. Blend in milk. Mix in onions and remaining ingredients. Pour into buttered 3-quart casserole. Bake about 1½ hours or until firm. Serve with lingonberry sauce or cranberry catsup.

SWEDISH LIVER PATÉ

(*Lefverpastej*)

The anchovies give this liver paté the characteristic Swedish touch.

1 lb. beef liver
milk
2 medium onions
½ lb. salt pork
6 drained anchovy fillets
1 slice white bread
½ cup milk
1 egg, well beaten
3 tablespoons flour
½ teaspoon pepper
6 slices bacon

Soak liver in milk to cover for 4 hours. Drain and dry. Grind liver with onions twice. Grind salt pork, anchovies and bread twice. Combine liver and salt pork mixtures. Add milk, egg, flour and pepper. Blend thoroughly. Line an 8½-inch by 4½-inch loaf pan with bacon slices. Press liver mixture firmly into pan. Bake in moderate oven (350°) 1 hour. Cover top to prevent overbrowning. Cool before unmolding. Chill before serving.

DANISH LIVER PATÉ

(*Leverpostej*)

Liver paté is part of the cold table in Scandinavia. There are many versions, since it is made at home, often from recipes passed from mother to daughter. This recipe is a Danish one, and it makes paté that is very rich and easy to spread on sandwiches.

1 lb. calf, beef, or pork liver
2 onions
1 lb. fresh pork fat
¼ cup cognac (optional)
1 tablespoon salt
1 tablespoon pepper

If beef liver is used, soak in milk to cover 4 hours, drain and dry. Grind liver finely with onions. Grind pork fat twice. Combine liver, fat, cognac, salt and pepper and blend thoroughly. Place in a 1-quart baking dish. Cover dish to prevent overbrowning during baking. Bake in slow oven (325°) 1 hour. Cool before unmolding.

For Danish open-faced sandwiches, spread liver paté on buttered dark bread. Top with slices of pickled cucumber and strips of jellied consommé.

NORWEGIAN KIDNEYS IN WHITE WINE

(*Nyrer i Hvitvin*)

4 veal kidneys
¼ cup butter
1 tablespoon chopped parsley
½ lb. mushrooms, sliced thin
2 tablespoons flour
1 cup dry white wine

½ cup bouillon
salt and pepper to taste

Trim kidneys and cut into thin slices. Place in cold water and let stand half an hour, changing water twice. Drain and wipe kidneys dry. Heat butter in skillet, and brown kidneys rapidly on all sides. Sprinkle with parsley and add mushrooms. Cook 1 minute, stirring constantly. Sprinkle with flour and add white wine and bouillon. Cook over medium heat 5 minutes, stirring all the time. If too thick, add a little more bouillon. Serve very hot, with steamed potatoes.

Reindeer Meat

Reindeer for meat are raised by the nomad Lapps of Northern Norway and the meat is sold throughout the country either fresh or frozen. Like venison, the meat is dark, lean and tangy. It is usually marinated before cooking. Any venison recipe can be used for reindeer meat.

The following recipe comes from the Grand Hotel in Tromsø, the capital of Northern Norway and an important cultural, fishing and sporting center. It is also the starting point for Arctic expeditions. The Grand Hotel is as comfortable as any good American hotel, with excellent food and dancing every night—as in most Norwegian hotels. When I was there, an old Lapp woman brought a whole reindeer and skinned and cut it up in no time, while squatting in the hotel yard.

REINDEER POT ROAST WITH MUSHROOMS, TOMATOES, GRAPES AND PINEAPPLE

(Reinsdyrmedaljong med champignons, tomat, druer og ananas)

1 5-lb. roast of reindeer, boned and rolled
1 quart dry red wine
1 large onion, sliced
1 stalk celery
10 peppercorns
1 tablespoon salt
2 bay leaves
½ lb. salt pork or bacon, cut in slices
½ cup butter
1 cup sour cream
½ cup heavy cream, whipped
paprika

Garnish

1 lb. mushrooms caps, sautéed in butter
6 tomatoes, cut in halves and grilled
½ lb. dark blue grapes, stemmed
1 cup chopped pineapple, sautéed in butter

Place meat in deep bowl. Combine wine, onion, celery, peppercorns, salt and bay leaves. Pour over meat and marinate for 24 to 48 hours. Turn meat several times. Drain and wipe dry. Strain marinade and reserve.

Lard meat with salt pork or bacon, or wrap larding around meat, tying with string. Heat butter in large heavy casserole or Dutch oven. Brown meat on all sides. Reduce heat to lowest possible. Pour half of the marinade over meat. Simmer, covered, about 2 to 3 hours (depending on toughness of the meat) or until meat is tender. To test for doneness, lift meat and test with a skewer: it should not draw blood. Baste occasionally during cooking time with pan juices; if necessary, add a little more marinade. When done, transfer meat to hot platter and keep hot. Remove string and salt pork or bacon. Make gravy by swirling sour cream in pan in which meat was cooked, but do not boil. (If necessary, thicken gravy with a little flour mixed with water to a smooth paste. Begin with 1 tablespoon and cook 2 to 3 minutes on lowest possible heat.) Add whipped cream to finished gravy and spoon a little over meat on platter. Surround meat with mushroom caps in rows and alternate mounds of grilled tomatoes, grapes and pineapple. The arrangement should be decorative. Serve remaining gravy separately. Serve with browned potatoes.

Whale Meat

Whaling is a major Norwegian industry, carried on in supermodern ships that are floating factories for the processing of the whole animal. Whale meat is readily available throughout Norway, and inexpensive. The meat is dark red and looks like meat, not fish. Properly prepared, it tastes like beef, and not like fish. It is important to soak the whale meat several hours (3 hours or more) in iced water to remove any possible fishy taste. Change water several times.

WHALE MEAT IN BROWN SAUCE

2 lbs. whale meat
¼ cup flour
1 teaspoon salt
½ teaspoon pepper
¼ cup butter, bacon or other fat
2 medium onions, sliced
1 cup or more boiling bouillon or water
2 bay leaves

Soak whale meat in iced water for at least 3 hours, changing water several times. Drain; dry thoroughly. Cut meat across the grain into 3- or 4-inch square pieces. Pound pieces with meat pounder or rolling pin. (Or sprinkle with meat tenderizer according to directions.) Combine flour, salt and pepper. Dredge meat pieces in flour mixture. Heat butter and brown onions in it. Push onions to one side of the skillet or casserole, and brown whale meat on all sides. Cover with boiling bouillon or water and add bay leaves. Simmer covered for 1 hour or until meat tests tender. Check gravy consistency; thicken, if necessary, with a little more flour. For a richer gravy, stir in ½ cup sour cream.

WHALE MEAT COOKED LIKE VENISON

- 2 lbs. whale meat
- ½ lb. salt pork or bacon, cut into thin strips
- ¼ cup butter
- 1 cup milk
- 1 cup water
- 5 peppercorns
- 1 teaspoon salt
- 1 teaspoon sugar
- 2 bay leaves
- ⅔ cup sour cream

Soak whale meat in iced water for 3 or more hours, changing water several times. Drain; dry thoroughly. Lard meat with salt pork, using larding needle, or make holes in meat with thick knitting needle and push pork strips through the holes. Or wrap strips around meat, tying with string. Brown meat in hot butter on all sides. Place in casserole or Dutch oven and cover with milk and water. Add peppercorns, bay leaves, salt and sugar. Cover tightly and simmer about 1 hour or until meat is tender. Turn meat several times during cooking. Place meat on hot serving platter; remove strings and pork. Keep hot. Strain pan juices and stir in sour cream. If a thicker gravy is desired, stir 1 or 2 tablespoons flour moistened with water to a smooth paste into pan juices. Cook for 3 minutes and proceed as above.

MORE ABOUT WHALE MEAT

After soaking in iced water (see above), whale meat can be prepared as pan-fried steak, as boneless birds, and ground for patties and meatballs, just like beef. Leftovers can be used in any standard way.

Vegetables, Sauces

FINNISH BARLEY PUDDING
(*Uunipuuro*)

The Finnish country people traditionally eat many of the grains that grow in their lattitudes (such as barley, oats, rye and buckweat) in the form of gruels and puddings. The use of these dishes goes back for many centuries, and most of them would appear strange to Americans. However, this typical barley pudding is excellent and can be served as a side dish in lieu of potatoes. In the Finnish countryside the pudding is served with hot milk as a lunch or supper dish.

1¼ cups barley (large grain)
4 cups water
6 cups boiling milk
⅓ cup butter

Set oven at 250°.

Soak barley in water overnight or for several hours. Cook in the same water. As barley begins absorbing water, gradually add boiling milk, stirring constantly. Cook barley over lowest possible heat for about 30 minutes. Stir frequently to prevent scorching. Or cook in top of double boiler over boiling water. Transfer barley to buttered 1½- or 2-quart baking dish. Dot with butter and bake until golden brown, about 2 hours.

NORWEGIAN CABBAGE WITH SOUR CREAM

I had this on the train that took me to Bodø in Northern Norway, and it seemed an excellent way to alleviate the dullness of cabbage. By the way, Norwegian trains are very cozy and comfortable, both in the way of passengers and personnel. The conductors even announce over the loudspeaker such notable sights as Sigrid Undset's farm!

1 medium cabbage, shredded (about 4 cups)
water
1½ teaspoons salt
½ teaspoon pepper
⅔ cup sour cream
1 tablespoon dill seeds

Cook cabbage in just enough water to keep it from burning. Stir frequently. The cabbage should be tender, but still crisp. Stir in salt, pepper, sour cream and dill seeds. Cook, covered, over lowest possible flame 5 to 10 minutes, stirring frequently to prevent scorching. If necessary, add a little more sour cream.

NOTE: This dish is even better when made with Savoy cabbage.

SWEDISH, NORWEGIAN HOT CAULIFLOWER WITH SHRIMP

This makes a good luncheon entrée.

1 large cauliflower
boiling salt water

Sauce

2 cups milk
1 thin slice onion or 1 teaspoon powdered onion
2 sprigs dill or parsley
4 tablespoons butter
4 tablespoons flour
1 teaspoon salt
¼ teaspoon white pepper
2 cups cooked cold shelled shrimp, chopped or whole
¼ cup heavy cream, whipped
minced fresh dill or parsley

Trim cauliflower, wash thoroughly, and cook whole in boiling salt water. Meanwhile, make sauce. Combine milk, onion and dill or parsley and bring to a boil. Remove dill or parsley. Melt butter, stir in flour and cook 2 minutes stirring constantly. Do not let brown. Stir hot milk into mixture, stirring all the while. Cook, stirring constantly, until mixture is thickened and smooth. Cook 2 minutes longer. Season with salt and pepper. Add shrimps and cook over lowest possible heat until shrimps are heated through. Fold whipped cream into sauce. Place hot cauliflower on serving dish and pour sauce over it. Sprinkle with minced fresh dill or parsley.

SWEDISH CAULIFLOWER WITH EGG SAUCE

(Blomkål med ägg)

Cauliflower grows well in the Scandinavian latitudes; hence it is a favorite vegetable.

1 large cauliflower
boiling salt water
¼ cup butter
⅔ cup minced onion
2 tablespoons fine dried breadcrumbs
2 hard-cooked eggs, chopped fine
¼ cup minced parsley or dill
1 teaspoon salt
¼ teaspoon pepper

Boil cauliflower whole or broken in flowerets. While it is cooking, make the sauce. Melt butter in skillet and cook onion in it until soft and golden. Stir in breadcrumbs, eggs, parsley or dill, and salt and pepper. Toss lightly until blended. Place cauliflower in serving dish and pour sauce over it.

DANISH RED CABBAGE

Very good and even better if made the day before it is to be served, and then reheated. This is a sweet–sour dish and, according to taste, a little more sugar and vinegar may be added.

3 lbs. red cabbage
3 tablespoons butter
1 tablespoon sugar
1 tablespoon cider vinegar
½ cup water
½ cup red currant jelly
2 peeled and cored apples, chopped
salt
pepper

Remove tough outer leaves and core from cabbage. Shred fine. In heavy saucepan, heat butter and melt sugar. Do not brown. Add cabbage, cook 3 minutes, and add vinegar and water. Simmer, covered, for 2 to 3 hours, or until very tender. Stir occasionally and, if needed to prevent scorching, add a little more hot water. Half an hour before cabbage is done, add red currant jelly, apples, salt and pepper. Continue cooking, stirring occasionally.

NORWEGIAN COLD CAULIFLOWER WITH SHRIMP

This makes an attractive dish for a smörgasbord. From the Hotel Continental in Oslo.

1 large cauliflower
boiling salt water
1½ cups mayonnaise (or more, depending on size of cauliflower)
1 lb. cooked cold shelled shrimp
1 hard-cooked egg, sliced
dill or parsley sprigs

Trim cauliflower, wash thoroughly, and cook whole in boiling salt water. Drain; cool and transfer to serving dish. Spread cauliflower with mayonnaise. Arrange shrimps on it in decorative design. Garnish with hard-cooked egg slices and dill or parsley sprigs.

NOTE: For a festive occasion, the cauliflower may be garnished as elaborately as you like with olives, pimento strips, tomato slices etc., etc.

BRITT'S STUFFED CAULIFLOWER

Britt Axelson is a dashing Swedish lady farmer who cooks this for her people. The dish is good family fare and can be made with any favorite meat loaf combination. The quantities don't have to be exactly in accordance with those given here.

2 medium cauliflowers
1 lb. ground meat (beef, pork, veal, or any combination)
½ cup fine dry breadcrumbs
¾ cup chopped parsley
1 egg
1½ teaspoons salt
½ teaspoon pepper
dash Tabasco
⅔ cup butter
aluminum foil

Set oven at 350°.

Trim cauliflowers of green leaves. Turn upside down and with sharp knife scoop out main stalk to make cavity. Take care not to break off buds. Wash cauliflowers and cook in boiling salt water until just tender. Combine all other ingredients and blend thoroughly. Line baking dish with aluminum foil and butter heavily with half of the butter. Fill cauliflower cavities with meat mixture. Place on aluminum foil, meat side down. Dot with remaining butter. Cover tightly with more aluminum foil so that cauliflower is completely covered. Bake about 30 to 40 minutes. Place on hot platter and serve with tomato or mushroom or curry sauce.

Finnish Mushroom Cookery

I was introduced to the wonderful world of Finnish mushrooms by Pan American's Paul P. Suni. In all of my gastronomical wanderings, I have never met with such a variety of mushrooms nor tasted better ones. To us, used to one kind of cultivated mushroom, the subtle and different tastes of the various Finnish mushrooms is a revelation.

Mushrooms are part of the standard Finnish diet. They are eaten fresh, and they are smoked and pickled for preservation. During the mushroom season, which begins at the end of August, the Finns, in family groups, go mushrooming in the incredibly beautiful woods which cover a great part of the country. There are over 100 edible mushrooms, all different, all wonderful.

The following recipes are popular ones, and of course, they taste very different depending on the kind of mushroom used.

FINNISH BAKED MUSHROOMS À LA SUNI

1 lb. mushrooms
lemon juice
2 tablespoons grated onion or 1 large shallot, minced
¼ cup butter
salt
pepper
2 tablespoons flour
2 cups heavy cream
4 egg yolks, lightly beaten
¼ cup fine dry breadcrumbs
¼ cup butter

Set oven at 425°.

Trim mushrooms and slice thinly. Sprinkle with lemon juice to keep white. Simmer, tightly covered, with onion and butter. Season with salt and pepper and stir in flour. Cook about 3 minutes. Place in buttered 1½-quart or 2-quart baking dish. Beat together cream and egg yolks. Pour mixture over mushrooms. Sprinkle with breadcrumbs and dot with butter. Bake 10 minutes or until golden brown.

FINNISH MUSHROOMS WITH SOUR CREAM

¼ cup butter
2 tablespoons grated onion or 1 medium shallot, sliced thinly
1 lb. mushrooms, sliced
1 teaspoon salt
¼ teaspoon white pepper
⅛ teaspoon nutmeg
1 cup sour cream

Melt butter and cook onion or shallot in it for 3 minutes. Add mushrooms, salt, pepper and nutmeg. Cook over medium heat until mushrooms are browned and pan liquid almost evaporated. Remove from heat and stir in sour cream. Heat through again, but do not boil. Serves 3.

SCANDINAVIAN GLAZED ONIONS

1 lb. small white onions
1 tablespoon sugar
1 teaspoon salt
2 tablespoons butter
1 cup bouillon or water

Place peeled onions in heavy skillet. Sprinkle with sugar and salt. Add butter and bouillon. Simmer until bouillon has been absorbed. Fry in skillet over low heat until onions are golden brown and glazed, shaking pan frequently to avoid sticking. Serve with roast meats.

MADELEINE HAMILTON'S POTATO–MUSHROOM RAGOUT

From a former Swedish skiing champion who is also an excellent cook.

4 cups hot mashed potatoes
2 eggs, beaten
1 teaspoon salt
½ teaspoon pepper
⅛ teaspoon cardamom
1 lb. mushrooms, sliced
¼ cup butter
2 tablespoons melted butter
⅓ cup chopped chives or parsley

Set oven at 425°.

Combine potatoes, eggs, salt, pepper and cardamom and mix thoroughly. Sauté mushrooms in hot butter until just limp. They must be still firm. Place mushrooms into the bottoms of individual well-buttered baking dishes. Top with a border of mashed potatoes piped through a tube in decorative swirls. Or else, use a fork and score the border with the fork to make a pattern. Paint potatoes with melted butter and sprinkle with chives. Bake until potatoes are slightly browned. Or broil under medium broiler.

NOTE: This dish can also be baked in a shallow baking dish and brought to the table in it.

NORWEGIAN BUTTER-STEAMED NEW POTATOES

Delicious with fresh boiled salmon. I first had this combination at the Grand Hotel in Tromsø, an important and very civilized Norwegian city well above the Arctic Circle.

20 to 24 tiny new potatoes, about 1 inch or less in diameter
6 to 8 tablespoons butter
salt and pepper
3 tablespoons fresh chopped dill

Scrub potatoes with wire brush, but do not peel. Melt butter in heavy casserole. Add potatoes and season with salt and pepper. Cover casserole tightly so that no steam willl escape. Cook over lowest possible heat until potatoes are tender. Shake casserole frequently to prevent sticking. Sprinkle with dill before serving.

DANISH SUGAR BROWNED POTATOES

(*Brunede Kartofler*)

A favorite Danish way with potatoes.

12 small potatoes
¼ cup sugar
¼ cup butter

Cook potatoes in boiling salt water until tender. Drain and peel. Cook sugar in a skillet over low heat until sugar turns brown. Add butter. Stir constantly until smooth. Add potatoes. Roll potatoes in sugar–butter mixture until coated and golden brown. Serve with pork, poultry, ham, and all meats.

BROWNED POTATOES THE SCANDINAVIAN WAY

2 lbs. hot boiled potatoes (very small potatoes are best)
2 tablespoons butter
⅓ cup dry breadcrumbs
1 teaspoon salt
½ teaspoon sugar

Peel potatoes and if necessary shape into small balls. Melt butter in heavy skillet and brown breadcrumbs, salt and sugar in it. Add potatoes and shake continuously until potatoes are covered with breadcrumbs and golden brown. Remove from pan and serve piping hot.

SWEDISH CREAMED POTATOES

(*Skånsk potatis*)

From Southern Sweden, and far better than most creamed potatoes.

6 tablespoons butter
2 medium onions, sliced thin
6 cups peeled and diced raw potatoes
1½ teaspoons salt
¼ teaspoon white pepper
1 cup light cream, or more
3 tablespoons minced parsley or fresh dill

Heat 2 tablespoons of the butter in skillet and cook onions in it until soft and golden. Transfer onions to casserole. Heat remaining butter and sauté potatoes in it until golden brown and half cooked. Transfer potatoes to casserole. Season with salt and pepper and mix thoroughly with onions. Add cream. Simmer covered over lowest possible heat until potatoes are done, about 15 minutes. The cream should be absorbed, and the potatoes creamy. Stir occasionally and check for dryness; if necessary add more cream, a little at a time. Before serving, sprinkle with parsley or dill.

NOTE: It is impossible to give accurate amounts for cream. Different kinds of potatoes will absorb different amounts of cream, and the absorption of cream depends also on the shape of the casserole. However, the dish is very easy to make; all it needs is a little attention.

FINNISH RUTABAGA PUDDING

An old-time dish served at Christmas with the Christmas ham, and a very good way of using a neglected winter vegetable.

8 cups, peeled and diced rutabagas or swedes
water
1½ teaspoons salt
¼ teaspoon pepper
⅛ teaspoon nutmeg
2 teaspoons sugar or dark syrup or molasses
¼ cup fine dry breadcrumbs
¼ cup light cream
2 eggs, beaten
¼ cup butter

Set oven at 375°.

Cook rutabagas in water to cover until soft. Drain but reserve stock. Mash rutabagas as for mashed potatoes. Beat in reserved stock, salt, pepper, nutmeg and sugar. Soak breadcrumbs in light cream. Beat eggs into breadcrumb mixture. Combine with rutabagas and blend thoroughly. Place in well-buttered baking dish. Smooth surface and dot with butter. Bake about 1 hour or until pudding tests done and is gently browned on top. Serve with meats.

Scandinavian Compound Butters

These butters are used in all good Scandinavian restaurants with meats, fish and vegetables. They do a world of good to everyday hamburgers and the eternal broiled chicken, and I recommend their use at home. Compound butters are extremely easy to make, either by hand or in a blender, and they keep well in the refrigerator, provided they're wrapped up tight or covered, as with any butter.

When using a blender, scrape off sides frequently with a rubber spatula, and use the spatula also to guide the ingredients into the processing blades. To all of these butters add salt to taste.

Shape the compound butter into a roll 1 inch in diameter and wrap in aluminum foil or waxed paper. At serving time cut off ½-inch pats (or pats of any desired size) and serve.

GARLIC BUTTER

(for French bread, meat, fish and vegetables)

Cream 1 cup butter and beat in 2 or 3 cloves of crushed garlic. Or add whole garlic cloves to blender while making butter.

BLUE CHEESE BUTTER

Cream 1 cup butter and beat in 4 tablespoons crumbled Blue cheese. Or combine butter and Blue cheese in blender and blend at high speed.

ANCHOVY BUTTER

(for fish and seafood)

Cream 1 cup butter and beat in 3 to 5 minced anchovy fillets, or 2 to 3 teaspoons anchovy paste. Or blend together in blender.

PAPRIKA BUTTER

(*for fish and broiled chicken*)

Cream 1 cup butter and beat in 2 teaspoons paprika, 1 tablespoon lemon juice, 2 teaspoons wine vinegar and ½ teaspoon salt. Or combine all ingredients in blender and blend at high speed.

CURRY BUTTER

(*for sandwiches, seafood, fish and vegetables*)

Cream 1 cup butter and beat in 1 teaspoon curry powder, ¼ teaspoon freshly ground pepper, and a dash of Tabasco. Or combine ingredients in blender and blend at high speed.

MAÎTRE D'HOTEL BUTTER

(*for steak and broiled meats*)

Cream 1 cup of butter and beat in ¼ cup each minced parsley and chives and 3 tablespoons lemon juice. Or combine ingredients in blender and blend at high speed.

Blender Butter

Scandinavian, especially Danish, butter is infinitely superior to almost all butter sold in American markets. The reason for this is that the butter has, by law, a higher fat content and a lower water content than American butter, and that it is made much more carefully. The better quality of the Scandinavian butter also accounts for the unparalleled excellence of baked foods, which cannot be matched here at home. It is the reason why a Danish pastry in Denmark is a winged delight, whereas an American one plods on the ground.

In order to have butter that resembles the Scandinavian kind, one has to make it oneself, an easy enough task with a modern blender—in fact, it couldn't be easier. Blender butter is the sweetest butter imaginable and quite a revelation for those who never tasted it.

SWEET BUTTER

2 cups heavy sweet cream
½ cup ice water

Pour cream into blender container. Cover and turn control to high speed. As soon as the cream is whipped, remove cover and pour in ice water. Blend a few seconds longer until butter forms. Pour into strainer and drain thoroughly. Knead with clean hands to extract any water that might be left in the butter. Makes 1 cup unsalted whipped butter.

SALT BUTTER

Add ¼ teaspoon salt to ice water and proceed as above.

DANISH BLUE SALAD DRESSING

Serve it on a salad of cold mixed vegetables, such as a combination of peas, carrots, cauliflower, celery knob cut in strips, boiled baby onions and potatoes. Cook all vegetables separately before mixing for salad.

½ cup sour cream
¼ cup mayonnaise
1 tablespoon fresh lemon juice
⅓ cup crumbled Danish Blue cheese

Combine all ingredients and chill before using.

NORWEGIAN BROWN ONION SAUCE

Good with meatballs, boiled meats, and cold leftover meat, and with boiled potatoes.

4 slices bacon, minced
1 medium onion, sliced
1½ tablespoons flour
2 cups hot bouillon
½ cup cider vinegar
1 teaspoon salt
¼ teaspoon pepper
¼ teaspoon sugar
dash of Kitchen Bouquet (optional)

Place bacon in cold saucepan and cook over medium heat until transparent. Add onion and cook until browned, but not burned. Stir in flour and cook until flour is browned, stirring constantly. Gradually stir in combined beef bouillon and vinegar. Season with salt, pepper and sugar. If sauce is not sufficiently brown, add a dash of Kitchen Bouquet. Cook over medium heat 5 minutes, stirring constantly. Strain through fine sieve or purée in blender; the sauce should be the consistency of thick cream. Makes about 2½ cups sauce.

SCANDINAVIAN CAPER SAUCE

For pork chops and for fried fish and meats.

- 1 small onion, chopped
- 1 tablespoon butter
- 3 anchovy fillets, minced, or 2 teaspoons anchovy paste
- 3 tablespoons capers
- 3 tablespoons chopped parsley
- 1½ teaspoons flour
- ½ cup bouillon
- ½ cup mild vinegar

Brown onion in butter. Add anchovies, capers and parsley. Stir in flour. Add bouillon and vinegar and simmer, covered, for 10 minutes, stirring frequently. (For a thinner sauce, add a little more bouillon.) Makes about 1⅓ cups sauce. If made for pork chops, pour sauce over chops before serving. If for fried fish or meats, serve separately.

SWEDISH COLD SAUCE FOR LOBSTER AND SEAFOOD

- 1 cup mayonnaise
- 2 tablespoons heavy cream
- 1 tablespoon catsup
- 3 tablespoons cognac

Combine all ingredients and blend thoroughly. Chill. Makes about 1½ cups sauce.

SCANDINAVIAN COLD CUCUMBER SAUCE

For fish, shellfish, especially lobster, or meat

- 1 large cucumber
- ¾ cup heavy cream

1 tablespoon white vinegar
½ teaspoon salt
¼ teaspoon white pepper

Peel, seed, and finely chop cucumber. Whip the cream until stiff and slowly add vinegar. Season with salt and pepper. Drain cucumber; fold gently into whipped cream. Makes about 1½ cups of sauce.

Danish and Norwegian Sauces

HORSERADISH

Horseradish is especially popular in Denmark and Norway. Usually it is used fresh, since fresh horseradish is infinitely superior to the bottled or dehydrated variety. However, if you can't get the fresh horseradish, use the others. Try reconstituting dehydrated horseradish with lemon juice rather than vinegar.

HORSERADISH CREAM FOR FISH AND SHELLFISH

Simple and excellent. Serve with boiled cod, haddock, shrimp, or lobster. Better not use it with trout or salmon, since the horseradish tends to overwhelm the unique delicate flavor of the fish.

1 cup heavy cream
¼ cup white vinegar
3 tablespoons finely grated horseradish
salt and white pepper to taste
1 tablespoon finely chopped chives (optional)

Whip cream until stiff. Gradually add vinegar, stirring constantly. When cream has reached the consistency of thick mayonnaise, add horseradish, salt and pepper. Sprinkle with chopped chives. Makes about 1¼ cups horseradish cream.

NOTE: A blander sauce, much to the taste of many Scandinavians, is made by omitting the vinegar.

BOTTLED HORSERADISH CREAM

Combine 3 parts whipped cream with 1 part bottled horseradish. Season with salt and pepper to taste.

HORSERADISH CREAM SAUCE

Very popular in Scandinavia for nearly everything that is complemented by horseradish, such as boiled or fried meats and fish.

3 tablespoons butter
3 tablespoons flour
1½ cups light cream, hot
horseradish to taste
⅓ cup heavy cream, whipped (optional)

Melt butter and add flour, stirring constantly until mixture is blended and smooth. Add hot cream all at once and cook until sauce is thickened and smooth, stirring all the time. Season with horseradish. Just before serving fold in whipped cream.

Makes about 1½ cups sauce.

SOUR CREAM HORSERADISH SAUCE

For smoked fish, cold seafood, or meats

1 cup sour cream
horseradish to taste (begin with 3 tablespoons)
1 teaspoon sugar
⅛ teaspoon salt
1 to 2 tablespoons minced fresh dill

Combine all ingredients except the dill. Chill, and just before serving add freshly minced dill.

Mayonnaise

Scandinavian cooking, especially Danish cooking, uses lots of mayonnaise. Buy the best kind you find, or make your own, which is a matter of minutes with an electric blender. Since every standard cookbook will give you a good mayonnaise recipe, I limit myself to the way of making it with a blender.

BLENDER MAYONNAISE

Use a measuring cup with a lip; this will enable you to pour the olive oil in a thin, steady stream, which is important for success.

juice of 1 large lemon
½ teaspoon dry mustard
½ teaspoon salt
1 egg
1 cup olive oil

Place lemon juice, mustard, salt, egg and ¼ cup of the olive oil into the container of an electric blender. Cover; turn on the motor at low speed. Uncover immediately. Pour in remaining ¾ cup oil in a thin, steady stream. Scrape sides of blender with spatula. Mayonnaise will thicken almost immediately. If all the oil has not been incorporated into the thickened mayonnaise, flick on high speed and flick off at once. Repeat if necessary. Makes about 1½ cups mayonnaise, which keeps 2 to 3 weeks under refrigeration.

Quick Mayonnaise Sauces

All of Scandinavia adores mayonnaise. If you don't want to make your own, buy the kind that tastes like real mayonnaise. Here are just a few of the quick sauces that start with a cup of mayonnaise and that will do a great deal to brighten everyday food.

COGNAC MAYONNAISE

For lobster or shrimp salads.

Combine 1 cup mayonnaise with 1 small peeled, chopped and seeded tomato and I tablespoon cognac.

ANCHOVY MAYONNAISE

For fish or shellfish salads.

Combine 1 cup mayonnaise with 1 tablespoon anchovy paste.

CUCUMBER MAYONNAISE

For fish, shellfish or aspics.

Combine 1 cup mayonnaise with ½ to ⅔ cup finely diced cucumber. Season with more salt and pepper if needed.

REMOULADE MAYONNAISE

For fried fish, shellfish, fish or cold meats.

Combine 1 cup mayonnaise with ½ clove crushed garlic, 2 teaspoons fresh or 1 teaspoon dry tarragon, 1 hard-cooked egg, finely chopped, ½ teaspoon prepared mustard, ½ teaspoon anchovy paste and 1 tablespoon chopped parsley.

SCANDINAVIAN CURRY MAYONNAISE

For lobster, seafood or chicken salads. A mild curry flavor is much appreciated by all the Scandinavians.

1½ to 2 teaspoons mild curry (or more, according to taste)
1 cup mayonnaise
1 to 2 tablespoons lemon juice (or more, according to taste)
1 teaspoon sugar
½ cup heavy cream, whipped
salt
pepper

Stir curry into mayonnaise. Blend in lemon juice, sugar and heavy cream. Taste; if necessary, add more curry and lemon juice, very little at a time. (Scandinavians like their sauces blander than Americans.) Season with salt and pepper to taste. Chill. At serving time spoon over salad and toss gently.

SCANDINAVIAN MUSHROOM SAUCE

For fish and other nonsweet soufflés; for fish and shellfish.

1 cup thinly sliced mushrooms
2 tablespoons butter
1 cup heavy cream
1 tablespoon cognac
salt
pepper

Cook mushrooms in hot butter until just tender. Add cream and cognac and season to taste with salt and pepper. Heat through thoroughly, but do not boil. Makes about 1½ cups sauce.

SCANDINAVIAN MUSTARD SAUCE

For Gravad Lax or other fish.

9 tablespoons olive or salad oil
3 tablespoons white vinegar
2½ tablespoons prepared mustard
¾ teaspoon salt
¼ teaspoon white pepper
¼ cup sugar
⅛ teaspoon cardamom

Combine ingredients and blend thoroughly. The sauce should be made at least 2 hours before serving. Beat with wire whip or fork before serving. Makes about 1 cup.

DANISH SHARP SAUCE

For lobster, shrimp, or cold fish.

1 hard-cooked egg yolk
1 raw egg yolk
2 teaspoons prepared mustard (1 teaspoon if mustard is sharp)
2 teaspoons sugar
2 tablespoons white vinegar
salt
pepper
1 cup heavy cream, whipped

Sieve hard-cooked egg yolk. Mix it to a smooth paste with the raw egg yolk, the mustard, sugar and vinegar. Season with salt and pepper to taste. Fold into whipped cream.

NOTE: If this sauce accompanies fish or shellfish cooked with dill, sprinkle 1 tablespoon minced fresh dill on sauce before serving.

SCANDINAVIAN SIMPLE VANILLA SAUCE

For every kind of fruit pudding, for Swedish and Danish apple cake.

- ¼ cup sugar
- 1 tablespoon cornstarch
- ¼ teaspoon salt
- 2 egg yolks
- 2 cups light cream or milk
- 1 teaspoon vanilla

Combine sugar, cornstarch and salt in top of double boiler. Add egg yolks and blend thoroughly. Gradually stir in cream. Cook over boiling water about 5 minutes or until mixture is thickened. Stir constantly. Do not overcook. Remove from heat; cool and add vanilla. Chill before serving. Makes 2 cups sauce.

SCANDINAVIAN FROSTED GRAPES

Used in elegant restaurants and homes to decorate platters of cold ham, reindeer roasts, cold cuts.

Stem, wash and dry perfect big blue grapes. First dip each individual grape in slightly beaten white of egg; then roll in a bowl of sugar. Or else, place sugar in paper bag and roll grapes in it. Shake free of excessive sugar.

SCANDINAVIAN FANCY VANILLA SAUCE

- 6 egg yolks, beaten
- 4 tablespoons sugar
- 2 cups heavy cream, heated

3 teaspoons vanilla
½ cup heavy cream, whipped

Combine egg yolks and sugar in top of double boiler. Beat until thick. Slowly add the heated cream, stirring constantly. Cook over hot, not boiling, water until thick, stirring all the time. Remove from heat; stir in vanilla. Cool, beating occasionally. At serving time, fold in whipped cream.

Desserts, Breads, Cakes, Cookies, Drinks

DELICATE NORWEGIAN ALMOND PUDDING

¼ cup cornstarch
1 cup milk
2 eggs, separated
1 cup heavy cream
½ cup sugar
¼ cup finely ground almonds
1 tablespoon rum or 1 teaspoon rum flavoring

Mix cornstarch with ¼ cup milk to a smooth paste. Beat in egg yolks. Combine remaining milk, heavy cream, sugar and almonds in saucepan. Bring to a boil. Lower heat and stir in cornstarch mixture. Cook 5 minutes over low flame, stirring constantly. Remove from heat and stir in rum. Fold in stiffly beaten egg whites. Pour into serving dish and chill. Serve with a warm fruit sauce.

NORWEGIAN APPLE PUDDING

The reason apples are used so much in Scandinavia is that they are one of the fruits that will grow well in those Northern latitudes.

The apples for this pudding must be tart and well-flavored or the pudding will be flat. Blueberries or cherries can also be used.

1½ cups flour
1 teaspoon baking powder
½ teaspoon baking soda
½ teaspoon salt
2 eggs
1 cup sugar
1 cup sour cream
1 teaspoon vanilla or ½ teaspoon almond flavoring
4 large apples, peeled, cored and sliced

Set oven at 350°.

Sift flour with baking powder, baking soda and salt. Beat eggs until thick; gradually add sugar, a little at a time. Stir in sour cream and flavoring. Fold in flour. In well-buttered 8- by 8- by 2-inch baking dish place alternate layers of batter and apples. Bake for 40 minutes or until top is golden brown. Serve warm with plain or whipped cream.

SCANDINAVIAN RED FRUIT PUDDING

(*Rødgrød*)

Perhaps the most famous of all Scandinavian desserts, and especially popular in Denmark. It is most delicious and refreshing and can be made with frozen berries as well. A mixture of berries is best, but you can also make *Rødgrød* with one kind of berries only.

1 pint currants
1 pint raspberries
1½ cups water
1 cup sugar
¼ teaspoon salt
⅓ cup cornstarch
½ cup water
1 tablespoon lemon juice
⅓ cup blanched almonds (optional)

Trim and gently wash fruit. Drain; place in deep kettle with 1½ cups water. Simmer, covered, 10 minutes. Strain through fine sieve. Measure juice in kettle and, if necessary, add water to make 2½ cups liquid. Add sugar and salt. Heat to boiling point, stirring constantly. Mix cornstarch and ½ cup water; stir into fruit juice. Bring to a boil and cook 3 minutes, stirring constantly. Remove from heat; blend in lemon juice. Pour into glass serving dish and chill. Split blanched almonds into halves and decorate top of *Rødgrød* in a star pattern. Serve with whipped cream.

ICELAND CHOCOLATE CAKE DESSERT

Inherently, there is nothing of ancient Iceland in this very good dessert. But the recipe comes from Iceland, and is very popular there, deservedly so.

½ cup butter
1 4-ounce bar dark sweet chocolate (not milk chocolate)
1½ cups ground blanched almonds
4 eggs, separated
butter
fine dry breadcrumbs

Set oven at 350°.

In top of double boiler melt butter and chocolate. Cool; stir in almonds. Beat egg yolks and blend into chocolate mixture. Beat egg whites until stiff but not dry and fold into batter. Butter a 1-quart ring or other mold heavily and coat with breadcrumbs. Pour cake batter into it and bake about 45 minutes or until cake tests done. Cool on rack. Invert on serving plate and fill with sweetened whipped cream. Or serve with Vanilla Sauce.

SCANDINAVIAN APPLE CAKE

All the Scandinavians love this cake, which, to our mind, is a pudding rather than a cake. In Denmark it is eaten at Christmas, handsomely swirled with whipped cream.

4 cups breadcrumbs or zwieback crumbs
2 tablespoons sugar
½ cup butter
2½ to 3 cups thick applesauce
Set oven at 375°.

Combine crumbs and sugar. Melt butter in skillet, and brown crumbs in it. Butter a 9-inch spring-form pan. Line the baking dish with a layer of crumbs, then alternate layers of applesauce and crumbs, ending with crumbs on top. Bake 25 to 30 minutes. Cool before unmolding. Decorate with whipped cream and dabs of red jelly, or serve with Vanilla Sauce (Plain or Fancy).

Swedish Variation

Add 1 tablespoon cocoa to crumbs. This makes for a more interesting flavor.

My Own Variation

Use thick apricot purée instead of applesauce. Cook dried apricots in very little water and sugar to taste. Strain through a sieve or purée in a blender.

RED FRUIT PUDDING MADE WITH FROZEN BERRIES

(Rødgrød)

2 10-ounce packages frozen raspberries, thawed
2 10-ounce packages frozen strawberries, thawed
⅓ cup cornstarch
½ cup water
1 tablespoon lemon juice
⅓ cup blanched almonds

Combine berries in saucepan and bring to a boil, stirring occasionally. Strain through fine sieve or purée in blender. Mix cornstarch with water. Bring fruit back to boiling point. Stir cornstarch into fruit juice. Bring to a boil and cook 3 minutes, stirring constantly. Remove from heat; blend in lemon juice. Pour into glass serving dish and chill. Split blanched almonds into halves and decorate top of *Rødgrød* in a star pattern. Serve with whipped cream.

NOTE: The recipe may be doubled.

NORWEGIAN EGGEDOSIS

Eggedosis is the national dish served in Norway on May 17th, a date which corresponds to our Fourth of July. It is a thick egg cream, eaten from a dish with a spoon. The grownups cheer their *eggedosis* with a little brandy. Eggedosis is served with cookies.

Eggedosis, which would make a simple dessert for American homes, is best made with an electric beater, since beating the eggs is the main trick. The basic proportions are 1 egg yolk beaten with 1 tablespoon of sugar. Some people add an egg white to a whole recipe of *eggedosis,* but it isn't really necessary.

Beat 8 egg yolks with 8 tablespoons sugar for 10 minutes with electric beater at medium speed. Spoon into glasses or small individual dishes and serve immediately. Children get their *eggedosis* plain, but for grownups pour a tablespoon of brandy into each glass before filling it with *eggedosis.*

FINNISH FRUIT PUDDING

A pudding widely eaten in all of Scandinavia.

1 11-ounce package mixed dried fruits
2 cups water
1 cup light or dark corn syrup
¼ cup quick cooking tapioca
¼ teaspoon cinnamon
¼ teaspoon nutmeg
⅛ teaspoon salt
whipped cream

Combine fruit and water; simmer over low heat 30 minutes. Do not boil. Drain; reserve liquid and fruit. Add enough water to fruit liquid to make 1½ cups. Add syrup. Combine tapioca, cinnamon, nutmeg and salt, and stir into fruit liquid. Let stand 5 minutes. Bring to a boil over medium heat, stirring occasionally. Remove from heat and let stand until slightly thickened. Pour half of the tapioca into a serving dish. Arrange fruit over tapioca. Cover with remaining tapioca. Cool. Garnish with whipped cream or serve with Vanilla Sauce.

SWEDISH LEMON CHIFFON CREAM

(*Citronkräm*)

Lemon creams turn up in all Scandinavian countries. This one is Swedish.

4 eggs, separated
½ cup sugar
grated rind of 2 lemons
juice of 2 to 3 lemons
½ cup dry white wine
1 cup heavy cream, whipped

In top of double boiler beat together egg yolks, sugar and lemon rind until white and fluffy. Stir in lemon juice and wine, a little at a time, beating constantly. Place over hot, not boiling, water and beat with a wire whip or a rotary beater until mixture rises and thickens. Remove from heat and continue beating until cooled. Just before serving time fold in stiffly beaten egg whites and whipped cream. Serve with ladyfingers or macaroons.

NOTE: For festive occasions the Lemon Chiffon Cream may be decorated with swirls of whipped cream topped with candied cherries.

BITTAN'S ORANGE CREAM

Bittan Valberg is a beautiful Swedish woman who designs and weaves beautiful rugs, and cooks for fun.

12 small almond macaroons
¼ cup curaçao liqueur

3 egg yolks
3 tablespoons sugar
1 cup light cream
grated rind of 1 orange
grated rind of 1 lemon
1½ tablespoons gelatin
¼ cup cold water
1 cup fresh orange juice
1 cup heavy cream, whipped
whipped cream and drained canned mandarin orange slices for decorating (optional)

Line bottom of glass serving dish with macaroons, and sprinkle with curaçao. Combine egg yolks with sugar and beat until light and fluffy. Add light cream, a little at a time, and mix thoroughly. Stir in orange and lemon rinds. Cook over low heat until mixture thickens, stirring constantly. Be careful not to boil, or cream will curdle. Remove cream from heat. Dissolve gelatin in cold water. Add to warm cream and stir until thoroughly dissolved. Cool cream as quickly as possible by placing saucepan into bowl of iced water and stirring until cool. Add orange juice and fold in heavy cream. Pour mixture over macaroons. Chill until set. Decorate with alternate swirls of whipped cream and drained canned mandarin orange slices.

DANISH PRUNE CUSTARD

(*Bagt Kraembudding med Svedsker*)

The Norwegians, too, are fond of this dessert.

1 14-ounce package prunes, cooked
whole blanched almonds
3 eggs, separated
¼ cup sugar
1 cup light cream
1 teaspoon vanilla
1 cup heavy cream, whipped

Set oven at 325°.

Pit prunes and replace pits with whole blanched almonds. Place in 1- or 1½-quart deep baking dish. Beat egg yolks with sugar. Bring cream to a boil and stir into egg yolks. Add vanilla. Fold in stiffly beaten egg whites. Pour custard over prunes. Bake about 35 to 40 minutes, or until a knife inserted in the center comes out clean. Serve hot or cold with a topping of whipped cream.

NORWEGIAN PRUNE PUDDING

Another good dessert made with one of Norway's favorite fruits. It is inexpensive, easy to make, and children like it.

⅓ cup sugar
3 tablespoons cornstarch
¼ teaspoon cinnamon
½ cup prune juice
1½ cups pitted and chopped cooked prunes
1 tablespoon lemon juice

Blend sugar, cornstarch and cinnamon in top of double boiler. Stir in prune juice and chopped prunes. Cook over boiling water until mixture thickens, stirring constantly. Cover and cook 10 minutes, stirring occasionally. Remove from heat, stir in lemon juice, and chill. Serve with vanilla sauce or whipped cream.

NOTE: For a softer pudding use ¾ cup prune juice.

SWEDISH CHRISTMAS RICE PORRIDGE
(*Risgrynsgröt*)

Traditional dessert for Christmas Eve. The person who finds the almond will be married before the next Christmas comes around.

1 cup rice (Do not use converted rice.)
2 tablespoons butter

1 cup water
4 cups milk
½ teaspoon salt
½ cup heavy cream
1 whole blanched almond
cinnamon (optional)
sugar
cold milk

Wash rice under running cold water. Boil the 1 cup water and add rice and 1 tablespoon butter. Cook uncovered over medium heat until water has disappeared. Stir frequently. Add milk and salt to rice. Simmer covered, over lowest possible heat (or in top of double boiler over boiling water) until rice is tender and milk absorbed. Remove from heat and stir in heavy cream and almond. Place in serving dish and sprinkle with cinnamon and sugar. Serve with cold milk.

FINNISH RICE–APPLE PORRIDGE

(*Riisi-omenapuuro*)

6 medium tart apples
⅔ cup ordinary rice, washed in cold water
⅔ cup sugar
grated rind and juice of 1 large lemon
¼ teaspoon salt
1 quart cold water

Peel, core, and thinly slice apples. Combine with all other ingredients in heavy saucepan. Simmer covered until rice is very soft and of a porridge consistency, stirring occasionally. Depending on the kind of rice used, this may take from 30 minutes to 1 hour. The finished dish should be translucent and clear. Pour into dish and chill thoroughly. Serve with whipped cream and a fruit sauce, or with either alone.

DANISH, NORWEGIAN RHUBARB PUDDING

(*Rabarbergrød, Rabarbragrøt*)

Rhubarb, one of the first green things to grow after the long Scandinavian winter, is greeted with joy, especially in Denmark and Norway, and made into this favorite pudding.

1½ lbs. rhubarb
1½ cups water
½ cup sugar
½ teaspoon vanilla
3 tablespoons cornstarch
1 cup heavy cream
¼ cup sugar
1 teaspoon vanilla

Trim rhubarb and cut into ½-inch slices. Combine with water and sugar and simmer until soft. Stir in vanilla. Blend cornstarch with a little cold water to make a smooth, stiff paste. Stir into rhubarb, and cook for 5 minutes, or until thick and clear. Stir constantly. Pour into glass serving dish; chill. Whip cream; when frothy, add sugar and vanilla. Whip until stiff. Pipe through pastry tube in decorative swirls on rhubarb pudding, or cover top of pudding with spoonfuls of whipped cream.

RUM PUDDING

(*Romfromage*)

The Danes, and also the Norwegians, are extremely fond of this pudding. A *fromage,* by the way, is a Danish pudding thickened with gelatin and enriched with whipped cream, and not a cheese, as one might think, considering that *fromage,* in French, means cheese.

1 envelope unflavored gelatin
1¼ cups light cream or milk
⅛ teaspoon salt
1 cup sugar
4 eggs, separated
¼ cup dark rum
1 cup heavy cream, whipped
Raspberry Sauce

Sprinkle gelatin on cream in heavy saucepan. Mix well; add ½ cup of the sugar. Bring to a boil. Beat egg yolks and pour a little of the cream mixture on eggs. Blend and return to saucepan. Cook over low heat until custard coats a spoon, stirring constantly. Remove from heat. Stir in rum; chill. Beat egg whites until foamy. Gradually add remaining ½ cup of sugar, beating until egg whites are stiff and stand in peaks. Fold into chilled custard and also fold in whipped cream. Rinse a 2-quart mold with cold water. Pour pudding into it and chill for 4 hours or overnight. To unmold, dip quickly in hot water and invert on plate. Serve with Raspberry Sauce.

Raspberry Sauce

Strain 1 box frozen raspberries through fine sieve or purée in blender. Gradually stir juice into 1½ teaspoons cornstarch. Cook over low heat until thickened, stirring constantly. Chill before serving.

RØMMEGRØT, THE NORWEGIAN NATIONAL CREAM PORRIDGE

The most famous of all the porridges that reach back into Norway's dark ages. It still is eaten in the countryside at weddings and other feasts. I think it is an excellent dish, provided the butter (see recipe below) is left out, and certainly worth-while making just to see what a century-old festive dish is like.

This Cream Porridge cannot be made with our commercial sour cream, which is processed to prevent the butter separation that is so essential to the original dish. If noncommercial sour cream is not available, make your own, as described in recipe.

2 cups heavy cream or 2 cups noncommercial sour cream
2 tablespoons white vinegar or lemon juice
1 cup flour
½ teaspoon salt
2 cups hot milk
salt

Pour heavy cream into saucepan and stir in vinegar or lemon juice. Let stand 15 minutes. Bring cream or noncommercial sour cream to a boil and boil gently for 5 minutes. Sprinkle with ½ cup of the flour and blend thoroughly. Continue cooking over low heat for 10 or more minutes, until butter comes to the surface. Beat constantly. Skim off butter and keep hot. When no more butter oozes out of the porridge, sprinkle in remaining flour. Add hot milk, a tablespoon at a time, stirring all the time until porridge is thickened and smooth. Salt mildly to taste. Serve hot, with hot butter, black currant juice, cinnamon and brown sugar.

DANISH VEILED COUNTRY LASS

(*Bondepige med Slør*)

A popular Danish dessert that is surprisingly good. It must be made with very dark rye bread or pumpernickel.

1 tablespoon butter
4 cups finely grated rye breadcrumbs
2 tablespoons sugar
2 cups thick, well-flavored applesauce
1 cup raspberry jam
1 cup heavy cream, whipped

Melt butter in skillet. Add crumbs and sugar and cook over low heat until crumbs are crisp, stirring frequently to prevent lumping. Cool crumbs. Line the bottom of a serving dish with a layer of crumbs. Cover with a layer of applesauce. Top with more crumbs and a layer of raspberry jam. Repeat procedure; the last layer should be crumbs. Chill. At serving time decorate with whipped cream piped through a pastry tube.

Baking Tips

The Scandinavian women are great bakers, and there are literally hundreds of excellent recipes for breads, cakes and cookies of all kinds. Many of these recipes resemble each other closely; the cookies, for instance, are almost always rich in butter and flavored with almonds. Then too, most Scandinavian baking was produced with an eye for its keeping qualities since in the old days the heating of the ovens was quite a production. Hence the hardtack breads, the rich cookies, that will stay fresh in air-tight tins.

Many of the Scandinavian baking recipes crop up in all of the four countries. In the following chapter, I have chosen—and it was a most difficult choice—the ones that my friends and I, both here and in Scandinavia, found most suited to our American tastes.

Potato starch, or potato flour, is much used in Scandinavian baking. It gives the baked foods a long-lasting quality. Here, in the United States, potato starch is usually only available in Scandinavian neighborhoods and in Jewish food stores. Cornstarch can be substituted, without any change of proportions or baking method, for potato starch. Any recipe made with cornstarch in place of potato starch will have the same long-lasting quality for good eating. The recipes in this book have all been tested with cornstarch.

The old-time traditional Scandinavian raising agent, before baking powder became common, was hartshorn salt. This was made from the horns of the male deer which roamed the forests in profusion. Hartshorn salt makes cookies much crisper and lighter. The equivalent can be bought in any drugstore under the name of ammonium carbonate. Any reader eager for experimentation might try to add 1/8 to 1/4 teaspoon of it to the baking powder in a recipe, provided she is not deterred by the strong ammonia odor. Her cookies will be crisper and lighter.

The flour used in the following recipes is all-purpose flour, sifted before measuring.

As for the almonds or nuts in the recipes, the instructions are to be interpreted literally. If a recipe, for instance, says: "1/3 cup sliced blanched almonds," the almonds were measured after slicing. But if the recipe says: "1/3 cup blanched almonds, sliced," the almonds were measured whole first, and then sliced. There is a difference in the volume of the almonds, depending on the way they are prepared.

Far too few cooks realize the importance of heating the oven properly. It takes any oven about 10 to 20 minutes to achieve the desired temperature. The correct temperature, right from the start of baking, is of the utmost importance to the success of the product. I cannot sufficiently recommend that my readers follow exactly the instructions given in the recipes as to when to light the oven.

Finally, some of the tortes in this book require a little practice. That means that a reader better try them out on the family before making them for company. And as the very last word, I suggest that the reader, before embarking on any baking project (or any cooking), read through the whole recipe and assemble all the ingredients before starting her work.

SWEDISH RYE BREAD

A very good, easy bread.

1 cup milk
1 package dry yeast or 1 cake compressed yeast
2 tablespoons sugar
1 cup lukewarm water
4½ cups flour
¾ cup dark corn syrup
1 teaspoon fennel seed
1 teaspoon anise seed
⅓ cup butter or margarine
grated rind of 1 orange
1½ teaspoons salt
3 cups medium rye flour
lukewarm water

Scald milk and cool to lukewarm. Dissolve yeast and sugar in lukewarm water and stir in milk. Beat in 3 cups flour. Cover and let rise until double in bulk, or about 1 to 1½ hours. Combine syrup, fennel and anise in saucepan and bring to boiling point. Cool to lukewarm. Beat syrup, butter, orange rind and salt into risen batter. Stir in rye flour and 1 cup of the remaining flour. Use remaining ¼ cup flour for kneading. Sprinkle some of ¼ cup flour on bread board and turn dough on it. Knead with floured hands until smooth and elastic. Place in greased bowl, turn to grease on all sides and let rise until double in bulk, from ½ to 2 hours.

Set oven at 375°.

Shape dough into 2 loaves. Grease 2 9- by 5-inch bread loaf pans, and place loaves in pans. Cover and let rise until double in bulk, or about 50 minutes. Bake about 45 minutes. Brush with lukewarm water and bake 5 minutes longer.

SWEDISH CARDAMOM COFFEE CAKE

1¼ cups milk
1 package dry yeast
¼ cup lukewarm water
¾ cup sugar
6¼ cups sifted flour
½ cup butter, at room temperature
¼ teaspoon salt
3 egg yolks
2 to 3 teaspoons cardamom
topping

Scald milk and cool to lukewarm. Dissolve yeast in ¼ cup lukewarm water. Add to milk, with 1 tablespoon of the sugar. Beat in 3 cups of the flour. Cover and let rise until double in bulk, or about 1 to 1½ hours. Add butter, remaining sugar, salt, egg yolks, cardamom and 3 cups flour. Reserve remaining ¼ cup flour for kneading. Turn dough onto floured surface and knead with floured hands until smooth and elastic. Place in greased bowl and turn to grease on all sides. Cover; let rise until double in bulk, or about 1 to 1½ hours. Divide risen dough into two halves, to make two cakes. Divide each half into 3 pieces and roll each piece into a strip 16 inches long. Pinch the 3 rolls together at one end, braid and pinch ends together. Place cakes on ungreased cookie sheet. Let cakes rise until double in bulk, or about 45 minutes. Set oven at 375° 20 minutes before braids are ready to be baked. Brush with topping. Bake 25 to 30 minutes.

Topping

Combine 2 teaspoons cinnamon, 2 tablespoons sugar and ¼ cup chopped nuts. Brush cakes with milk and sprinkle with topping.

FINNISH BROWN BREAD

(*Hiivaleipä*)

The Finnish country people are great bakers. The old-time ovens used to be built into the wall behind the stove like a tunnel, about a yard wide and sometimes as deep as six feet. At baking time, a wood fire was lit in the oven, and when it had burned down to red and glowing embers, these were raked forward into the stove with a long pole that ended in a kind of iron shovel. The oven was then cleaned with a broom dipped in water. A ventilator at the back of the stove drew off the smoke, and was closed as the fire was raked out. A damper regulated the heat.

Since heating an oven was a time-consuming business, the Finnish farm wives baked in large quantities. The following bread has a textured grain and a light brown color. The shape is round, and it is eaten cut in wedges, which are split and buttered. The bread also toasts extremely well.

1½ cups hot water
2 tablespoons butter, at room temperature
1 tablespoon sugar
2 teaspoons salt
1 package dry yeast
½ cup lukewarm water
3 cups whole wheat or rye flour
2½ cups unsifted flour (about)
melted butter

Pour hot water into a large mixing bowl. Stir in butter, sugar and salt. Cool to lukewarm. Stir yeast into lukewarm water and dissolve completely. Add to first mixture and blend well. Beat in whole wheat or rye flour. Add 2 cups other flour. Use remaining ½ cup to flour pastry board. Turn dough onto floured pastry board and knead 10 minutes. Add more flour to board if dough sticks, but only a little at a time. Knead until dough is smooth and satiny. Grease a large bowl and place dough in it. Brush top with melted butter. Cover with a lightly dampened kitchen towel. Allow to rise in a warm place (85°) about 45 minutes to 1 hour or until almost doubled in bulk. Twenty minutes before time is up set oven at 400°. Punch down dough and divide into 2 halves. Grease a baking sheet. Form each half of dough into a round loaf. Place on baking sheet; press down with hands until the loaf is about 1 inch thick. Bake about 30 minutes or until the crust of the bread is light brown. Remove from baking sheet and cool on racks.

SCANDINAVIAN CHRISTMAS BREAD

(*Julekaka*)

This is baked especially in Norway, Sweden and Finland, in any number of variations. The bread is a nice change from fruitcake, and good buttered or nonbuttered, fresh or toasted. Serve it with coffee, or, even more pleasantly, with a glass of sherry or any sweet or dry wine.

½ cup milk
½ cup butter
1 package active dry yeast (or 1 cake)
½ cup lukewarm water
¼ cup sugar
1 teaspoon salt
1 egg, slightly beaten
1 tablespoon powdered cardamom
1 cup light raisins
¼ cup chopped candied orange peel
¼ cup chopped candied cherries
¼ cup chopped blanched almonds
3½ cups to 4 cups sifted flour
1 egg white, beaten
lemon icing
candied orange peel, sliced
candied cherries
angelica

Heat milk; melt butter in it. Cool to lukewarm. In large mixing bowl (3-quart size or larger) sprinkle yeast on lukewarm water. Stir until dissolved. Stir in sugar, salt, egg, cardamom, raisins, orange peel, cherries and almonds. Gradually add flour, beating well after each addition, until the dough is stiff. Cover; let rise in warm place (85°) until double in bulk, about 1½ to 2 hours. Turn dough on a lightly floured board and knead until no longer sticky, but smooth and elastic. Grease a 2-quart deep cake pan (or 2 1-lb. coffee cans). Shape dough in round loaf; place in pan. Brush with shortening, cover and let rise until double, about 1 hour. Set oven at 350° 20 minutes before bread is ready to be baked. When the bread has risen, brush with beaten egg white. Bake 50 minutes to 1 hour. (If the bread is baked in the 2 coffee cans, bake about 35 minutes.) Remove bread from pan immediately; cool on rack. Frost with lemon icing and decorate with slices of orange peel, candied cherries and angelica, arranged in flower patterns.

FINNISH VIIPURI TWIST

A Finnish coffee bread baked in the shape of an enormous pretzel. It is said that the first Viipuri Twist was baked for Christmas in a Finnish monastery in 1433. The Twist, which is as large as a cookie sheet, is not only outstandingly decorative and most unusual, but also delightful to eat. At Christmas time it is served filled with gingerbread men and other cookies.

1 package dry yeast
¼ cup lukewarm water
¼ teaspoon salt
1 egg, well beaten
7 tablespoons sugar
¾ cup lukewarm milk
2 tablespoons butter, at room temperature
¼ teaspoon nutmeg
½ teaspoon cardamom
4 cups sifted flour

Sprinkle yeast on lukewarm water and stir until dissolved. Add salt, beaten egg, sugar, lukewarm milk, and butter. Beat in nutmeg and cardamom. Beat in flour gradually to make stiff dough. Knead dough until smooth and elastic. Place dough in a greased bowl. Cover and let rise in warm place until doubled in bulk. Punch down and knead well. Shape dough into a long 36-inch roll. The middle of the roll should be ½ inch thicker than the ends. Place roll of dough on a greased and floured cookie sheet. Shape dough into twist on the cookie sheet. Keeping the shape of a pretzel in mind, twist both ends of the roll around each other and turn inwards to form the middle of the twist. Separate the ends again and join each on either side of the thick part of the roll, to form a triangular opening in the middle of the twist. Brush with boiling water. Let rise 1 hour. Just 20 minutes before the hour is up, set oven at 375°. Brush twist with boiling water and place in oven. Bake 40 to 50 minutes or until twist is deep brown. Remove from oven and brush again with boiling water.

SWEDISH SHROVE TUESDAY BUNS

(*Semlor*)

Traditionally served on Shrove Tuesday and throughout Lent. These large light buns are good with coffee, though in Sweden they are often accompanied by hot milk with cinnamon.

1 package dry yeast
¼ cup lukewarm water
1 egg, slightly beaten
⅔ cup light cream, lukewarm
¼ cup sugar
¼ teaspoon salt
½ teaspoon cinnamon
½ cup butter, at room temperature
3 to 3¼ cups sifted flour
Almond Paste (see page 230)
whipped cream
confectioners' sugar

Sprinkle yeast on warm water and stir until dissolved. Stir in half of the beaten egg (reserve other half), lukewarm cream, sugar, salt, cinnamon and butter. Mix thoroughly. Add flour, a little at a time, and beat to make a soft dough. Turn out dough on floured surface and knead about 10 minutes, or until dough is smooth and elastic. Place dough in greased bowl and turn to grease on all sides. Cover and let rise until double in bulk, or about 1 to 1½ hours. Punch down risen dough and knead on floured board until smooth. Shape dough into 10 or 12 round buns. Place buns on greased cookie sheet. Let rise until almost double in size. Set oven at 400° 20 minutes before buns are ready to be baked. Brush with reserved egg. Bake 10 to 12 minutes or until golden brown. Cool on racks. Cut off tops of buns with a sharp knife. Insert a wafer-thin piece of almond paste into each bun. Top with whipped cream. Replace top of bun and sprinkle with confectioners' sugar.

SWEDISH SAFFRON BUNS OR LUCIA BUNS

These buns are traditionally served on St. Lucia's Day, December 13, the beginning of the Christmas season. On that day a young daughter of the house puts on the traditional white robe and crown of evergreens and lighted candles, and goes from bedroom to bedroom serving saffron buns and fresh hot coffee. Before coming into the room, she sings the St. Lucia song outside the door.

¾ cup milk
⅓ cup sugar
1 teaspoon salt
¼ cup butter
1 teaspoon saffron
2 tablespoons boiling water
½ cup warm water
2 packages active dry yeast or 2 cakes compressed yeast
1 egg, beaten
3½ cups sifted flour (about)
¼ cup yellow raisins
1 egg white, slightly beaten
¼ cup finely chopped blanched almonds
2 tablespoons sugar

Scald milk; stir in sugar, salt and butter. Cool to lukewarm. Meanwhile combine saffron and boiling water; let stand. Pour warm water into large mixing bowl. Sprinkle yeast over water; stir until dissolved. Add milk mixture, egg, saffron and 2 cups of the flour, and beat until smooth. Stir in remaining flour to make soft dough. Turn on floured surface. Knead with hands until smooth and elastic, about 8 to 10 minutes. Place in greased bowl and turn so that dough will be greased on all sides. Cover and let rise in warm place, free from draft, until doubled in bulk. This takes about 1 hour. Punch down; turn out on floured surface. Cover and let rest 10 minutes.

Set oven at 375° 20 minutes before buns are ready to be baked.

Divide dough into 18 pieces. Roll each piece into a strip 10 to 12 inches long and cut in half. Coil both ends of each strip into the center of the strip. Place two coiled strips back to back to make one bun. Place on greased baking sheet. Cover and let rise in warm place, free from draft, until doubled in bulk, or about ½ hour. Press a raisin deep into center of each coil. Brush with white of egg. Combine almonds and sugar and sprinkle a little on each bun. Bake about 20 minutes. Makes about 18 buns.

FINNISH MAY DAY CRULLERS

(*Tippaleivät*)

> May Day, the First of May, is the Finnish national holiday. Everybody who has ever graduated from high school or college dons his white student cap and gives himself over to frolicking. The national drink for this day is *Sima* (see page 232), and with it are served the following crisp and delicious crullers.

3 eggs
5 tablespoons sugar
1¾ cup sifted flour
1 cup heavy cream
fat for deep frying
powdered sugar

Beat eggs with sugar until thick. Alternately stir in flour and heavy cream. Beat until smooth. Heat fat or oil for deep frying to 380°. Spoon batter into pastry tube. Squeeze batter into fat in a criss-cross stream to make a circle the size of a doughnut.

Fry on both sides about 2 to 3 minutes or until browned. Drain on paper towels and sprinkle with powdered sugar. Serve hot with *Sima*. Makes about 20 crullers.

FINNISH KARELIAN PASTIES

(*Karjalan Piiraat*)

Karelian pasties are an old, old Finnish national dish, the substantial food of people who have to work hard outdoors in a cold climate. Though I don't believe that they will be popular in America, I feel they have a place in this book because they are so very unusual, in appearance and in taste, with an air of history, so to speak.

Filling

1 cup rice (do not use converted rice)
2 cups water
1 tablespoon butter
1 teaspoon salt
2 cups milk
3 hard-cooked eggs, chopped

Wash rice under running cold water. Combine 2 cups water, butter and salt in a saucepan. Bring to a boil and add rice. Cover and simmer until water is absorbed. Add milk. Cover and simmer until milk is absorbed, stirring occasionally. Cook until rice is tender. Fold hard-cooked eggs into rice. Make pastry.

Pastry

1 cup water
1 teaspoon salt
2 cups rye flour
2 cups all-purpose flour

Combine water and salt. Stir in rye flour first and then other flour. Knead until dough is smooth and elastic. Divide dough into 20 equal parts. On floured board roll out dough into wafer-thin rounds. Place rounds on top of each other, sprinkling a little flour between them to avoid sticking. Place a heaping tablespoon of filling on each pastry round. Spread the filling into an oval shape, from one end of round to the other, leaving the opposite sides uncovered to the width of 1 inch each. Turn in edges and fold uncovered pastry sides over filling. Do not cover filling entirely; leave an uncovered strip about 1/4 inch wide. Crimp the edges of each pasty with finger and thumb to resemble pleats.

Set oven at 425°.

Place pasties on greased and floured baking sheets. Bake about 15 to 20 minutes or until golden. While pasties are baking, make Dipping.

Dipping

1 cup boiling water
6 tablespoons butter
Combine water and butter and keep hot.

Dip baked pasties into buttered water as soon as they are baked and while still hot. Place dipped pasties on top of each other and cover with a clean kitchen towel. Let stand covered about 15 minutes. Spread with butter and eat while still warm.

NOTE: To store Karelian Pasties, wrap them tightly in aluminum foil. To heat, place them in top of double boiler over boiling water, or warm, tightly wrapped, in hot oven (425°) for 3 to 5 minutes. As a variation Karelian Pasties can also be filled with mashed potatoes or medium barley. The barley should be cooked in the same fashion as is the rice in the above recipe.

DANISH, NORWEGIAN ALMOND RING CAKE
(*Kransekake*)

This cake is really a tower of graduated almond paste rings, rising from the largest ring at the bottom to the smallest on top. It is popular in Denmark, and even more so in Norway, where it is served at Christmas, weddings and other festive occasions. Since the almond paste can be bought, the cake is surprisingly easy to make and an excellent show piece. It is garnished with candy, cookies, and Norwegian or Danish flags.

Cake

3 lbs. almond paste
4 to 5 egg whites, unbeaten

Icing

5 cups confectioners' sugar, or more, sifted
4 to 5 egg whites

Set oven at 300°.

Heat almond paste over low heat until lukewarm, to make it pliable. With wooden spoon blend in egg whites. Knead with hands until firm and very smooth. (Knead hard; almond paste is not delicate.) Cover pastry board or any surface with confectioners' sugar. Coat palms of hands with confectioners' sugar, and keep them coated throughout shaping of almond paste rings. Roll dough with palms into 12 rolls ½ inch thick and in these lengths: 5, 6, 7, 8, 10, 12, 14, 16, 18, 20, 22, and 24 inches. Grease well and lightly flour brown paper the size of a cookie sheet. Place paper on cookie sheet. Place one roll at a time on paper and shape into a ring, pinching the ends together. Gently pinch each ring with thumb and forefinger with an upward movement so that rings will slope off into a sharp crease on top. Be careful to keep rings perfectly round. Bake about 20 minutes until light golden. Remove and cool on a smooth surface.

To make icing, gradually stir confectioners' sugar into egg whites. Beat until mixture is smooth. Reserve one third. With decorating tube number 3 or 4, make loops of icing on each ring. Or drizzle icing over each ring with a spoon or a brush.

To assemble, place largest ring on large serving plate or cake plate. Thinly spread top with reserved icing. Pile next largest ring on top, and repeat process. The icing helps the rings to stay on top of each other. End with smallest ring.

To serve, divide larger rings into sections and serve smaller ones whole. Makes about 12 servings or more.

ICELAND ALMOND CAKE DESSERT

(*Mondlukaka*)

Food in Iceland resembles very much the food of the other Scandinavian countries. This cake is good and easy, and it will keep well if wrapped in aluminum foil—without the filling and topping, of course.

1 cup butter
1 cup sugar
4 eggs, separated
1 teaspoon vanilla
1 cup blanched almonds, ground fine
1 cup sifted flour
½ teaspoon baking powder
½ cup strawberry jam
1 cup heavy cream, whipped and sweetened to taste

Set oven at 350°.

Cream butter and gradually add sugar. Beat in egg yolks, one at a time, beating well after each addition. Stir in vanilla and almonds. Sift together flour and baking powder and gradually stir into batter. Beat egg whites until stiff but not dry, and fold into batter. Bake in 3 8-inch buttered and floured layer pans about 30 minutes, or until golden brown. Cool 5 minutes before removing from pans. Spread strawberry jam between cooled layers and cover top and sides with swirls of whipped cream.

SWEDISH CREAM MERINGUE CAKE

Meringue confections are one of the glories of Swedish baking. This torte can be put together with a cream filling, or with sweetened whipped cream and fruit, such as raspberries, strawberries, or blueberries.

Cake

¾ cup butter
¾ cup sugar
6 eggs (yolks are used for cake, whites for meringue)
1 teaspoon vanilla
½ teaspoon almond flavoring
1¼ cups plus 1 tablespoon sifted flour
1½ teaspoon baking powder
¼ teaspoon salt
½ cup milk

Set oven at 300°.

With electric blender at low speed cream together butter and sugar for 3 minutes. Beat in egg yolks, one at a time, and then beat 3 minutes longer. Stir in vanilla and almond flavorings. Sift together flour, baking powder and salt. Add to batter alternately with milk. Grease and flour 3 9-inch layer pans. Distribute batter into pans and smooth with knife or spatula.

Meringue

6 egg whites
1 cup sugar
½ teaspoon vanilla
½ cup finely ground almonds or walnuts

Beat egg whites until stiff and dry. (Use an electric beater.) Gradually beat in sugar. Add vanilla and ground nuts. Continue beating until the meringue stands in stiff peaks. Spread meringue evenly on tops of the cake batter in the three pans. Bake 45 to 50 minutes or until cakes test dry. Cool on racks. Remove carefully from pans and brush free of crumbs.

Orange Filling

- 1/3 cup flour
- 1 cup sugar
- 1/8 teaspoon salt
- 1/4 cup water
- 1 1/2 cups orange juice
- 1/4 cup lemon juice
- 2 tablespoons grated orange rind
- 1 tablespoon grated lemon rind
- 4 egg yolks, beaten

Combine flour, sugar, salt and water and blend until smooth. Add orange and lemon juice and orange and lemon rinds. Cook until mixture thickens and is smooth and almost transparent, stirring constantly. Stir a small amount of the hot filling into the egg yolks. Return to saucepan and cook over low heat 3 minutes longer, stirring constantly. Remove from heat and beat until cool.

Topping

- 2 cups heavy cream, chilled
- 2 tablespoons sugar
- 2 teaspoons vanilla
- 1 cup toasted almonds, cut in slivers

In chilled bowl and with chilled beater whip cream until stiff. As cream begins to thicken, beat in sugar and vanilla.

Assembling the Meringue Torte

Just before serving, place one cake layer on cake plate, meringue side up. Cover with 1/3 of the filling. Top with second layer, meringue side up. Repeat process, always placing layers meringue side up. Frost the top and sides of the torte with whipped cream topping and sprinkle with toasted almond slivers. Serve as soon as possible, and keep under refrigeration until serving time. Makes about 8 servings.

FANCY LEMON FILLING FOR MERINGUE CAKE

1 tablespoon cornstarch
½ cup sugar
½ cup water
grated rind and juice of 2 small lemons
4 egg yolks, beaten

Combine cornstarch and sugar. Blend with water to a smooth paste. Stir in lemon rind and juice. Blend in beaten egg yolks. Cook over lowest possible heat until filling is thick, stirring constantly. Beat until cooled.

PLAIN FILLING FOR MERINGUE CAKE

Use prepared pudding mix in any desired flavor, such as vanilla, lemon, chocolate, etc. Cook according to directions.

APRICOT FILLING FOR MERINGUE CAKE

Combine ¾ cup thick apricot sauce, made from stewed, sweetened and strained apricots (flavored with a little kirsch or brandy, if desired) and 1 cup heavy cream, whipped.

This is an excellent filling for any kind of layer cake.

SWEDISH CHOCOLATE DREAM CAKE

(*Drömtårta*)

A jelly roll with a delicious filling.

½ cup flour
⅓ cup cocoa, preferably Dutch type
1½ teaspoons baking powder
½ teaspoon salt

¼ teaspoon soda
3 eggs
3 tablespoons water
1 teaspoon vanilla
¾ cup sugar
confectioners' sugar

Set oven at 350°.

Sift together flour, cocoa, baking powder, salt and soda. Combine eggs, water and vanilla and beat until thick and lemon colored. Add sugar gradually, a tablespoon at a time, beating thoroughly after each addition. Slowly sift flour mixture into egg mixture and fold in carefully, but thoroughly. Grease a 15- by 10-inch jelly roll pan and line with waxed paper. Spread batter evenly in pan and bake 30 minutes or until cake tests done. Touch cake lightly with finger tip. If the dough springs back quickly, the cake is done. Sprinkle a kitchen towel heavily with confectioners' sugar. Turn cake onto towel and peel off waxed paper. Trim off crisp edges. Roll warm cake lengthwise in towel into a roll. Cool on rack, seam side down. Unroll and spread with Dream Filling. Reroll and refrigerate until serving time.

DREAM FILLING

This filling is much creamier if made in an electric mixer.

¾ cup sweet butter
1 egg yolk
¼ cup cocoa, preferably Dutch type
3 cups confectioners' sugar
3 tablespoons rum or cognac

Cream butter with egg yolk and cocoa. Beat in sugar gradually, alternating with rum. Keep at room temperature for spreading.

EAT-SOME-MORE DANISH TEA CAKE

From Mrs. Arne Christiansen who lives in America but cooks in the best Danish manner. This cake is quick and easy to make.

½ cup butter or margarine
1 cup confectioners' sugar
2 eggs
grated rind of 1 lemon
2 cups sifted flour
2 teaspoons baking powder
¼ cup milk
3 apples, peeled and thinly sliced
⅔ cups blanched chopped almonds
sugar to taste

Set oven at 350°.

Cream together butter and sugar until mixture is fluffy. Beat in eggs, one at a time. Stir in lemon rind. Sift flour with baking powder. Add flour to batter, alternately with milk. Spread batter into buttered and floured 9-inch square baking pan. Arrange apple slices on top of batter in overlapping rows. Sprinkle with almonds. Sprinkle with sugar; the amount depends on the sweetness of the apples. Bake 50 minutes or until cake tests clean. Serve with sweetened whipped cream.

Danish Pastry (*Wienerbrød*)

Danish pastry is the glory of Danish baking. The tourists who return from Denmark with a heart full of nostalgia for the flaky, melting pastries need not despair, for they can be made here.

If Danish pastry is not perfect, it is not worth eating. Here are a few tricks to help you to make Danish pastries. These tricks are the results of experimenting with a great many recipes. First of all, use unsalted margarine rather than butter, the way the Danes do. They use much margarine for their baking, because they feel it gives better results in achieving flakiness of pastry. Margarine has a greater malleability than butter, and can be rolled out thinly and evenly, a most important step in making Danish pastry. The margarine should be *unsalted* for best results. Second, keep your pastry cool. The Danes say you can't make good pastry on a hot day. To produce flakiness be conscientious about chilling the dough between rollings. Third, work as quickly as possible, with cool hands.

All Danish pastry should be eaten as soon after baking as possible. Danish pastries are not made to keep. But they freeze very well after baking. Cool and wrap tightly in foil or freezer wrap. Thaw before serving or reheat slightly in 375° F oven 2–3 min. to restore crispness. Do not keep in your freezer longer than 6 months.

DANISH PRUNE CAKE

A very good coffee cake and very nice for festive breakfasts. Like the Danish pastry, it is better made with unsalted margarine than with sweet butter.

¼ cup milk
2 cups unsifted flour
¼ cup sugar
½ teaspoon salt
¼ cup unsalted margarine
½ cup warm water (105° to 115° F)
2 packages active dry yeast or 2 cakes compressed
1 egg, beaten
1½ cups chopped stewed prunes or other preserves, such as raspberry
3 tablespoons sugar
3 tablespoons lemon juice
1 teaspoon grated lemon peel

Scald milk; cool to lukewarm. Combine flour, sugar and salt. Cut in margarine with a pastry cutter or 2 knives. Pour warm water into large bowl. Sprinkle with yeast. Stir until dissolved. Stir in lukewarm milk, beaten egg and flour mixture. Stir until well blended. Place in greased bowl and turn to grease top. Cover; let rise in warm place, free from draft, until doubled in bulk. This will take about 40 minutes.

If prunes are used, combine prunes, sugar, lemon juice and peel. Set aside. Grease a 15- by 10- by 1½-inch pan. Punch down dough and turn out on well-floured board. Divide in half. Roll each half to a 16- by 12-inch rectangle. Place one half in greased pan. Spread with prune mixture or with preserves. Cover with second half of dough. Seal edges well. Cover; let rise in warm place, free from draft, until doubled in bulk, or about ½ hour. Set oven at 350° 20 minutes before cake is ready to be baked. Bake about 20 minutes. Turn out of pan at once. When cool, frost with lemon icing.

DANISH PASTRY

- ¾ cup milk
- ½ cup sugar
- 1½ teaspoons salt
- ¼ cup unsalted margarine
- ½ cup warm water (105° to 115°)
- 2 packages active dry yeast or 2 cakes compressed yeast
- 2 eggs, separated
- 1 tablespoon grated lemon rind or 2 teaspoons ground cardamom
- 3½ cups unsifted flour
- 2 tablespoons cornstarch
- 1½ cups unsalted margarine
- sugar
- jelly, preserves, or thick cream filling

Scald milk; add sugar, salt and ¼ cup margarine. Cool to lukewarm. Pour warm water into a large bowl. Sprinkle or crumble in yeast. Stir until dissolved. Add lukewarm milk mixture. Beat together egg yolks and 1 egg white; reserve remaining egg white. Add yolk mixture and lemon rind to yeast mixture. Add 1 cup flour and mix well. Combine cornstarch and remaining flour; stir into batter until just mixed. Refrigerate.

Cream 1½ cups margarine. Place on a piece of waxed paper. Cover with a second piece of waxed paper. Roll to a 10- by 12-inch rectangle. Chill 1 hour.

Roll chilled dough into a 12- by 16-inch rectangle. Remove top sheet of waxed paper from margarine. Hold margarine uncovered side down over the dough. Place the sheet of margarine on the dough with the 12-inch side of the dough and the 12-inch side of the margarine together, leaving one third of the dough uncovered. Remove the sheet of waxed paper. Fold the uncovered third of the dough over the margarine. Fold remaining third covered with margarine over this. Roll out dough to a 12- x 16-inch rectangle, fold into thirds. Chill one hour. Roll and fold dough.

Chill 1 hour. Roll and fold dough again. Chill 1 hour or overnight.

Shape half the dough at a time, and keep remainder refrigerated. Shape gently but quickly into spiral rolls or any other shape. Place 2 inches apart on greased baking sheet. Chill 1 hour. Set oven at 375° 20 minutes before pastry is ready to be baked. Beat reserved egg white with 1 tablespoon water. Brush dough with egg white mixture. Sprinkle lightly with sugar. Bake 15 to 20 minutes.

Spiral Roll

Roll half the dough to a 15- by 6-inch rectangle. Cut strips 15 by ½ inch long. Twist each strip and form into a spiral roll. Proceed and bake as above.

Spandauers

Roll half the dough to a 9- by 12-inch rectangle. Cut dough into 3-inch squares. Put ½ teaspoon red jelly or preserves or thick cream filling in the center of each square. Fold to form triangles, pressing down well on edges to seal. Or place filling in middle of square, and fold in the four corners towards the center, pressing down well on edges to seal. Brush dough with egg white mixture, sprinkle with sugar, and bake as above. This recipe makes about 24 pastries.

NORWEGIAN KING HAAKON'S CAKE

King Haakon VII was the first king of Norway after the country declared her independence from Sweden in 1905. The cake can only be described as a rich, important one.

Cake

1 cup butter
1 cup sugar

- 4 eggs, separated
- 1 teaspoon vanilla
- 1 cup sifted flour
- 1 cup sifted cornstarch
- 1 teaspoon baking powder
- ⅛ teaspoon salt

Set oven at 350°.

Cream butter and sugar until thoroughly light and blended, about 3 minutes with an electric blender at low speed. Add egg yolks and vanilla and beat 3 minutes longer. Sift together flour, cornstarch, baking powder and salt. Add to egg mixture, beating constantly for 3 more minutes. Best egg whites until stiff but not dry and fold into batter. The dough should be soft and fluffy. Grease and flour 3 9-inch layer pans. Divide dough into pans and smooth evenly with a knife or spatula. Bake about 25 to 30 minutes or until cake tests done and edges are slightly browned and shrink away from the pan. Cool cake in pans on cake rack for 5 minutes; invert on waxed paper.

Chocolate Cream

- 3 tablespoons flour
- 1 cup light cream
- ⅛ teaspoons salt
- ½ cup sugar less 1 tablespoon
- 4 egg yolks, beaten
- 1 teaspoon vanilla
- 5 tablespoons dark, unsweetened cocoa (Dutch type)
- ¼ cup heavy cream, whipped

Mix flour with ¼ cup of the light cream to a smooth paste. Gradually add remaining cream, salt and sugar, stirring constantly. Cook over medium heat until mixture thickens to the consistency of medium white sauce. Stir constantly. Stir a little bit of the sauce into the beaten egg yolks. Add egg yolk mixture to balance of sauce. Cook over lowest possible heat 3 minutes longer, stirring all the time. Be careful not to boil, or cream will curdle. Remove cream from heat and stir in vanilla and cocoa.

Cool as quickly as possible by placing saucepan in bowl of iced water and stirring until cool. Chill. Fold in whipped cream just before assembling cake.

Almond Paste

This can be bought in Scandinavian specialty stores, or it can be made at home.

Combine 1 cup finely ground blanched almonds with ½ cup sugar, 1 small egg, ¼ teaspoon vanilla and a few drops of yellow vegetable coloring. Mix thoroughly and knead with hands into a smooth paste.

Between 2 sheets of waxed paper, with rolling pin, roll out almond paste to the size of a 9-inch layer pan. Trim edges.

Royal Icing

3 cups sifted confectioners' sugar
2 egg whites
¼ teaspoon salt
2 teaspoons lemon juice
1 teaspoon vanilla
food coloring (optional)

Combine all ingredients except food coloring in a bowl. With electric mixer at high speed beat until mixture is light and fluffy and stands in stiff peaks. If necessary, add a little more egg white or sugar to achieve correct spreading consistency. Add food coloring and beat in thoroughly. Do not underbeat; this icing can hardly, if at all, be overbeaten. Cover with a damp cloth when not in use; this method will keep the icing for several days at room temperature.

Assembling King Haakon's Cake

Brush layers free of crumbs. Place one layer on cake plate. Spread with half of the chocolate cream and top with second layer. Spread with remaining chocolate cream and top with third layer. Peel the top piece of waxed paper from the circle of almond paste. Place almond paste on top layer of the cake and peel off the other piece of waxed paper, which is now on top. Frost cake with Royal Icing, beginning with the sides. Use knife or spatula dipped in cold water. The cake should be absolutely smooth.

Decorating King Haakon's Cake

Cut candied peel into 1/8-inch strips. With these make the letter "H" and the Roman numeral "VII" in the middle of the cake. Cut a small crown from candied peel and place above initial. Around edge of cake place a decorative border of candied cherries, pineapple, and peel cut into fancy shapes. If you are a Norwegian, or wish to honor Norway, decorate further with small Norwegian flags.

Makes about 12 servings.

SWEDISH MAZARIN TORTE

(*Mazarintårta*)

One of the most famous of Swedish cakes.

Dough

- 1⅓ cups sifted flour
- 1 teaspoon baking powder
- ⅓ cup sugar
- ½ cup butter
- 1 egg

Into deep bowl sift together flour, baking powder and sugar. Cut in butter and add egg. Mix together and knead with hands or spoon into a smooth dough. Chill while preparing filling.

Filling

- ½ cup butter
- ⅔ cup sugar
- 1 cup ground blanched almonds
- ½ teaspoon vanilla extract
- 2 eggs
- ⅔ cup raspberry jam

Cream butter; add sugar gradually and beat until fluffy. Add almonds and vanilla. Add eggs, one at a time, beating well after each addition.

How to Make Torte

Set oven at 350°.

Roll out chilled dough between 2 sheets of waxed paper to fit bottom of 9-inch spring form pan. Cut remaining dough into a strip and line sides of pan with it. Bring the dough at the bottom of the pan and the dough on the sides together so that they are tightly joined. (This is done to prevent filling from oozing out during baking.) Spread ⅓ cup of the raspberry jam over dough at bottom of the pan. Top with filling. Bake about 50 minutes or until torte tests done. Cool torte 10 minutes. Remove sides of spring pan and let torte cool entirely. When cold, spread with remaining ⅓ cup jam. Dribble Icing over jam.

Lemon Icing

Combine 1 cup sifted confectioners' sugar with 1 tablespoon lemon juice and 1 teaspoon water. Beat until smooth and of spreading consistency.

SWEDISH MERINGUE TART

A truly glorious creation. Meringues are easy to make if you have an electric beater and are willing to beat, beat, beat. They also must be baked in a slow, slow, slow oven. A proper meringue should be snow white for perfect taste, texture and appearance. A slow baking accomplishes this. This tart will make about 10 servings.

6 egg whites
¼ teaspoon cream of tartar
⅛ teaspoon salt
grated rind of 1 lemon

- 1½ cups sugar
- ½ cup blanched almonds, ground
- ⅔ cup sifted cornstarch

Combine egg whites, cream of tartar, salt, and lemon rind in large bowl. With electric beater at medium speed beat until egg whites hold soft peaks. Beat in 1 cup sugar, one tablespoon at a time, beating constantly. Beat about 5 to 10 minutes longer, or until meringue is very thick and dull. Combine remaining sugar, almonds and cornstarch. Sift into meringue and fold in quickly.

Set oven at 225°.

Grease and flour 2 large baking sheets. On plain, unwaxed brown paper, such as packing paper, trace and cut out 4 8- or 9-inch circles. Spread a thin layer of meringue on each circle, using spatula. Smooth to end of paper and flatten top. Bake layers about 40 to 45 minutes, or until they are crisp and dry, but still white. Cool; remove layers carefully from paper.

Fillings for Meringue Tart

You can fill a meringue tart with anything that takes your fancy. Creamy fillings and fruit fillings, plus whipped cream, and ice cream, combine well with the crispness of the tart, Here are two fillings the Swedes and other Scandinavians like.

Strawberry Filling

- 2 cups sliced sweetened strawberries, drained
- 3 cups heavy cream, whipped
- 2 tablespoons kirsch, cognac or Cointreau (optional)
- ½ cup blanched almonds, halved

Fold together strawberries and 2 cups of the whipped cream. Blend in liqueur. Spread on 3 of the meringue layers. Cover top layer with remaining whipped cream, preferably in an ornate design of swirls and rosettes. Use a pastry bag with a star tip. Stud whipped cream top with almonds. Chill tart before serving.

Chocolate Filling

- 1 package dark sweet chocolate pudding, made with half milk, half cream
- 1 cup heavy cream, whipped
- 1 cup toasted almonds, halved

Cook chocolate pudding according to directions. Chill; fold in ½ cup whipped cream. Spread pudding between meringue layers; leave top layer plain. Cover top layer and sides of cake with remaining whipped cream, tracing decorative swirls. Stud top and side of cake with toasted almond halves. Chill before serving.

NOTE: A meringue tart with chocolate filling is sometimes called a *Rolla Tårta.*

DANISH SAND CAKE

(Sandkage)

A very good and very popular rather dry cake that keeps for a long time in an air-tight tin. It has a fine, grainy quality which comes from including cornstarch in the ingredients. The cake does not need to be iced. For serving, Sand Cake should be cut into thin slices.

- 1 cup butter
- 1 cup sugar
- grated rind of 1 lemon
- 6 eggs, separated
- 2 tablespoons brandy
- 1 cup sifted flour
- 1 cup sifted cornstarch
- 1½ teaspoons baking powder
- ½ teaspoon salt
- confectioners' sugar

Set oven at 350°.

Cream butter until fluffy. Gradually add sugar, beating well after each addition. Stir in grated lemon rind. Beat in egg yolks, one at a time. Stir in brandy and beat again 3 minutes. Sift together flour, cornstarch, baking powder and salt. Stir flour mixture into batter, beating thoroughly. Whip egg whites until stiff but not dry. Fold egg whites gently into batter. Grease thoroughly and flour a 9-inch tube pan. Pour batter into it evenly. Bake about 45 minutes or until cake tests done. Cool cake before removing from pan. Dust cake with confectioners' sugar before serving.

NORWEGIAN SPONGE CAKE

(Bløtekake)

A favorite Norwegian cake, to be filled with whipped cream and jam, or with vanilla filling.

1 cup sifted confectioners' sugar
⅔ cup sifted cornstarch
3 eggs, separated
⅛ teaspoon cream of tartar
2 tablespoons water
½ teaspoon vanilla

Set oven at 350°.

Sift ½ cup of the sugar and the cornstarch together 3 times. Beat egg whites, cream of tartar and water in large bowl with rotary beater or electric mixer until mixture forms soft peaks. Beat in remaining ½ cup sugar a little at a time. Continue beating until stiff peaks form when beater is raised. Add egg yolks and vanilla; beat in just until well blended. Fold in sugar–cornstarch mixture a little at a time, and blend in thoroughly. Bake in 2 8-inch greased and floured layer cake pans 30 minutes or until top springs back when touched lightly with finger. Let cool before removing from pans. Cut sides of cake away from the pans with a sharp knife. Fill layers with filling and garnish with whipped cream.

Filling; Garnish

½ cup strawberry jam
⅔ cup heavy cream, sweetened and whipped
1 cup fresh or drained frozen whole strawberries

Spread strawberry jam on one sponge cake layer. Cover with one third of the whipped cream. Top with second layer and spread remaining whipped cream over top and sides of cake. Garnish with strawberries.

SWEDISH SPICE CAKE
(*Kryddkaka*)

¾ cup butter
1½ cups firmly packed brown sugar, sifted
3 eggs, separated
2¼ cups sifted flour
1½ teaspoons soda
1½ teaspoons cinnamon
¾ teaspoon nutmeg
¾ teaspoon cloves
1 cup sour milk or buttermilk
Cream Filling (about 1⅔ cups)
1 cup heavy cream, sweetened to taste and whipped

Set oven at 375°.

Cream butter; add sugar, a little at a time, and beat until fluffy. Beat in egg yolks, one at a time. Sift together flour, soda and spices. Add to egg mixture, alternately with sour milk. Begin and end with flour. Beat egg whites until stiff but not dry and fold into batter. Pour into 2 9-inch greased and floured layer cake pans. Bake about 20 to 25 minutes or until cake tests clean.

Cool and remove from pans. Sandwich together with Cream Filling before serving and cover top with whipped cream.

Cream Filling

- ½ cup sugar
- 1½ tablespoons cornstarch
- 1½ tablespoons flour
- ⅛ teaspoon salt
- 1½ cups milk or light cream
- 1 egg yolk, slightly beaten
- ¾ teaspoon vanilla

Sift together sugar, cornstarch, flour and salt. Mix with cold milk or cream into a smooth paste. Cook over low heat until mixture thickens, stirring constantly. Cook all in all about 7 minutes. Stir some of the hot mixture into egg yolk. Return egg yolk mixture to sauce and cook 2 minutes longer, stirring constantly. Remove from heat and beat in vanilla. Cool before using. Makes 1⅔ cups.

SWEDISH THOUSAND LEAVES TORTE

(*Tusenbladstårta*)

A rich, handsome and worthwhile Swedish specialty. It is important that the layers be very thin and crisp and that the applesauce used be of a tart and well-flavored variety. If the apples are too mild in flavor the Torte will be too bland.

Torte

- 2 cups sifted flour
- 1 cup cold butter
- 4 tablespoons ice water

Sift flour into mixing bowl. With pastry cutter or two knives, cut in butter until pieces are the size of peas. While mixing with fork, add ice water gradually. Toss until dough just holds together. With hands, and handling as little as possible, shape into a ball. Chill for 30 minutes to 1 hour. Meanwhile, make filling.

Fillings

1½ cups thick, tart and well-flavored applesauce

Custard Cream Filling

1½ teaspoons unflavored gelatin
2 tablespoons cold water
2 egg yolks
3 tablespoons sugar
1½ tablespoons cornstarch
1 cup light cream
1 teaspoon vanilla
1 cup heavy cream, whipped

Sprinkle gelatin on cold water to soften. In top of double boiler combine egg yolks, sugar, cornstarch and light cream. Cook over simmering, not boiling, water until smooth and thick, stirring constantly. Remove from heat and beat in gelatin and vanilla. Stir until gelatin is dissolved. Cool, beating occasionally. Fold in heavy cream. Chill. While Custard Cream Filling is chilling, make Icing.

Lemon Icing

2 tablespoons lemon juice
1 cup sifted confectioners' sugar

Stir lemon juice gradually into confectioners' sugar, a little at a time, beating constantly, until spreading consistency has been achieved.

Assembling Thousand Leaves Torte

Set oven at 425°.

Divide chilled dough into 6 portions. Use one portion at a time; keep others in refrigerator until used. Roll each portion between two sheets of waxed paper to a 9-inch circle. Use a 9-inch layer cake pan to measure circle, and trim off excess dough. Slide each layer onto a cookie sheet and peel off carefully the top sheet of waxed paper. (Or each portion may be rolled on bottom of 9-inch layer pan and trimmed.) Prick with fork all over, or layers will bunch during baking. Brush layers with iced water and sprinkle with 1 tablespoon sugar. Bake about 6 to 8 minutes or until golden brown. Cool on cookie sheets. Carefully peel off the bottom sheet of waxed paper. Sandwich layers together by spreading first layer with applesauce, second layer with Custard Cream Filling, third layer with applesauce, fourth layer with Custard Cream Filling and fifth layer with applesauce. Reserve top layer.

Garnishing Thousand Leaves Torte

½ cup candied orange peel
½ cup blanched almonds
1 cup heavy cream
1 teaspoon sugar
½ teaspoon vanilla

Cut orange peel into strips. Ice top layer with Lemon Icing and place on top of other torte layers. Arrange orange peel strips in star pattern in the middle of the top layer. Toast almonds and chop coarsely. Sprinkle almonds around outer edge of cake. Whip cream with sugar and vanilla. With a pastry tube make rosettes of whipped cream on sides of torte, or frost sides with a spatula. Makes 10 to 12 servings.

MARZIPAN COOKIES

Using the ingredients for almond macaroons, prepare a mixture that is stiff, using the minimum of egg white. Divide into portions, and color them with a few drops of food coloring. Sprinkle confectioners' sugar on baking board. Pat or roll out dough ¼ inch thick. Cut into desired shapes with cookie or truffle cutters dipped in confectioners' sugar. Bake as for almond macaroons. Decorate with candies, candied fruits, or any colorful or sparkling cake decorations.

SWEDISH TOSCA CAKE

A good cake for a coffee party.

Cake

- 2 eggs
- 1 cup sugar
- 1 teaspoon vanilla
- 1 cup sifted flour
- 1½ teaspoons baking powder
- ¼ teaspoon salt
- ¼ cup milk
- ½ cup butter or margarine, melted
- butter
- fine dry breadcrumbs

Set oven at 325°.

Beat together eggs, sugar and vanilla. Sift together flour, baking powder and salt. Stir into egg mixture alternately with milk. Begin and end with flour. Beat in melted butter. Butter a 9-inch pie pan and sprinkle with breadcrumbs. Pour batter into pan and bake 30 minutes or until cake tests done. While cake is baking, make topping.

Topping

- ¼ cup blanched almonds
- ¼ cup butter
- 3 tablespoons sugar
- 2 teaspoons heavy cream
- 1 tablespoon flour

Spread blanched almonds on baking sheet and warm in oven for 5 minutes. Slice warm almonds with a sharp knife. Combine almonds with all other topping ingredients and heat to boiling point, stirring constantly. Remove from heat and cool, stirring occasionally.

Finishing Tosca Cake

After cake has baked 30 minutes and tests done, remove from oven. Turn up oven to 375°. Spread almond topping over top of cake. Place cake on cookie sheet and return to oven. Bake 10 minutes longer or until top is golden brown and bubbly. Serve warm, with whipped cream.

ALMOND COOKIES

These very good cookies are a typical example of the rich, buttery cookies beloved by Scandinavians.

1¼ cups shelled almonds, blanched or unblanched, according to your taste
1 cup sweet butter
½ cup sugar
1 teaspoon vanilla or grated rind of 1 large lemon
½ teaspoon salt
2 cups sifted flour
vanilla sugar

Grind almonds fine in nutgrinder or electric blender. Cream butter and gradually add sugar. Stir in almonds, vanilla or lemon rind, salt and flour. Chill for about 2 hours. Set oven at 350°. Snip off small pieces of dough and shape into little loaves 1 inch long and ½ inch wide, or into tiny rings, or into crescents. Bake on buttered and floured baking sheets about 15 minutes or until cookies are beginning to be golden. They must not brown. Cool about 3 minutes. Dip in vanilla sugar.

Vanilla Sugar

Combine 2 cups sifted confectioners' sugar and 1 stick vanilla. Place in container with tight lid, and store, covered, for 2 days or longer before using.

SWEDISH ALMOND MACAROONS

½ lb. almond paste (about 1 cup)
1 cup sifted confectioners' sugar
½ teaspoon vanilla
½ teaspoon salt
2 to 3 egg whites
sugar

Set oven at 300°.

Knead almond paste until soft; work in sugar. Add vanilla and salt. Add egg whites, a little at a time, blending well after each addition. Use just enough egg whites to make a soft dough that will hold its shape when dropped from a teaspoon. Line cookie sheets with unglazed brown paper. Drop paste onto sheets by teaspoonfuls, about 2 inches apart. Or force through a cookie press into rounds. Sprinkle with sugar. Bake about 20 minutes. Place macaroons on damp towel to loosen the brown paper and remove paper. Cool on racks.

DANISH ALMOND PASTE COOKIES

The colored icing sugar can be bought in any market where sprinkles and other cake decorations are sold.

1 cup butter
¼ lb. almond paste
½ cup superfine sugar
1 egg, beaten
2 cups sifted flour
⅛ teaspoon salt
colored icing sugar

Set oven at 375°.

Cream butter with almond paste. Beat in sugar gradually; add egg. Stir in flour sifted with salt. Mix thoroughly. Shape through cookie press in the shape of daisies. Fill center with colored icing sugar. Bake 10 to 15 minutes or until golden.

LACY SWEDISH ALMOND WAFERS

(*Mandel flarn*)

These are usually served with a custard or with a molded dessert.

¾ cup unblanched almonds, finely ground
½ cup sweet butter, at room temperature
½ cup sugar
1 tablespoon flour
⅛ teaspoon salt
2 tablespoons heavy cream

Set oven at 350°.

Combine all ingredients in small heavy saucepan. Heat until butter melts, stirring constantly. Drop by teaspoonfuls on buttered and floured cookie sheet, about 4 inches apart. Don't bake more than 6 cookies at one time. Bake about 7 minutes or until edges are browning but center is still bubbly. Cool 1 minute. Loosen each cookie with a sharp knife and wrap immediately around the handle of a wooden spoon. Cool on racks joint side down. These cookies are very fragile and must be handled carefully.

NOTE: If cookies are too crisp to remove from cookie sheet, return to oven for a few seconds. These cookies can also be kept flat and sandwiched with any favorite filling.

NORWEGIAN BERLINER KRANSER

Scandinavians decorate their cookies with sparkling pearl sugar. The nearest approach to pearl sugar in America is crushed sugar cubes. They will sparkle in a way not even approximated by ordinary sugar.

To crush sugar cubes, place them in a paper bag and hit them with a hammer. This way, the sugar won't fly all over the kitchen.

1 hard-cooked egg yolk
1 raw egg yolk
½ cup confectioners' sugar
½ teaspoon vanilla
1¾ cups sifted flour
½ cup butter, at room temperature
1 egg white, slightly beaten
sparkling sugar

Combine hard-cooked and raw egg yolks and blend to a smooth paste; beat in sugar and vanilla. Work in flour and cut in butter. Mix thoroughly; this is best done by hand. Chill 4 hours. Set oven at 350°. Snip off small pieces of dough and roll between hands into strips, about 7 inches long and ½ inch thick. If dough sticks, flour hands. Shape strips into rings, looping ends, and let ends overlap a little. Brush with egg white and sprinkle with sugar. Bake about 8 to 10 minutes. These cookies must not brown.

SWEDISH ALMOND RUSKS
(*Mandelskorpar*)

A pleasant plain cookie.

⅓ cup butter
¾ cup sugar
2 eggs
½ teaspoon vanilla
½ teaspoon almond flavoring
⅔ cup blanched almonds, coarsely chopped

1¾ cups sifted flour
1½ teaspoons baking powder

Set oven at 375°.

Cream butter and sugar until light. Beat in eggs, one at a time; then add vanilla and almond flavorings and almonds. Blend until smooth. Sift together flour and baking powder and stir gradually into batter. Butter and flour cookie sheets. Spread batter in 1½-inch wide strips. Bake 8 to 10 minutes or until golden. Remove from oven and cut immediately into ½-inch slices. Turn off oven and return cookies to dry out for about 15 minutes.

FINNISH BREAD

Popular throughout Scandinavia, and an excellent, light cookie.

1 cup sifted flour
⅛ teaspoon salt
¼ cup sugar
½ cup ground unblanched almonds
½ cup butter
1 egg white, slightly beaten
⅓ cup chopped almonds
3 tablespoons sugar

In mixing bowl combine flour, salt, sugar and almonds. Cut in butter with pastry cutter or two knives. Stir mixture into a soft dough and divide into 4 parts. Chill 15 minutes. Set oven at 350°. With floured hands roll out the 4 parts of dough into 4 ½-inch wide strips. The strips must be of even length. On floured surface place strips parallel to each other. With sharp knife and using ruler as a guide, cut through all 4 strips at one time making 1½-inch pieces. Place cookies on buttered and floured cookie sheets. Brush with egg white. Combine chopped almonds and sugar and sprinkle over cookies. Bake 10 to 12 minutes or until golden. Cool on cookie sheets and remove carefully.

SWEDISH DREAM COOKIES

(*Drömmar*)

They are made extra crisp and flaky by the ammonium carbonate used in lieu of baking powder. (See notes on page 184.)

1 cup butter
½ cup sugar
½ teaspoon vanilla
2 cups sifted flour
1 teaspoon pulverized ammonium carbonate (hartshorn salt)
½ cup blanched almonds

Cream butter and gradually add sugar. Stir in vanilla. Sift flour with ammonium carbonate and add to butter mixture. Blend thoroughly. Chill dough for 1 hour. Set oven at 350°. Snip off small pieces of dough and roll into balls the size of a jumbo olive. Place on greased and floured baking sheets. Press down center with finger tip and place one whole almond or half an almond in each center. Bake about 12 to 15 minutes or until golden brown.

SWEDISH CINNAMON COOKIES

(*Kanalkakor*)

These cookies are not the usual Central European cinnamon stars which are made with white of egg. They are very tender and flavorful cookies.

⅔ cup butter
1 cup sugar
1 egg
1 teaspoon vanilla
1⅓ cups sifted flour
1 teaspoon baking powder

1 teaspoon cinnamon
½ cup walnuts, finely chopped
2 tablespoons cinnamon
2 tablespoons sugar

Cream butter and gradually add sugar. Beat in egg and vanilla. Sift flour with baking powder and cinnamon. Add to egg mixture and blend thoroughly. Chill for 30 minutes. Set oven at 350°. Combine walnuts, cinnamon and sugar. Roll chilled dough into balls the size of walnuts. Roll each ball into walnut–cinnamon sugar. Place cookies on greased and floured baking sheets about 3 inches apart. Bake 12 minutes.

NORWEGIAN HONEY COOKIES

Store for 2 weeks in an airtight container before using—but they will keep for much longer.

1 cup honey
1 cup sugar
2 tablespoons lemon juice
1 tablespoon chopped candied citron
1 tablespoon chopped candied lemon peel
1 tablespoon chopped candied orange peel
2⅔ cups blanched almonds
2 cups sifted flour
¼ teaspoon cinnamon
¼ teaspoon cloves
¼ teaspoon nutmeg
½ teaspoon cardamom

Heat honey, but do not boil. Stir in sugar, lemon juice and citron, lemon and orange peels. Grind 2 cups of the almonds in a nutgrinder or in electric blender. Add almonds to fruit mixture. Sift flour with spices. Add to fruits and blend thoroughly. Cover and chill 3 days. Set oven at 325°. On floured board, roll very thin. Cut with cookie cutters into any desired shapes. Bake on greased and floured cookie sheets 8 to 10 minutes. Cool and spread with Lemon Icing. Place 1 almond from remaining almonds on each cookie.

Lemon Icing

Stir about 2 tablespoons lemon juice into 1 cup sifted confectioners' sugar. Beat until spreading consistency.

GRANDMOTHER'S JELLY COOKIES

(Mormors' Syltkakor)

A traditional Swedish Christmas cookie, consisting of a large cookie topped with a smaller one.

½ cup butter, at room temperature
⅓ cup sugar
1 egg, separated
1¼ cups sifted flour
¼ teaspoon salt
2 tablespoons finely chopped blanched almonds
2 tablespoons sugar
currant jelly

Set oven at 375°.

Cream butter and gradually add sugar. Beat in egg yolk, flour and salt. Blend thoroughly. On floured surface roll out to about ¼-inch thickness. (The dough must be rolled thinly.) Divide dough. Cut one portion of the dough with 2⅓-inch round cookie cutter. Cut the other portion of the dough with a round or scalloped 2-inch cookie cutter. Remove center of 2-inch cookies with a thimble. Beat egg white slightly. Combine almonds and sugar. Brush each 2-inch cookie (those with the hole) with egg white and sprinkle with almond–sugar mixture. Place on buttered and floured cookie sheets almond side up. Bake all cookies about 6 to 8 minutes. Do not let brown. Cool cookies on racks. Place about ½ teaspoon currant jelly on bigger cookie and top with smaller cookie, almond side up. The jelly should appear in the hole in the center of the top cookie.

NORWEGIAN PEPPER NUTS

(Peppernøtter)

A wonderful old-fashioned recipe from the family of Kaptein Sverre Holck of the Bergen Line, who runs a fine and most abundant table on his ship.

1⁄3 cup butter
2½ cups confectioners' sugar
4 eggs, beaten
3 tablespoons lemon juice
1 tablespoon grated lemon rind
¼ cup chopped candied orange peel
½ cup chopped candied lemon peel
½ cup chopped candied citron
4 cups sifted flour
1 teaspoon cinnamon
1 teaspoon cloves
¾ teaspoon black pepper
1 teaspoon anise seed
1 teaspoon allspice
1 tablespoon ground cardamom
1 teaspoon baking soda
1 teaspoon salt
½ teaspoon almond flavoring

Cream butter and gradually add confectioners' sugar. Beat in eggs and blend thoroughly. Stir in lemon juice, lemon rind, and orange, lemon and citron peels. Sift flour with remaining ingredients except almond flavoring. Add to fruit mixture and stir in almond flavoring. Blend thoroughly. Shape into 1-inch balls and place on greased and floured cookie sheets. Chill overnight.

Set oven at 350°.

Bake peppernuts about 15 minutes or until browned. While still warm, brush with Lemon Icing, made by stirring 1 to 2 tablespoons lemon juice into 1 cup sifted confectioners' sugar and stirring to spreading consistency.

NOTE: The peppernuts should be shaped before chilling or the dough will be too stiff to handle.

SWEDISH PUNCH RINGS

½ cup butter or margarine
1 cup sifted flour
2 tablespoons Swedish punch or rum
1 egg, beaten
½ cup finely chopped almonds
2 tablespoons sugar

Set oven at 350°.

Cream butter until fluffy. Add flour and Swedish punch. Mix thoroughly with spoon or with hands. Roll out on waxed paper to strips 4 inches long and ½ inch wide. Shape strips into rings. Brush with egg. Combine almonds and sugar and sprinkle on top of cookies. Bake on buttered and floured cookie sheets for 8 to 10 minutes or until golden.

RYE RINGS

(*Rågkakor*)

Light and not too sweet, with a hole in the middle.

1 cup butter
½ cup sugar
1 cup sifted rye flour
1¼ cups sifted flour

Cream butter and gradually add sugar. Stir in rye flour first;

mix thoroughly. Then add other flour. Chill dough 30 minutes.

Set oven at 350°.

Work with a little of the dough at one time; keep remaining dough in refrigerator until ready to handle. Knead dough slightly and roll out as thinly as possible between 2 sheets of waxed paper. Prick surface with fork all over. Cut out rounds with 2- or 3-inch cookie cutter. Cut center from cookies with thimble. Place cookies on buttered and floured cookie sheet, using spatula. Bake about 8 to 10 minutes or until golden. Cool on cookie sheets.

SWEDISH GLÖGG

No Swedish Christmas is complete without plenty of *glögg*. It certainly is a heart-and-body warming drink.

3 whole cardamom seeds
8 whole cloves
1 stick cinnamon
1 4-inch strip orange rind (yellow part only)
1⅓ cups water
¼ cup blanched almonds
½ cup golden raisins
1 bottle Bordeaux wine
1 bottle port wine
½ bottle cognac
sugar to taste

Tie cardamom seeds, cloves, cinnamon and orange rind in a cheesecloth bag. Place in water and bring to a boil. Simmer, covered, 10 minutes. Add almonds and raisins and simmer 10 minutes longer. Add Bordeaux wine, port wine and cognac and bring to a quick boil. Remove from heat immediately. Cool and store, covered, overnight. At serving time, remove spice bag. Heat *glögg* but do not boil. Add sugar to taste. Serve in heated mugs or glasses, with a few almonds and raisins in each glass.

SWEDISH PUNCH
(*Svensk Punsch*)

An old-fashioned drink, with a sweet, innocent taste that lures the unwary to underestimate its potency. There are many recipes for it, though nowadays it is usually bought ready bottled. Whatever the recipe, Swedish punch must contain arrack. The following recipe, from Inga Norberg's *Good Food from Sweden* is a good one.

9 pints water
5½ lbs. sugar
2 bottles arrack
1 bottle cognac
1 bottle 100 proof vodka
2 teaspoons glycerine

In large heavy kettle boil together water and sugar to make 9 pints syrup. Cool. Stir in all other ingredients. Continue stirring punch for ¾ to 1 hour. Bottle in 7 quart bottles, cork and seal bottles. Store bottles lying on their sides. The punch improves with time, but it can be served after 5 days. Serve ice cold. Makes about 1¾ gallons of punch.

NORWEGIAN SPRITZ COOKIES OR *S* COOKIES

A universal Northern European cookie, usually shaped like an *S*.

1 cup butter at room temperature
⅔ cup sugar
3 egg yolks
1 teaspoon vanilla

2½ cups sifted flour
candied cherries

Set oven at 375°.

Cream together butter and sugar. Beat in egg yolks, one at a time. Stir in vanilla. Blend in flour. Force through cookie press or spritz gun into round swirls. Decorate middle with a candied cherry. Or shape into *S*. Bake 7 to 10 minutes or until golden. Sprinkle with vanilla confectioners' sugar.

FINNISH SIMA, THE MAY DAY DRINK

May Day, the First of May, is a great Finnish holiday with general rejoicing throughout the country. The students put on their traditional white caps, badge of their academic status, and dance, sing and drink *Sima* with their May Day Crullers (see page 193).

Sima is a pleasant, slightly acidulated, and refreshing drink. This recipe can be doubled or tripled.

1 lemon
4 quarts water
2 cups sugar
2 cups light brown sugar
1 12-ounce can beer or 2 tablespoons hops
¼ teaspoon dry yeast
raisins
sugar

With a sharp knife pare off the yellow part of the lemon rind and reserve. Peel off the white part and throw away. Slice the lemon and remove seeds. In a large kettle or enameled bucket combine water, sugars, lemon slices and lemon peel. Bring mixture to a boil. Remove from heat and add beer or hops. When mixture has cooled to lukewarm, dissolve yeast in ½ cup of mixture and stir into brew. Cover tightly and let stand overnight at room temperature. Strain *Sima* and prepare 4 quart bottles by rinsing them with boiling water. Place ½ teaspoon sugar and 3 to 4 raisins in each bottle. Fill bottle with *Sima* and cap. Store in a cool place. The *Sima* is ready when the raisins have risen to the surface. Serve chilled. Makes about a gallon.

ALMOND PASTE

Almond paste is much used in all Scandinavian baking. Imported almond paste can be bought in specialty shops, but it can also easily be made at home. The following recipe has an excellent flavor and a smooth, non-gritty texture.

1 cup blanched almonds
1 teaspoon almond flavoring
2 cups sifted confectioners' sugar
2 egg whites, slightly beaten

Grind almonds twice in nutgrinder, or grind very fine in electric blender. Combine almonds, almond flavoring and confectioners' sugar. Add egg whites, 1 teaspoon at a time, beating vigorously. Knead with hands until paste is absolutely smooth.

OLD-FASHIONED NORWEGIAN SOUR CREAM COOKIES

The recipe can easily be doubled.

½ cup butter
¾ cup sugar
1 egg
2¼ cups sifted flour
½ teaspoon baking soda
½ teaspoon baking powder
½ teaspoon salt

1 teaspoon cardamom or nutmeg
½ cup sour cream
vanilla sugar

Cream butter and gradually add sugar. Beat in egg. Sift flour with baking soda, baking powder, salt and cardamom. Stir into butter mixture alternately with sour cream, beginning and ending with flour. Chill overnight or until firm enough to roll. Set oven at 375°. Roll dough on floured board to about ¼-inch thickness. Cut with round 3-inch cookie cutter. Bake on ungreased cookie sheets about 12 minutes or until golden brown. Sprinkle with vanilla sugar.

Index to Recipes

THE ART OF DUTCH COOKING

***or* HOW THE DUTCH TREAT**

A culinary journey to Holland

THE ART OF DUTCH COOKING

or HOW THE DUTCH TREAT

by

C. *Countess van Limburg Stirum*

DRAWINGS BY THE AUTHOR

Library of Congress Catalog Card Number 61-6524

Printed in the United States of America

This edition published by
The Ladies' Home Journal Cook Book Club
by arrangement with Doubleday & Company, Inc.
a b c d e f g h

To NOJA
With many thanks

CONTENTS

Recipes capitalized in the text may be located by consulting the Index.

Life has not changed so very much

PREFACE

With this little book I hope to introduce to you "how the Dutch treat" in the best sense of this so often ill used expression.

Most people have seen a painting by an old Dutch Master (either a reproduction, or the original in a museum) of a family gathered round a sumptuous meal, of village people skating on the frozen canals, or of a woman busy in her house with its floor of black and white tiles and the sun streaming in through a high window. And since those days life in my country has not changed so very much, nor has the food the people eat.

A foreigner in Holland, as a tourist, has only too little chance to share this daily, rather homely life, which centers for the greater part around the family, from the day a beautiful new baby is introduced in its long dress (a family heirloom) to the friends of its mamma, to all the fun the family has with Sint Nicolaas on the fifth of December.

The restaurants in Holland give as a rule a good sample of international cooking, for the simple reason that the Dutch people eat their national dishes in their own homes and when they go out, they want to eat something different.

I have tried in this book not only to give you Dutch recipes but also to bring you some of the atmosphere of my country, where many ancient customs have survived and live on in the family circle.

For most people, Dutch food is an undiscovered territory, and I sincerely hope that the discovery of it will bring you joy and many pleasant meals.

INTRODUCTION TO DUTCH FOOD

Naturally every country has its own national food, depending on the climate and the products of the soil. The Russians have their caviar and vodka, the Italians their pastas and Chianti, and so on.

The Dutch have their meadows with cattle, which means milk, butter, and meat; their canals and the sea, meaning fish. Vegetables and fruit grow extremely well in this not-very-cold but rather dampish climate. The national drink is Genever, or Dutch gin.

It is not yet customary to have everything frozen or in cans and ready for use at any moment, as in America. Therefore the basis of the food is its freshness, and one could say that meals in Holland "go with the seasons." In spring the products are different and the preparation is lighter than that for food eaten in winter, which is heavier and richer.

Of course it is not possible to give a standard work on Dutch cooking, as there are so many ingredients that do not exist outside Holland, such as fresh herring or plovers' eggs, which are found by the farmer boys in the meadows during two weeks in April—the dates being fixed by the government—and are a rare and expensive delicacy.

I have tried to use only ingredients that are available in America, or the best equivalent I could find. Most food is not complicated to prepare, though perhaps entirely new for the United States, and is often cooked in advance, which makes it easier for the housewife, as she has only to reheat it.

A DAY IN HOLLAND AND THE MEALS TAKEN

It is customary to eat a lot of bread, all kinds of bread—white, brown, black, rye, rolls with raisins, and so forth—for breakfast and for lunch. The big meal is eaten in the evening.

8 A.M.: breakfast. Most people drink endless cups of strong tea (with sugar and a little milk) with this meal. The children eat porridge—*pap*, as it is called—with white or brown sugar, all different kinds of bread with cheese, a slice of cold meat, boiled or fried eggs, and jam. And everything with plenty of butter. Quite a meal to start the day!

10:30 A.M. Coffee with sugar and hot milk. Usually *koekjes* (cookies), or various biscuits baked at home or bought in a bakeshop, accompany the coffee. Everybody stops working. In offices, coffee is handed round at the desks; in shops and workshops, people drink it at a counter or in a canteen. It is customary for housewives to make a morning call on each other, a nice occasion for a little gossiping.

12:30 P.M.: lunch. One often finds the term *Hollandse Koffietafel* on the menu of a restaurant. It means all the various kinds of bread, sliced sausage, cheese and one little warm dish (for recipes, see Luncheon Dishes chapter), fresh fruit, and endless cups of coffee.

4 P.M. Tea with cakes and biscuits.

6 P.M. If one can afford it, this is the time for a little *apéritif*, a Genever (Dutch gin). There are many different brands, but the main difference is between "old" and "young." The old is a little more oily and stronger in taste. Genever cannot be used as "gin" and does not taste well diluted with water or used to make cocktails. It is very strong and must not be taken in great quantities, but as a quick pickup it is marvelous.

6:30 P.M.: dinner. This meal usually begins with soup, made with great quantities of meat, vegetables, and so forth. Then comes fish or meat, with potatoes and lots of gravy or sauce. For dessert there is usually a pudding or a sweet made of stale bread, macaroni, or the famous *Flensjes*, very thin pancakes (for recipes, see Desserts chapter). One usually drinks beer or water with this meal. Wine is a luxury for special occasions.

Before starting on the different recipes I want to tell you about the Dutch dish that is eaten practically at all hours of the day and night and is number one on the menus of restaurants and snack bars. This may be compared with the American hamburger; however it is eaten mostly by men, who have only a short time for a little food between business hours or are "en route" the whole day in their cars. The name of this special dish is Uitsmijter, and here follows the recipe.

UITSMIJTER
For one person

Butter
2 slices white bread
Slices boiled ham or roast beef
2 eggs
1 dill pickle

Butter the bread and cover with slices of ham or roast beef—a matter of taste. Fry the eggs and put them on top of the meat. Add the dill pickle.

When one is very hungry, one can fry the bread in butter and top with the cold meat and fried eggs.

THE ART OF DUTCH COOKING

or **HOW THE DUTCH TREAT**

Cheese market, Alkmaar

APPETIZERS and CHEESES

Although cheese is our national product, there exist very few original cheese dishes, like the famous Fondue in Switzerland, which is a meal in itself. Nor do we eat cheese as an after-dinner savory, as they do in England.

But as cheese is the most popular appetizer to nibble when drinking Genever, I'll tell you something about the different kinds of cheese that are made.

The three most important kinds are called after the

towns they are made in: 1) Gouda cheese, a large, flat, round cheese with a 12-inch diameter; 2) Edam cheese, a round ball, red outside (this one is well known, as it is exported all over the world); 3) Leiden cheese, the same shape as the Gouda cheese, but made with cuminseed and less fatty than the other two kinds.

The most important thing about these cheeses is their age. Some are made in spring, as soon as the cattle goes from the stables to the meadows after the winter, and is the so-called "May cheese," a very fat and creamy cheese. Some are made during the summer. They are stored for a certain time, becoming aged—more *belegen*, as they call it—and during this process they lose moisture. Therefore old cheese is much drier and sharper in taste than the young, freshly made cheese and is more expensive too. The various kinds are sold in the shops, thinly sliced or in one piece of the desired weight.

For dishes that require grated cheese, the "older" kinds are used; for sandwiches, the "younger" ones, as they are easier to slice and do not crumble. As an appetizer one uses a rather old cheese, diced and eaten with a sharp mustard.

A very nice appetizer is made in the following way.

Butter
4 slices black rye bread
3 slices creamy cheese

Butter the bread thickly and put the cheese in between, one layer on top of the other. Press between two plates so that bread and cheese adhere well together. Cut crosswise with a sharp knife.

CHEESE TRUFFLES
Kaastruffels

¼ pound butter
3 tablespoons grated cheese
Pepper, salt, celery salt, or paprika to taste
Slices stale pumpernickel, crumbled

These are very easy to make and do not need any cooking.

Cream the butter and mix with the cheese and the spices. Chill. Shape into little balls with a warm teaspoon and roll in the crumbled rye bread. Chill thoroughly and serve. Instead of rye bread, bread crumbs could be used.

STUFFED EGGS WITH CHEESE

Eieren gevuld met kaas

6 eggs
4 tablespoons butter
2 tablespoons grated Parmesan cheese
¼ teaspoon salt
¼ teaspoon pepper
½ tablespoon chopped parsley

Hard-boil the eggs. Chill and shell them. Cut them into halves lengthwise. Remove the yolks and rub them through a sieve. Melt the butter and mix with the cheese, egg yolks, salt, pepper, and parsley. Fill the eggs with this paste and chill.

MEAT BALLS

Bitterballen

3 tablespoons butter
4 tablespoons flour
1 cup milk or water
1 tablespoon very finely minced onion
1 teaspoon Worcestershire sauce
½ teaspoon grated nutmeg
½ teaspoon salt
1 tablespoon chopped parsley
1½ cups cooked, chopped meat
Bread crumbs
2 egg yolks
Fat for frying
Mustard

Melt the butter, stir in the flour, and add the milk or water. Make a thick sauce. Add the six following ingredients. Simmer for 5 minutes, stirring well. Spread this mixture on a plate, and when it is cool, shape into little balls. Roll these in the bread crumbs. Beat the egg yolks with 3 tablespoons water, roll the balls through this mixture, and see that they are covered well on all sides. Roll again through the bread crumbs. Let them stand for 1 hour; they must be dry. Drop them in hot fat, cook until they are brown, and drain them on absorbent paper. They are served with mustard, and usually it is very difficult to eat them without burning your mouth, but that is as it should be.

CHEESE CROQUETTES

Kaascroquetten

3 tablespoons butter
5 tablespoons flour
1 cup milk
1½ cups grated cheese
¼ teaspoon pepper
Sifted bread crumbs
2 egg yolks
Fat for frying

± 10 CROQUETTES OR
20 CHEESE BALLS

Melt the butter, stir in the flour, and slowly add the milk. Cook and stir the sauce with a wire whisk until it is smooth and boiling. Add the cheese and stir until it is melted. Season with pepper. Spread on a plate and cool. Shape with a spoon into croquettes and dip them in the bread crumbs. Beat the egg yolks with 3 tablespoons water and roll the croquettes through this mixture, then again through the bread crumbs, and fry in deep fat. Drain on absorbent paper. Instead of croquettes, one can make little balls and eat these as an appetizer with a drink.

CHEESE PUFFS
Kassballetjes

3 tablespoons butter
5 tablespoons flour
1½ cups grated cheese
3 egg yolks, beaten
3 egg whites, beaten stiff
¼ teaspoon pepper
Fat for frying

± 20 PUFFS

Melt the butter, stir in the flour, and add 1 cup water. Cook and stir the sauce with a wire whisk until it is smooth and boiling. Add the cheese and stir until it is melted.

Take the sauce from the fire, add the beaten egg yolks, and fold in the egg whites. Add pepper. With a small spoon take a part of this mixture and drop into hot fat. Drain on absorbent paper.

Served with tomato sauce and a green salad, these puffs make an excellent lunch dish.

WARM CHEESE-AND-BREAD DISH

Kaas en broodschoteltje

10 slices stale bread without crusts
5 slices cheese
2 eggs
1 cup milk
1 tablespoon butter

4 SERVINGS

Place 5 slices of bread in a buttered ovenproof dish. Cover with the cheese and top with the rest of the bread. Beat the eggs with the milk and pour over the bread and cheese. Let soak for ½ hour. Dot with butter and bake in a moderate oven (350° F.) for ½ hour. Serve warm or cold. This dish goes well with a green salad.

CHEESE SOUFFLÉ

Kaas soufflé

3 tablespoons butter
2 tablespoons flour
1 cup milk
½ cup grated cheese
3 egg yolks, beaten
¼ teaspoon salt or celery salt
Pinch of pepper
3 egg whites, beaten stiff

4 SERVINGS

Melt the butter, stir in the flour, and slowly add the milk. Cook and stir the sauce with a wire whisk until it is smooth and boiling. Add the cheese and stir until it is melted. Add 3 beaten egg yolks and salt and pepper. Cool. Fold in 3 egg whites. Pour into a lightly greased baking dish, 7 inches in diameter. Bake for ½ hour in a moderate oven (350° F.), without opening the oven door to have a look. Serve at once.

I will end this chapter with a popular appetizer.

Put some shelled peanuts in a hot frying pan and shake them well. Serve with a liberal amount of salt.

Soups

SOUPS

Soups play an important role in the Dutch cuisine, as the climate is rather damp and cold, and one likes to start a meal with something warm. Therefore cold soups are not on the national menu. Some soups, such as pea soup and bean soup, are eaten as a whole meal. They simmer the whole day over a slow fire and are eaten the next day, which improves their taste highly.

Leftover vegetables such as cauliflower or asparagus are

always used for soup too, with the water they are cooked in. So there are lots of vitamins in these soups and very few calories.

PEA SOUP
Erwtensoep

3 cups green split peas
2 pigs' feet
1-pound slab fresh bacon
3 leeks
2 onions
2 tablespoons butter
2 tablespoons chopped parsley
1 cup chopped celery stalks with leaves
1 celery root or celeriac
1 can frankfurters
Salt and pepper to taste
Pumpernickel

6 SERVINGS, AS THIS IS CONSIDERED TO BE THE WHOLE MEAL

Cook the peas in 3 quarts water till tender, and if necessary rub them through a sieve. Add the pigs' feet and simmer for 2 hours. Add the bacon. Wash and slice the leeks and the onions. Fry them in butter and add to the soup with the parsley and celery root (cut into cubes). Simmer for 1 hour or more. Cut the frankfurters into pieces and add them with their juice to the soup. Let stand overnight. Reheat this soup the next day. Add salt and pepper. Stir well, as it will have become much thicker. Take the bacon out and cut into slices. Serve these on the pumpernickel with the soup.

From what is left of the soup make next day a

GREEN SOUP

Groene soep

Add as much water as necessary to give each person a cup.

2 tablespoons chopped parsley
Croutons fried in butter

Boil the soup, and sieve. If there is any meat left on the pigs' feet, cut this in small pieces and put back in the soup. Adjust seasoning. Fry croutons—enough for each person to add 2 spoonfuls to his cup of soup. Garnish with parsley.

BEAN SOUP

Bruine bonen soep

2 cups dried beans
1 teaspoon salt
4 whole cloves
6 peppercorns
1 bay leaf
2 leeks, sliced
¾ cup sliced celery with leaves
2 medium-sized onions, chopped
¾ cup sliced carrots
4 tablespoons fat or lard
2–3 tablespoons soya sauce
2–3 tablespoons catchup

8 SERVINGS

Soak the washed dried beans overnight in 10 cups water. Next day add to the same water the salt, cloves, peppercorns, and bay leaf. Bring to the boiling point and simmer for 4 hours. Rub through a sieve. Fry the leeks, celery, onions, and carrots in the fat. Add to the soup and simmer for 2 hours more. Before serving, add the soya sauce and the catchup. This is a spicy soup. Of course cans of beans with water added may be used.

CURRY SOUP

This is made of what is left of the Bean Soup.

6 cups Bean Soup (water added if necessary)
2 medium-sized onions, chopped finely
3 tablespoons butter
3 tablespoons flour
1 tablespoon curry powder
Parsley
¾ cup croutons fried in butter

6 SERVINGS

Heat the Bean Soup. Fry the onions in the butter until golden brown. Blend in the flour and the curry powder. Mix well. Slowly add the soup to this mixture and cook for about 10 minutes. Rub through a sieve. Add the parsley and serve with the croutons.

MEAT BALLS, BEEF OR VEAL, FOR SOUP
Soepballetjes

Meat balls are often added to soup. In this case it is not necessary to use meat for the stock.

- 2 slices white bread without crusts, soaked in very little milk
- ½ pound ground fresh beef or veal
- 1 egg
- ½ teaspoon salt
- ¼ teaspoon grated nutmeg

Mix all ingredients well and roll into small balls. Drop into the simmering soup and cook till done (± 10 minutes).

VEGETABLE SOUP WITH MEAT BALLS
Groentesoep met balletjes

- 3 cups diced fresh vegetables (leeks, carrots, beans, peas, parsley, celery, etc. No tomatoes)
- 3 tablespoons butter
- 1 teaspoon salt
- 2 tablespoons rice
- Beef Meat Balls

6–8 SERVINGS

Fry the vegetables lightly in the butter and add 6 cups water, salt, and rice. Cook slightly, until they are done. Add the Beef Meat Balls, and simmer for 10 minutes.

VERMICELLI SOUP WITH MEAT BALLS

Vermicelli soep met balletjes

⅔ cup vermicelli
1 teaspoon salt
Little piece of mace
Veal Meat Balls

6 SERVINGS

Cook the vermicelli in 6 cups water with the salt and mace (this gives the extra flavor) for about ½ hour. Add the Veal Meat Balls and simmer for 10 minutes.

EEL SOUP

Paling soep

This is eaten during Lent.

1 tablespoon salt
6–8 peppercorns
½ bay leaf
1½-pound eel, cleaned and cut into 1-inch pieces
6 tablespoons butter
6 tablespoons flour
1 tablespoon chopped parsley
2 egg yolks

8 SERVINGS

Bring 8 cups water to a boil with the salt, peppercorns, and bay leaf. Add the eel and simmer for 20 minutes. Take the eel out. Fry the butter with the flour and add the eel stock. Simmer for 15 minutes. Sieve. Add the eel and the parsley. Reheat the soup. Take the soup from the fire. Beat the egg yolks with a little of the liquid and add to the soup.

KIDNEY SOUP
Nier soep

1 veal kidney
4 cups stock or 4 cups water with 4 bouillon cubes
1 tablespoon finely chopped onions
3 tablespoons butter
3 tablespoon flour
1 cup cream
1 small can champignons
2 tablespoons Madeira
6 SERVINGS

Soak the kidney in water for 2 hours. Change this water two or three times and cook in the stock until done (½ hour). Drain kidney and dice. Fry the onion in the butter, and add the flour. Add the cream, stirring well, and, slowly, the stock to this mixture. Simmer for 15 minutes. Then add the champignons and the diced kidney. Just before serving, stir in the Madeira.

CHERVIL SOUP
Kervel soep

5 tablespoons butter
6 tablespoons flour
6 cups veal stock
3 tablespoons chopped chervil
3 egg yolks
6–8 SERVINGS

Melt the butter and stir in the flour. Slowly add the stock. Stir well and simmer for 10 minutes. Add the chervil. Take the soup from the fire. Beat the egg yolks with a little of the liquid and add to the soup.

Hollandse Koffietafel

LUNCHEON DISHES

and recipes for leftover food as part of the Hollandse Koffietafel

It may not sound very hospitable to give your guests a dish made of leftovers, instead of rushing to the store to buy everything fresh. But still, the best luncheon dishes are often made from refrigerator scraps. It is not the custom to have a hot meal in the middle of the day, although one luncheon dish is usually part of the *Hollandse Koffietafel.*

This last is served in the following way. All dishes are put on the table at the same time—various kinds of bread, such as white, brown, rye, pumpernickel, rolls, rusks, zwieback, and currant bread, and various kinds of meat, such as ham, liver, sausages, roast beef, etc. These are all sliced and put on separate dishes. For the children there is a variety of sweet things: jams, and an amazing assortment of sugar and chocolate products to sprinkle on the buttered slices of bread. But these are all bought ready-made. Cheese is never omitted. All this is accompanied by a seasonal salad, lettuce, tomato, or cucumber. These are prepared in a special way.

DRESSING FOR LETTUCE SALAD
Slasaus

1 hard-boiled egg
½ teaspoon salt
½ teaspoon pepper
½ teaspoon sugar
1 teaspoon mustard
3 tablespoons oil
1 tablespoon vinegar, or juice of ½ lemon
1 thin leek or spring onion, shredded

Mash the hard-boiled egg with a fork. Add salt, pepper, sugar, and mustard. Stir in the oil, vinegar or lemon juice, and the leek. The dressing should be of a smooth consistency.

The lettuce, cleaned and dried, is added gradually to this sauce in the salad bowl and thoroughly mixed.

TOMATO SALAD
Tomatensla

1 tablespoon oil
1 teaspoon salt
½ teaspoon pepper
1 teaspoon chopped onion
½ teaspoon sugar
4 tomatoes, sliced
½ tablespoon chopped parsley

Mix oil, salt, pepper, onion, and sugar. Pour this mixture over the sliced tomatoes. Sprinkle with the chopped parsley.

CUCUMBER SALAD
Komkommersla

1 cucumber
2 teaspoons salt
2 tablespoons wine vinegar
1 tablespoon chopped parsley

Peel and slice the cucumber thinly. Sprinkle with the salt and put the cucumber for 1 hour in a colander to drain off excess moisture. Add vinegar and parsley and mix well.

MACARONI WITH HAM AND CHEESE
Macaronischoteltje

1½ cups macaroni (when boiled, this becomes twice this amount)
1 cup chopped boiled ham
1 cup grated Parmesan cheese
3 tablespoons butter
1 tablespoon bread crumbs

3 SERVINGS

Break macaroni into 2-inch pieces. Bring to the boil in 6 cups water. Boil 15 minutes, turn off the heat, and let the macaroni stay in the water for about 15 minutes. Drain well. Add the ham, cheese, and 2 tablespoons butter. Mix, stirring with 2 spoons. Put in a greased ovenproof dish. Dot with the rest of the butter; sprinkle with the bread crumbs. Bake in a moderate hot oven (350° F.) for ½ hour.

One can vary this dish by adding sautéed chopped onions, pepper, celery salt, Worcestershire sauce, or tomato paste.

STUFFED TOMATOES
Gevulde tomaten

6 large tomatoes
½ pound meat (beef, veal, pork, or a combination of these), ground or chopped
1 slice white bread without crust, soaked in a little milk
1 teaspoon grated onion
½ teaspoon salt
¼ teaspoon pepper

¼ teaspoon grated nutmeg
½ tablespoon chopped parsley
2 tablespoons butter

6 SERVINGS

Cut a slice off the top and empty each tomato with a small spoon. Keep the slices and insides for further use. Prepare the stuffing by mixing together all ingredients, except the butter. Stuff the tomatoes and put them in a greased ovenproof dish. Press a little lump of butter in each tomato. Now rub through a sieve the parts of the tomatoes you have reserved, pour this liquid between the tomatoes in the dish, and add the rest of the butter. Bake in a moderate oven (350° F.) for ½ hour.

STUFFED CUCUMBER
Gevulde komkommer

1 large cucumber
1 bouillon cube
½ pound meat (beef or veal), ground
1 slice white bread without crust, soaked in a little milk
1 teaspoon grated onion
½ teaspoon salt
¼ teaspoon pepper
¼ teaspoon grated nutmeg
2 tablespoons bread crumbs
2 tablespoons grated cheese
1 tablespoon butter

Peel and slice the cucumber lengthwise in halves and crosswise into three pieces. Take the pulp out with a spoon. Cover the six pieces with water and parboil for 8 minutes. Dissolve the bouillon cube in 1 cup of the stock. Drain the cucumber. Mix the meat with the soaked bread, onion, salt, pepper, and nutmeg. Stuff the pieces with this mixture. Put them in a greased ovenproof dish. Pour in the bouillon. Sprinkle with bread crumbs and cheese and dot with butter. Bake in a moderate oven (350° F.) for ½ hour.

HUNTERS' DISH
Jachtschotel

This dish is called Hunters' Dish because left-overs of game can be used instead of meat.

3 onions, sliced
3 tablespoons butter or fat
1 pound cooked chopped meat
Meat drippings diluted with water to make 2 cups
½ teaspoon salt
½ teaspoon pepper
¼ teaspoon grated nutmeg
1 tablespoon Worcestershire sauce
3–4 medium-sized potatoes, mashed
4 apples, peeled and sliced very thin
1 tablespoon bread crumbs

6 SERVINGS

Sauté the onions in 2 tablespoons butter. Add the meat, liquid, and spices. Mix well. Fill a greased oven-proof dish with alternate layers of mashed potatoes, the meat-and-onion mixture, and a layer of apple slices. The top layer should be potatoes. Dot with the rest of the butter and sprinkle with bread crumbs. Bake in moderate oven (350° F.) for ½ hour.

CURRY DISH

Kerryschoteltje

3 onions, chopped
3 tablespoons butter or fat
2 teaspoons curry powder
½ teaspoon salt
1 pound cooked meat, diced
3 cups boiled rice
Meat drippings diluted with water to make 2 cups
1 tablespoon bread crumbs

4–6 SERVINGS

Sauté the onions in 2 tablespoons butter. Stir in the curry powder and salt. Add the meat, rice, and liquid. Mix well. Put into a greased ovenproof dish and dot with the rest of the butter. Sprinkle with bread crumbs. Bake in moderate oven (350° F.) for ½ hour.

HUZARENSLA

A cold salad for Hussars

1 head lettuce (use inner leaves only)
1 pound cold cooked meat, diced
3 sour apples, diced
3 hard-boiled eggs, chopped
1 cooked beet, diced
6 boiled potatoes, mashed
4 dill pickles, sliced
4 tablespoons small pickled onions
3 tablespoons oil
3 tablespoons vinegar
Pepper and salt to taste
Mayonnaise

8 SERVINGS

Decorate an oblong dish with lettuce leaves. Mix all ingredients except the mayonnaise with the oil and vinegar and with pepper and salt. The result must be a rather solid mass. Spread this on the lettuce leaves like a pudding. Cover with a thick coating of mayonnaise.

For decoration:
2 hard-boiled eggs
Slices of dill pickle
1 tablespoon chopped parsley

Chop the whites of the eggs and rub the yolks through a sieve. Use these with round slices of the pickle and the parsley in strips or squares on top of the mayonnaise.

EGGS IN CURRY SAUCE

Eieren in kerrysaus

2 onions, chopped
4 tablespoons butter
2 teaspoons curry powder
4 tablespoons flour
1 cup milk
1 apple, diced
1 tablespoon raisins
1 teaspoon salt
8 hard-boiled eggs
1 tablespoon chopped parsley

8 SERVINGS

Sauté the onions in the butter. Add the curry powder and flour. Stir in the milk and 1 cup water and make a smooth sauce. Add the apple and simmer until the pieces are nearly dissolved. Add the raisins and salt. Slice or quarter the eggs. Put them in a dish, cover with the sauce, and sprinkle parsley on top.

Serve this dish with mango chutney, fried bananas, and rice. A cucumber salad might be served with it.

FRIED EGGS WITH CHEESE

Spiegeleieren met kaas

6 thick slices Edam cheese
3 tablespoons butter
6 eggs
Pepper or paprika
6 SERVINGS

Sauté the slices of cheese for a few minutes in butter,

turning over once. Fry the eggs in the usual manner. Put one on each slice of cheese. Sprinkle with pepper or paprika powder, depending on the taste of the cheese.

Serve with toast, butter, and a green salad. Fresh radishes go very well with this dish.

BAKED EGGS WITH ONIONS AND CHEESE

Gebakken eieren met uien en kaas

1 onion, grated
4 tablespoons butter
4 tablespoons grated cheese
6 eggs
½ cup cream

6 SERVINGS

In a shallow ovenproof dish, sauté the onion in the butter till golden brown. Sprinkle with 2 tablespoons cheese. Break the eggs over these ingredients, keeping the yolks whole. Cover with the cream and the rest of the cheese. Bake the eggs in a moderate oven (350° F.) until they are firm.

OMELETTE WITH RAGOUT OF SHRIMPS

Omelet met garnalen ragout

4 eggs
Pinch of salt
4 tablespoons butter
2 tablespoons flour
¾ cup milk
½ cup shrimps
Pinch of grated nutmeg
½ tablespoon chopped parsley

4 SERVINGS

Beat 4 eggs with 4 tablespoons water until well blended. Add salt. In a skillet, melt 2 tablespoons butter. Add the egg mixture, cook over a slow fire, and prick with a fork until the eggs are firm. The omelette should be a delicate brown underneath.

For the ragout: Melt 2 tablespoons butter and add 2 tablespoons flour. Stir in the milk and make a smooth sauce. Add shrimps, nutmeg, and parsley. Mix well. Spread this mixture lengthwise over the middle of the omelette and fold over.

Serve with a green salad.

EGGS IN MUSTARD SAUCE
Kamper steur

This dish originates from the town of Kampen.

4 tablespoons butter
4 tablespoons flour
2 cups bouillon
1½ tablespoons mustard
1 tablespoon capers (optional)
6 hard-boiled eggs

6 SERVINGS

Melt the butter, add the flour, and stir until well blended. Stir in the bouillon and make a smooth sauce. Mix in the mustard and capers. Quarter the eggs and pour the sauce over them.

RUSSIAN EGGS (cold)
Russische eieren

2 hard-boiled eggs
Lettuce leaves
1 tablespoon sliced cucumber, marinated
1 tomato, quartered
½ tablespoon chopped parsley
½ tablespoon chopped celery stalks
Mayonnaise

1 SERVING

Cut the tops off the eggs, so that they can stand. Put them in the middle of a plate. Surround with lettuce leaves. Decorate with cucumber and tomato. Mix the parsley and the celery stalks with the mayonnaise and pour over the eggs.

Scheveningen harbor

FISH

Bordering on the North Sea, Holland has a lot of fish which is different from that of other countries. Although salmon and lobster are not on the menu, we have various other kinds of sea food that enjoy great popularity. As a rule we use only fish which is brought in fresh nearly every day and we are therefore quite dependent on the seasons. In winter, fish is rather scarce and expensive. Oysters from the Province of Zeeland (the famous Imperiales) are eaten only when there is an "R" in the name of the month beginning with SeptembeR and ending with ApRil. They are very expensive and considered a great luxury, always eaten on the half shell, on ice, with toast and butter, a little ground pepper, and a piece of lemon. To add catchup or any other sauce is considered a sacrilege. It is an old Dutch custom to consume dozens of oysters (and nothing else) on New Year's Eve, with a bottle of champagne to celebrate the coming of the New Year.

Herring—"the poor man's oyster," as it is sometimes called—is certainly a national dish and forms the basis of an important industry. Therefore the beginning of the herring season calls for some extra celebration, and the consumption of fresh, young, and fat herrings is a tradition in Holland that has no counterpart anywhere else.

On a certain date in May the herring fleet from the various seaports, such as Katwijk, Ymuiden, and Scheveningen sail out and parade along the coast for an afternoon, gaily decorated with bunting. From all over the country, people come to watch from the dunes; and, with its full sails and flags flying in the breeze, the fleet is indeed a unique sight.

When evening falls, the ships return to port, and now the serious work begins: getting ready for the big race. The skipper who brings in the first catch within twenty-four hours wins the race, and as a special honor, he is allowed to present the first herrings of the season (packed in a cask of traditional design) to Her Majesty, the Queen. His photograph appears in all the newspapers, and everybody is delighted.

And from that moment on, the whole nation eats herring—"green" herring, as it is called. The most elegant and expensive restaurants as well as the little cafés put it on their menus as a number-one specialty. The herrings are usually served on ice, with toast and butter, more or less like oysters. But the best way to eat them is from a little cart on the streets (see jacket illustration). They are decorated with the national tricolor and carry the proud announcement: *Hollandse Nieuwe* (Holland New Ones).

It is an amazing spectacle to see all classes of people flock to the herring stalls in the season: the workingman as well as the dignified businessman passing by in his car, who just cannot resist the temptation to stop and buy. But it really takes skill to eat them like this: the vendor cuts off the head, rips out the inner "works," but leaves the tail on. So take the herring between the thumb and finger of your right hand, swish it through some raw chopped onions (optional), toss your head, open your mouth—and eat (or swallow is the correct expression for this strange performance).

For the rest of the year herrings are salted or pickled in vinegar and herbs.

A salad is made of them that is rather popular in Holland and very nice as a little hors d'oeuvre to start a meal.

HERRING SALAD
Haringsla

1 head lettuce (use inner leaves only)
3 pickled herrings, chopped
3 apples, diced
3 hard-boiled eggs, chopped
2 boiled beets, diced
8 cold boiled potatoes, mashed
3 dill pickles, sliced
½ medium-sized onion, chopped very fine
Oil
Vinegar
Pepper and salt
Mayonnaise

8 SERVINGS

Decorate an oblong dish with the lettuce leaves. Mix all the ingredients with oil and vinegar, and pepper and salt to taste. The result must be a rather solid mass. Spread this on the lettuce leaves like a pudding. Cover with a thick coating of mayonnaise.

For decoration:
2 hard-boiled eggs
Slices of dill pickle
1 tablespoon chopped parsley

Chop the whites of the eggs and rub the yolks through a sieve. Use these with round slices of the pickle, and the parsley cut in strips or squares on top of the mayonnaise.

After oysters and herring, shrimps take the third place as a popular sea food. Although they are much smaller than their big American cousins, they can be eaten in the same way. In Holland they are caught fresh and eaten on slices of bread with a little lemon juice or vinegar and some pepper.

SHRIMP CROQUETTES
Garnalen croquetten

3 tablespoons butter
2½ tablespoons flour
1 cup milk
2 cups minced shrimps
1 tablespoon chopped parsley
½ teaspoon grated nutmeg
1½ cups bread crumbs
1 egg
Oil for frying

± 12 CROQUETTES

Make a thick and smooth sauce of the butter, flour, and milk. Add the shrimps, parsley, and nutmeg and stir well. Spread on a dish and let cool. Take about a heaping tablespoon of this mixture and shape in the form you wish. Roll in the bread crumbs. Beat an egg with 2 tablespoons water on a plate. Roll the croquettes through this mixture and again through the bread crumbs. The croquette must be well covered on all sides. Let them set for ½ hour. Then fry them in deep oil, at 390° F., until brown. Drain on absorbent paper. Should it be necessary to reheat them, put them for a short time in a very hot preheated oven.

SHRIMP SALAD

Garnalensla

2 cups shrimp
1 apple, diced
2 cold boiled potatoes, diced
1 tablespoon chopped celery
1 tablespoon chopped parsley
4 tablespoons oil
2 tablespoons vinegar
1 teaspoon pepper

6 SERVINGS

Mix together all ingredients and chill.

SHRIMP SAUCE

Garnalen saus

3 tablespoons butter
3 tablespoons flour
1½ cups milk or fish stock
Little piece of mace
½ tablespoon chopped parsley
1 cup shrimps
1 egg
¼ teaspoon ground pepper

Make a smooth sauce of the butter, flour, and the milk or fish stock. Add the mace, the parsley, and the shrimps. Simmer until all is blended well, but do not let the shrimps become soft. Stir in the egg and pepper. This is an excellent sauce with boiled or fried fillets of sole.

FISH CAKES

Viskoekjes

1 cup prepared fish
1 slice bread, softened in milk
1 egg
½ teaspoon salt
1 tablespoon chopped parsley
Bread crumbs
3 tablespoons butter

6 CAKES

These cakes may be made of any kind of fish or fish leftovers. Boil the fish and remove all the bones. Mince very fine. Mix all the ingredients to form cakes. Roll them through the bread crumbs and fry in butter.

BAKED FILLETS OF HADDOCK OR COD

Gestoofde kabeljauw of schelvis

4 tablespoons butter
4 tablespoons flour
2 cups milk
¼ teaspoon salt
¼ teaspoon grated nutmeg
2 egg yolks, beaten
2 egg whites, beaten stiff
6 fillets of haddock or cod
½ cup bread crumbs

6 SERVINGS

Melt the butter, add the flour, and stir in the milk. Add salt and nutmeg to this cream sauce. Take the sauce from the fire and add the egg yolks. Fold in the beaten egg whites. Put the fillets in a greased, ovenproof dish. Pour the sauce over the fish, sprinkle with the bread crumbs, and bake in a 350° F. oven for ½ hour.

Various ingredients can be added to this sauce, such as: chopped parsley, small mushrooms, shrimps, and capers. Or one can use different kinds of fish at the same time; pieces of salmon may be added to give a touch of color.

BAKED FILLETS OF HADDOCK OR COD WITH POTATOES

Gestoofde kabeljauw of schelvis met aardappelen

2 onions, chopped
3 tablespoons butter
6 fillets of haddock or cod
1 pound potatoes
3 eggs
½ teaspoon salt
1 cup sour cream
Bread crumbs

6 SERVINGS

Fry the onions in the butter. Flatten out the fish. Boil the potatoes for 10 minutes and slice them. Put in a greased ovenproof dish a layer of fish, cover with a layer of potatoes and some of the fried onions; then a layer of fish, and so forth. End with a layer of potatoes. Beat the eggs with the salt for a few minutes. Add the sour cream and pour over the fish. Sprinkle with bread crumbs and bake in a moderate oven (350° F.) for about ¾ hour. Any kind of fish can be used for this recipe.

Volendam fishermen

FRIED SOLE
Gebakken tong

4 soles (not fillets)
Salt
1 cup bread crumbs
½ cup butter
1 lemon, quartered

4 SERVINGS

Rub the soles with some salt and after ½ hour dry them thoroughly. Roll them through the bread crumbs. Brown the butter in a skillet and fry the soles on both sides till golden brown, moving them around so they don't stick to the bottom. Serve them with lemon quarters.

These may be eaten with boiled potatoes and a salad of lettuce or cucumber and melted butter.

FILLETS OF SOLE IN WHITE WINE
Tong filets in witte wijn

½ teaspoon salt
12 fillets of sole
2 cups white wine
6 tablespoons butter
3 tablespoons flour

4 SERVINGS

Salt the fillets and put them in a greased ovenproof dish. Add the wine and 3 tablespoons butter. Cover and put for 20 minutes in a moderate oven (350° F.). Fry the rest of the butter with the flour and make a sauce with the wine drained from the fish. Sieve if necessary and pour back over the fish.

FILLETS OF SOLE WITH SPINACH AND CHEESE SAUCE

Tong filets "Florentine"

12 fillets of sole
1 teaspoon salt
2½ tablespoons butter
2 cups cooked spinach
2 tablespoons flour
1 cup milk
2 tablespoons grated Parmesan cheese

4 SERVINGS

Place the fillets in boiling salted water and simmer till nearly tender. This goes quickly. Drain well and put them in a greased ovenproof dish. Cover with the spinach. Make a cream sauce of 2 tablespoons butter, the flour and the milk. Stir in the cheese and cover the spinach with the sauce. Dot with butter and put for 10 minutes in a hot oven (400° F.).

If this dish is prepared in advance, bake the fish in a moderate oven (350° F.) for ½ hour.

QUICKLY FRIED FRESH FISH

Use any kind of fillets or small, cleaned fish. Sprinkle them with salt and let stand for ½ hour. Dry and roll them 1) through flour; 2) through beaten egg; and 3) through bread crumbs. Pour enough oil in a heavy skillet so that the bottom is well covered. Heat the oil for about 4 minutes and fry the fish, turning once.

PIKE
Snoek

The trouble with pike is that there are so many small bones in it. Therefore, cut the fish open over the whole length, take out the entrails, and clean thoroughly. Now cover the fish with a mixture of 3/4 vinegar and 1/4 water and let stand overnight. Most of the very small bones will be dissolved.

PIKE WITH WHITE-WINE SAUCE
Snoek in witte wijn saus

1 pike of about 4 pounds
1/4 cup and 4 tablespoons butter
1 tablespoon chopped parsley
1 medium-sized onion, chopped
1 tablespoon chopped celery
1 teaspoon salt
1/4 teaspoon pepper
1/4 teaspoon grated nutmeg
1/4 teaspoon mace
1 cup white wine
Bread crumbs
1 lemon, sliced
4 tablespoons flour
1 tablespoon capers
2 egg yolks, beaten

8 SERVINGS

Cut the cleaned pike (see rule for cleaning under Pike) in pieces and arrange these in the original shape of the fish in a greased ovenproof dish. Fry in 1/4 cup butter the parsley, onion, and celery, add the other spices, wine, and 1 cup water, and pour over the fish. Sprinkle with bread crumbs and put the slices of lemon on top. Put the fish in a 375° F. oven till tender—about ½ hour. Fry the 4 tablespoons butter with the flour, add the liquid from the fish, and make a cream sauce. Simmer for 10 minutes. Add the capers, take the sauce from the fire, and stir in the beaten egg yolks. Serve this sauce with the fish.

PIKE IN CREAM SAUCE WITH CHEESE

Snoek "au gratin"

1 pike of about 3 pounds
1 cup white wine
1 teaspoon salt
½ cup and 4 tablespoons butter
1 medium-sized onion, chopped
5 tablespoons flour
1½ cups cream
¼ teaspoon pepper
5 tablespoons grated Parmesan cheese
2 egg yolks, beaten
Bread crumbs

8 SERVINGS

Simmer the cleaned pike (see rule for cleaning under Pike) in the wine, 1 cup water, salt, and ½ cup butter till tender. Remove skin and all the bones. The meat should be in fairly large pieces. Fry the onion in the rest of the butter till golden brown. Add the flour and make a cream sauce with the cream, and about 1½ cups of the liquid from the fish, and the pepper. Simmer for 10 minutes. Stir in 3 tablespoons cheese, the egg yolks, and the fish. Pour into an ovenproof dish and sprinkle with the rest of the cheese and the bread crumbs. Let brown in moderate oven (375° F.) for ½ hour.

PIKE BALLS
Snoek balletjes

3 cups ground pike
2 thick slices white bread without crust, softened in a little milk
¾ teaspoon salt
2 eggs
¼ teaspoon pepper
½ cup ground smoked, fat fish (such as smoked eel)

8 SERVINGS

Mix all the ingredients well and form 1-inch balls. Drop them in 5 cups boiling water with salt. After 10 minutes they will be done. Drain. Served with boiled potatoes sprinkled with chopped parsley and melted butter, these balls taste exceptionally good.

STOCKFISH
Dried codfish

This is a very popular dish in the winter months, when other fish is rather scarce. It is sold dry or already softened in water by the fishmonger. First I'll give you the recipe showing how to cook it and then I'll tell you the way it is eaten in Holland.

STOCKFISH
Stokvis

1 pound dried codfish

Soften the fish overnight in plenty of water. Clean them next day and cut in long strips. Roll these up and fasten with a piece of string. Bring sufficient water to a boil—the fish must be covered. Immerse the fish in the water and reduce the heat. The fish must not boil, but simmer for about 1 hour. The time depends very much on the quality of the fish. Test it with a fork—the fish must not get soft. Drain and take the strings off.

Now we can start eating. Everybody gets a soup plate and takes a piece of fish.

Add to this for each person:

a) 2–3 boiled potatoes
b) 2–3 spoonfuls boiled rice
c) 2 spoonfuls fried onions
d) Liberal amount of butter sauce
e) The same amount of a sharp mustard sauce, and—but this is for the very brave—
f) top with a fried egg

Mix everything on your plate and eat with a fork and spoon. It tastes excellent.

PAN FISH
Pan vis

As one always makes the dishes that go with the stockfish, such as rice, onions, sauce; etc., in rather large quantities, there are a fair amount of leftovers the next day. Of these we prepare Pan Fish. Fry some extra onions, mix all the leftovers together, heat them topped with a liberal amount of butter, in a ovenproof dish in the oven. Served with a salad made of lettuce, cucumber, or tomato, this makes a whole meal.

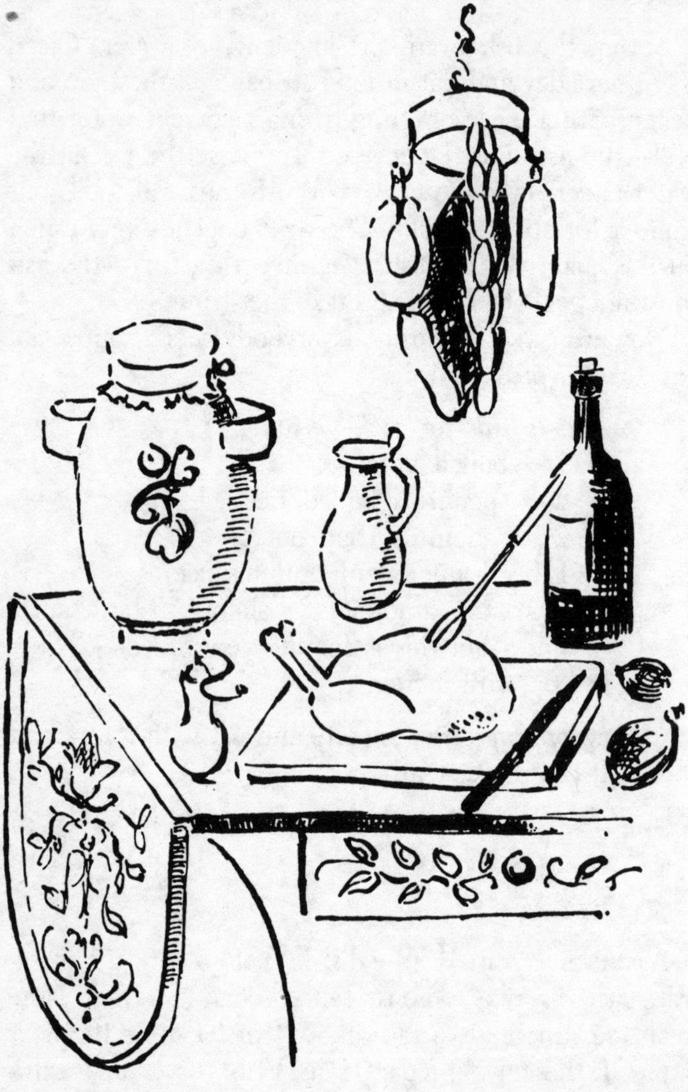

Meat, poultry, and game

MEAT, POULTRY, AND GAME

The meat in America is superb, but is cut by the butcher in quite a different way from that in Holland. Nevertheless, since it plays such an important role on our daily menu in both countries, I thought that it might be a good idea to give you some of our recipes, based on similar ways of cutting the meat.

FILLET OR TENDERLOIN OF BEEF
Ossenhaas

1 fillet of beef of about 2 pounds
3 ounces lard
6 tablespoons butter
Salt and pepper

6 SERVINGS

Remove the surplus fat and skin and pound the fillet with the back of a knife, against the grain. Lard the meat with narrow strips. Pour a kettle of boiling water over the meat. Melt the butter in a roasting pan in the oven and brown slightly. Bake the fillet in the butter, basting all the time. (Oven temperature, 350° F.) It takes about 20 minutes to the pound, but never longer than 80 minutes. Salt and pepper are added afterward, as salt toughens the meat.

FILLET OF BEEF WITH VEGETABLES (warm)
Ossenhaas à la Jardinière

1 fillet of beef of about 2 pounds
6 tablespoons butter
Various vegetables: cauliflower, asparagus, peas, small carrots, champignons, Brussels sprouts, small tomatoes stuffed with spinach, etc.

2 tablespoons butter
2 tablespoons flour
¾ cup bouillon
¼ cup Madeira
¼ teaspoon salt

6 SERVINGS

This is a very nice dish for a dinner party. Prepare the fillet as in the previous recipe. Cut the fillet in thin slices and arrange them in the middle of the dish. Prepare all the vegetables separately and arrange them around the meat in piles, making a pleasant color combination. Fry the butter with the flour and make a smooth sauce with the bouillon. Add the meat gravy and simmer for 5 minutes. Just before serving, add the Madeira and salt. Garnish the meat with a few tablespoons of the gravy and serve the rest separately. Mashed potatoes—stir in some grated cheese—go very well with this dish.

FILLET OF BEEF WITH VEGETABLES (cold)

Prepare the fillet of beef as in Fillet of Beef with Vegetables (warm). Prepare the vegetables. Let everything cool first, then slice the meat. Marinate some of the vegetables, such as asparagus, cauliflower, and champignons. Decorate with chopped parsley and serve with mayonnaise sauce and potato salad.

MARINATED BONELESS CHUCK ROAST
Stoofvlees

1 piece of boneless chuck roast of about 4 pounds
1 bottle red wine
3 onions, sliced
1 bay leaf
6 cloves
1 carrot, sliced
6 peppercorns
1 teaspoon salt
1 cup butter
2 tablespoons flour
Worcestershire sauce

12 SERVINGS

Two days before you intend to eat this dish, let the meat soak in a marinade of the wine with the herbs, only partly covering the meat. Turn two or three times a day. Dry the meat. Melt the butter in a casserole, put in the meat, and turn constantly until it is a golden brown. Sprinkle with the flour and add half of the marinade. Simmer slowly with the lid on, for 1 hour, stir, and turn often. Now take the cover partly off, so that the liquid can evaporate and the sauce thickens. Simmer for 1½ hours more, adding marinade if necessary. Slice the meat and strain the sauce, adding some Worcestershire sauce or more salt.

HÂCHÉ (stewed meat)
Hâché

4 medium-sized onions, chopped
4 tablespoons fat
2 pounds round steak, cut into 1-inch cubes
3 tablespoons flour
2 tablespoons vinegar
2 bay leaves
5 cloves
1 teaspoon salt
1 tablespoon Worcestershire sauce

6 SERVINGS

Brown the onions in the fat in a heavy pan. Remove the browned onions from the pan and sauté the meat in the same fat. Add the onions, and sprinkle with the flour. Add 2 cups water and all the other ingredients. Cover the pan and simmer for about 2 hours, stirring from time to time.

This dish is eaten with boiled potatoes and red cabbage.

BEEFSTEAK
Biefstuk

1 pound beefsteak, 2 inches thick
½ cup butter
¼ teaspoon salt
Grated pepper
Milk or water

4 SERVINGS

Rub the steak with some butter. Heat the frying pan over a good flame until it is very hot. Sear the steak quickly, first on one side, then on the other side. Reduce the flame, add the rest of the butter, season with salt and pepper, and broil each side for 5 minutes more. Put the steak on a hot plate, reheat the gravy, and pour a little milk or water in the middle of the frying pan. As soon as the foam on the surface has disappeared, the gravy is done. Pour over the meat.

You will find this dish on all the menus of the restaurants in Holland.

Serve with fried potatoes, a vegetable dish, and a green salad.

BEEFSTEAK TARTARE (Cold)
Tartare biefstuk

1 pound ground round steak
1 egg yolk
1 tablespoon oil
1 teaspoon salt
1 teaspoon Worcestershire sauce
¼ teaspoon pepper
¼ teaspoon paprika
1 tablespoon chopped pickled gherkins
1 tablespoon finely chopped onions (optional)
1 tablespoon capers
1 teaspoon mustard

4 SERVINGS

Mix all the ingredients thoroughly. It is impossible to give the exact amount of pepper, etc., as this is a dish made according to one's own taste. Some people like to add lemon juice or a little vinegar, catchup, and chopped parsley.

Serve with hot toast and butter.

BEEFSTEAK TARTARE, FRIED
Hamburger

1 pound ground round steak
1 egg yolk
1 teaspoon salt
¼ teaspoon pepper
Paprika
1 tablespoon finely chopped onions (optional)
Bread crumbs
Fat for frying
4 eggs

4 SERVINGS

Mix the meat with the egg yolk, salt, pepper, paprika, and onions. Shape into balls. Roll them in bread crumbs and fry quickly in very hot fat. The outside should be brown, but the inside raw. Top each meat ball with a fried egg. Serve with mustard.

FRESH BEEF TONGUE—BOILED
Gekookte ossetong

1 beef tongue
1 onion
1 large carrot
Sprigs of parsley and celery
½ tablespoon salt

Cover the tongue with warm water and add the other ingredients. Bring to the boil and simmer for about 3 hours. Remove the skin while still warm, starting at the point and pulling down. Put the tongue back in the liquid until you are ready to serve it, because it soon dries out. The liquid makes a very good stock for soup.

The tongue is eaten with Sour Sauce (see below) and white beans.

SOUR SAUCE
Zure saus

8 tablespoons butter
6 tablespoons flour
2 cups stock from the tongue
Juice of 1 lemon
1 egg yolk, beaten

Melt 6 tablespoons of the butter and blend in the flour. Add the stock and make a smooth sauce. Add the lemon juice and fold in the beaten egg yolk. Add the rest of the butter in small lumps, and stir until melted.

SMOKED BEEF TONGUE, BOILED
Gekookte, gerookte tong

1 smoked beef tongue
1 onion
2 bay leaves
Sprigs of parsley and celery

Soak the tongue overnight in cold water. Cover with fresh water and add the other ingredients. Bring to the boil and simmer for about 3 hours. Remove the skin (see Fresh Beef Tongue, boiled).

The tongue is eaten with Raisin Sauce.

RAISIN SAUCE

Rozijnen saus

½ cup brown sugar
1 cup stock from the tongue
½ cup raisins
Juice of ½ lemon
½ cup white wine
1 teaspoon grated lemon rind
2 tablespoons butter

Dissolve the brown sugar in the stock. Add the raisins and the lemon juice and simmer for 10 minutes. Add wine and lemon rind and stir in the butter. Slice the tongue, and serve the sauce separately.

STUFFED BREAST OF VEAL

Gevulde kalfsborst

1 pound ground veal
3 slices white bread, soaked in milk
2 eggs
1 teaspoon salt
¼ teaspoon grated nutmeg
1 breast of veal of about 4 pounds
½ pound butter
Small can champignons (optional)

Make a stuffing of the ground veal with the bread, eggs, salt, and nutmeg. Make a cut in the breast and loosen the skin carefully. Fill with the stuffing. Brown the butter in a roasting pan and bake the meat in a slow oven (300° F.) about ½ hour to the pound. Baste every 10 minutes, adding a little cold water when the butter gets too dark, but not more than 1 cup in all. A small can of champignons may be added to the stuffing. *For the gravy:* Brown 2 tablespoons flour in 2 tablespoons butter. Add 1 cup hot stock or hot water with the drippings in which the meat has been baked. Season the gravy with salt, pepper, powdered herbs to taste (orégano, tarragon, etc.), and simmer for 10 minutes. Strain the gravy and add 1 tablespoon Madeira or sherry.

BREAST OF VEAL, STEWED
Gestoofde kalfsborst

1 breast of veal
12 tablespoons butter
8 cups bouillon
4 carrots
Sprigs of parsley and celery
Piece of mace
1 teaspoon salt
½ lemon, cut in thin slices
5 tablespoons flour
Juice of ½ lemon
1 small can champignons

6 SERVINGS

Pound the meat with the back of a knife until tender, place in colander, and pour boiling water over it. Bake in 8 tablespoons butter for 15 minutes in a moderate oven. Add the hot bouillon, carrots, parsley, celery, mace, salt, and the lemon slices. Simmer for 1¼ hours, covered.

Melt 4 tablespoons butter, blend in the flour, and make a smooth sauce with 2½ cups of the meat stock. Cook for 10 minutes; strain. Add the lemon juice and the champignons. Instead of breast, one can use other parts of veal, cut in 2-inch squares.

This dish is served with rice.

VEAL CUTLETS
Kalfscoteletten

6 veal cutlets, each ½ inch thick
Salt
Grated nutmeg (optional)
2 eggs
Bread crumbs
5 tablespoons butter

6 SERVINGS

Pour hot water over the cutlets, dry them, and sprinkle with salt and nutmeg. Drip them in the eggs diluted with 2 tablespoons water. Cover them with bread crumbs on both sides. Brown the cutlets in the butter over a low flame until they are tender, about 20 minutes, turning them six times.

FILLET STEAKS OF VEAL
Kalfsoesters

6 slices of veal cut from the round
Parsley
Lemon slices
Anchovies

6 SERVINGS

These are prepared like Veal Cutlets. When they are done, sprinkle each one with chopped parsley and top with a slice of lemon and a rolled anchovy.

STUFFED FILLETS OF VEAL

Blinde vinken

6 slices of veal cut from the round
¼ pound ground veal
1 egg
1 slice white bread, soaked in milk
Pinch salt, pepper, and nutmeg
4 tablespoons butter
2 lemon slices
6 SERVINGS

Pound the slices of veal until very thin. Mix the ground veal with the egg, bread, salt, pepper, and nutmeg. Divide into six pieces, and place each on a slice of veal. Roll the slices and tie with thread. Brown quickly in butter on all sides, add 1 tablespoon water and the lemon slices, cover, and simmer until tender, about ¾ hour.

Do not forget to take the thread off. Instead of meat stuffing, one can roll the slices around a boiled egg or use a filling of fried onions and chopped parsley.

VEAL KIDNEYS, SAUTEED

Gebakken kalfsnieren

2 veal kidneys
2 cups bouillon
½ bay leaf
¼ teaspoon salt
¼ teaspoon pepper
½ small onion
1 egg
Bread crumbs
3 tablespoons butter
4 SERVINGS

Soak the kidneys in water for 2 hours, changing the water twice. Simmer for ½ hour in the bouillon with the bay leaf, salt, pepper, and onion. Cut them into slices. Sprinkle with salt and pepper. Dip them in the egg diluted with 2 tablespoons water, roll in the bread crumbs, and sauté them in butter.

RAGOUT OF VEAL KIDNEYS ON BREAD

Nierbroodjes

2 veal kidneys
½ bay leaf
¼ teaspoon salt
½ small onion
½ cup butter
3 tablespoons flour
½ cup cream
1 tablespoon soy sauce
1 tablespoon chopped parsley
Bread crumbs
12 slices stale white bread without crusts

12 SERVINGS

Soak the kidneys in water for 2 hours, changing the water twice. Bring fresh water to a boil with the bay leaf, salt, and onion. Add the kidneys and boil for ½ hour.

Melt 3 tablespoons butter and blend in the flour. Add 1 cup liquid (½ cream, ½ stock), soy sauce, and parsley. Cook and stir until the sauce is smooth and thick. Chop the kidneys and add to the sauce. Fry the slices of bread in butter. Divide the kidney ragout in twelve parts. Put one part on each slice of bread, sprinkle with bread crumbs (rather a thick layer), dot with butter, and put for 10 minutes in a moderate oven (325° F.).

SWEETBREADS
Zwezerik

There are many ways to prepare sweetbreads—broiled, braised, etc.—but this old recipe may be of interest to you.

SWEETBREAD PUDDING
Zwezerik pudding

2 sweetbreads
Sprigs of parsley and celery
Piece of mace
½ teaspoon salt
2 slices stale white bread, without crusts, soaked in a little cream
3 egg yolks
2 tablespoons butter, creamed
Pinch of salt and pepper
1 tablespoon chopped parsley
3 egg whites, whipped stiff

4 SERVINGS

Put the sweetbreads in a pan with water. Warm, but do not bring to a boil. Repeat this three times, using fresh water every time. Rinse them in cold water; remove the fat and membrane. Bring water to the boiling point with the parsley and celery, the piece of mace, and the salt. Simmer for 20 minutes. Drain and rinse. Reserve the stock. Remove the skin and cut the sweetbreads into small pieces. Mix these with the bread and the egg yolks;

add the butter, salt, pepper, and chopped parsley. Fold in the beaten egg whites. Pour the pudding into a greased baking dish, put in a pan with hot water, and steam in a moderate oven (350° F.) for ½ hour. Serve with Sweetbread White Sauce.

SWEETBREAD WHITE SAUCE
Witte saus

Stock from the sweetbreads
4 tablespoons butter
4 tablespoons flour
1 tablespoon brandy

Boil the sweetbread stock until reduced to 2 cups. Melt butter, add flour, and stir in the stock until the sauce is smooth and boiling. Add brandy.

PÂTÉ OF CALF'S LIVER (a cold dish)
Pâté van Kalfslever

2 pounds calf's liver
½ pound fresh fat bacon
1 small can truffles
2 tablespoons Madeira
½ pound butter
1 teaspoon salt
½ teaspoon pepper
½ teaspoon marjoram or orégano
½ teaspoon ground cloves
10 slices smoked fat bacon

8 SERVINGS

Remove the skin and veins from the calf's liver and wash in cold water. Put the liver, with ½ pound fresh bacon, through a meat chopper twice. Soak the truffles in the Madeira. Melt the butter and add all the spices, the sliced truffles, and the Madeira to the liver mixture. Mix well. Cover the bottom and sides of a pudding mold with slices of bacon, put the mixture in, and cover with the rest of the slices of bacon. Cover the pudding mold well and put in a pan of hot water. Steam in a moderate oven (350° F.) for 3 hours.

JELLIED VEAL
Kalfsvlees in gelei

2 calf's feet
1 teaspoon salt
½ bay leaf
5 ounces smoked tongue
1 small can truffles
4 dill pickles
1 envelope unflavored gelatine
¼ cup vinegar

4–6 SERVINGS

Cover the calf's feet with water, add the salt and bay leaf. Bring to a boil and simmer for 3 hours. Take the meat off the bones and put through the meat grinder. Shred the smoked tongue. Slice the truffles and dill pickles. Soften the envelope of unflavored gelatine in ½ cup cold water. Dissolve in 1 cup hot stock of the calf's feet. Add the vinegar and all the other ingredients. Mix well. Pour into moist mold, chill, and unmold.

Decorate with lettuce leaves, sliced tomato, and mayonnaise.

This is a very nice dish for a cold supper.

ROLLED RIB
Varkensschijf

4 pounds rolled rib
½ cup butter or fat
1 apple, sliced
1½ teaspoons salt
1 teaspoon marjoram or orégano
½ teaspoon pepper

8 SERVINGS

Pour a kettle of boiling water over the meat. Brown the butter or fat in a pan in the oven, add the meat, and bake in a 350° F. oven for 2 hours. After 1 hour add the sliced apple and the spices. If the roast gets too brown, add a little water to the gravy. Allow about ½ hour to the pound. Baste often.

Serve warm with cabbage or Brussels sprouts or, when cold, with fried potatoes and a green salad.

PORK CHOPS WITH PURÉE OF POTATOES AND ROBERT SAUCE
Varkenscarbonaden met purée en Robert saus

6 pork chops
Salt and pepper
4 tablespoons butter

6 SERVINGS

Sprinkle the chops with salt and pepper and spread them with butter. Heat a frying pan and sear the chops, reduce the heat, and add the rest of the butter. Cook them slowly until they are done, about 20 minutes. Heap Purée of Potatoes (see Potatoes chapter) in the middle of a dish and surround with the pork chops.

ROBERT SAUCE
Robert saus

1 tablespoon chopped onion
¼ teaspoon ground red pepper
1 bay leaf
4 cloves
2 teaspoons sugar
1 teaspoon mustard
Drippings of the pork chops and enough water to make 2 cups
4 tablespoons butter
4 tablespoons flour
1 tablespoon Madeira

Add the spices to the liquid and simmer for 20 minutes. Melt the butter, add the flour, and stir in the strained liquid, making a smooth sauce. Add the Madeira before serving.

HAM IN GELATINE

Ham-pudding

1 envelope unflavored gelatine
1½ cups bouillon
1 pound boiled ham, chopped
4 dill pickles, chopped
½ teaspoon salt
½ teaspoon pepper
2 hard-boiled eggs, chopped
Mayonnaise

Sprinkle the gelatine in cold water to soften and add to 1 cup hot stock. Stir in all the other ingredients. Put the mixture into a moist pudding mold, chill, and unmold. Serve with mayonnaise.

HAM BALLS

Hamballetjes

1 pound boiled ham, chopped
1 pound boiled potatoes, mashed
1 slice stale white bread without crust, softened in a little milk
3 eggs
1 teaspoon salt
1 teaspoon Worcestershire sauce
Bread crumbs
4 tablespoons butter or fat

12 BALLS

Mix all ingredients together and shape into balls. Roll them through the bread crumbs and sauté in butter.

Serve with a tomato or mustard sauce.

HAM TIMBALE

Timbale van ham

1 pound boiled ham, chopped
3 egg yolks
1 slice stale white bread without crust, soaked in a little milk
1 tablespoon chopped onion
½ cup bouillon
½ tablespoon chopped parsley
½ teaspoon salt
¼ teaspoon pepper
½ tablespoon Madeira
3 egg whites

Mix all the ingredients together except the egg whites. Beat these until stiff and fold into the mixture. Place this mixture in a greased pudding mold. Cover well and steam in a pan of hot water in a 350° F. oven for 1¼ hours and unmold.

LAMB

In Holland lamb is not a very popular dish, as it is in America and England. There are many people who have never eaten it at all, and as there is little demand, the supply is limited and the price is rather high. Therefore recipes for lamb are more suited for a dinner party. They take a little extra time to prepare, but the results make up for that.

ROAST CUSHION SHOULDER OF LAMB
Gevulde lamsborst

For the stuffing:

- 2 tablespoons butter
- 2 tablespoons flour
- 1 onion, chopped
- 1 teaspoon curry powder
- ½ apple, diced
- ½ tablespoon chopped parsley
- ½ cup water
- ½ cup milk
- ¾ cup boiled rice

For roasting:

- 1 shoulder of lamb
- 1 clove garlic
- 1 cup butter

6–8 SERVINGS

Make about 1 cup Curry Sauce (see Eggs in Curry Sauce in Luncheon Dishes chapter). Mix with the boiled rice. Rub the meat with a clove of garlic; one side of the meat must be open for inserting the stuffing. Stuff with the mixture of rice and Curry Sauce and secure with toothpicks. Roast the meat in the butter in a slow oven (300° F.), about 40 minutes to the pound. Baste often.

Serve with boiled rice, fried bananas, and a green salad.

LAMB CHOPS

Lamscoteletten

4 onions, chopped
4 tablespoons butter
8 lamb chops
2 tablespoons flour
1 cup bouillon
1 tablespoon vinegar
4 tomatoes, sliced
1 tablespoon chopped parsley
1 teaspoon celery salt
1 bay leaf
½ teaspoon salt
½ teaspoon paprika
2 teaspoons red currant jelly

8 SERVINGS

Sauté the onions in the butter and take them out of the skillet. Sauté the chops until they are half done; take them out too. Add the flour and make a smooth sauce, stirring in the bouillon. Place the chops in an ovenproof dish and pour the vinegar over them. Cover with the sliced tomatoes, parsley, celery salt, onions, and the sauce. Add bay leaf, salt, and paprika. Cook in a covered dish in a slow oven (300° F.) for about 3 hours. Just before serving, add the red currant jelly and some more salt if necessary.

Serve this dish with mashed potatoes and white beans.

LAMB TONGUES IN MADEIRA SAUCE
Lamstongetjes in Madeira saus

6 lamb tongues (1 per person)
1 bay leaf
Small piece of mace
Sprigs of parsley and celery
1 teaspoon salt
4 tablespoons butter
½ clove garlic, minced
4 tablespoons flour
2 tablespoons Madeira

6 SERVINGS

Cover the tongues with water. Add the spices and salt. Bring to a boil and simmer for ½ hour. Take the tongues out of the stock and trim the necks if necessary. Drain and cut into slices. Sauté these in the butter with the garlic. Add the flour and stir in 2 cups of the stock to make a smooth sauce. Add the Madeira. Sieve the sauce over the tongue.

Serve with boiled rice.

POULTRY AND GAME

In contrast with the fact that there is little taste for lamb in Holland, game and poultry are very popular here. There is still game in abundance, and great favorites of the cheaper kinds are rabbit (from the dunes) and hare (from the meadows). Since the shooting season is limited strictly by the government, the game stock is not deteriorating. Turkey is eaten a little more often at Christmas nowadays, although the traditional dish is goose.

Chicken too is still considered a Sunday treat, in spite of the fact that although it costs the same as meat, it takes a good deal more butter to prepare the necessary amount of gravy to go with the so-beloved potatoes.

ROAST CHICKEN
Gebraden kip

2 young chickens of about 2 pounds each
½ cup butter
Salt

4 SERVINGS

Chickens are often fried in a skillet on top of the stove, as many people do not have ovens. Before preparing, cut the necks and the underparts of the legs off. With the giblets, a pinch of salt, and a piece of mace, these make a delicious bouillon.

Pour boiling water over the insides and the outsides of the chickens. Season the insides of the chickens with a little salt and put a small lump of butter inside. Melt the rest of the butter in a skillet. Place the chickens in the butter and brown them for 5 minutes over a high fire, turning them often, so that they become a delicate brown on all sides. Reduce the fire, half cover the skillet with the lid, and go on roasting until the chicken is done. For a young chicken it takes 20 minutes. A fork should go in easily between the joints. Add the livers the last 5 minutes.

This dish is served with potatoes, boiled or sautéed, young green peas, and a compote.

FRIED YOUNG COCKERELS

(in Austria: Wiener Backhähndl)
Gebakken haantjes

4 young cockerels or young chickens
Pinch of salt
Flour
2 eggs
Bread crumbs
Oil

4 SERVINGS

Leave the chickens for 2 minutes in boiling water. Rinse with cold water. Cut open lengthwise and take out the largest bones. Now cut crosswise once. Sprinkle with salt and dredge them lightly with flour. Beat the eggs with 4 tablespoons water. Roll the pieces through the egg mixture, then through the bread crumbs. They should be well covered on all sides. Heat the oil and fry the pieces.

CHICKEN IN TOMATO SAUCE

Kip met tomaten saus

2 chickens of about 2 pounds each
½ cup butter
1¼ cups bouillon
2 tablespoons flour
4 tablespoons tomato purée
1 tablespoon chopped celery, stalks and leaves
1 teaspoon grated onion
1 teaspoon sugar
½ teaspoon salt
¼ teaspoon pepper

4 SERVINGS

Pour boiling water over the chickens, outside and inside. Sauté the chickens in butter until they are brown on all sides. Cut each in four pieces. Put them back in the pan and add the bouillon and the other ingredients. Cover and bake in a slow oven (325° F.) for about ¾ hour. Place the pieces of chicken on a dish and strain the sauce.

Serve this dish with macaroni or spaghetti and grated cheese.

GALANTINE OF CHICKEN
(Pressed chicken)
Galantine van kip

1 stewing chicken of about 5 pounds

For the stuffing:

¾ pound veal
3 ounces lard
1 3-ounce slice smoked ox tongue
1 small can truffles
1 slice stale white bread without crust, soaked in a little milk
4 egg yolks
1 teaspoon salt
2 dill pickles, sliced
2 tablespoons Madeira
Salt and pepper

For cooking:

5 thin slices fat bacon
6 cups bouillon
3 carrots
Sprigs of parsley and celery

Put the veal and the lard through the meat chopper. Dice the tongue and the truffles. Mix all the ingredients for the stuffing very well. Pour boiling water over the chicken. Cut the breast open and disjoint it. Sprinkle a little salt and pepper in the chicken and put the stuffing inside. Close the breast by sewing it together.

Fasten the slices of bacon onto the breast with thread. Roll the chicken in a piece of cheesecloth. Put in a pan with the bouillon, carrots, parsley, celery, and salt. The chicken should be covered; otherwise, add some water. Bring to a boil and simmer for 2 hours. Let cool in the stock.

Place the chicken between two boards with a weight on top—a vase filled with water will do—and let stand for 3 hours. Remove the cheesecloth and take off the thread and bacon.

Decorate this dish with quartered tomatoes, eggs, lettuce leaves, etc. Serve with a light Mayonnaise (see Sauces chapter).

ASPIC (for decoration)
Aspic

2 envelopes unflavored gelatine
2 cups stock, strained
2 bouillon cubes
2 tablespoons vinegar
1 tablespoon sherry

Soften the gelatine in ½ cup water. Bring the stock to a boil. Add the bouillon cubes, vinegar, and sherry. Stir in the gelatine and water until dissolved. Pour into a shallow dish and chill thoroughly. Cut into different shapes and break up what is left with a fork.

PARTRIDGES WITH CABBAGE

Patrijzen met kool

4 partridges
Salt
12 slices fat bacon
½ cup butter
1 big or 2 small heads cabbage
2 onions, chopped
1 teaspoon pepper
¼ teaspoon grated nutmeg

6 SERVINGS

Pour boiling water over the birds and rub them with salt. Place the slices of bacon, 3 to each bird, over the breasts and tie with thread. Melt the butter in a baking dish and roast the partridges like chickens in a moderate oven (350° F.) for 40 minutes, basting often.

Shred the cabbage, cook for 10 minutes, and drain well. Put half of it in a casserole. Remove the bacon from the partridges and cut the birds lengthwise in halves. Place them on the cabbage in the casserole and cover with the rest of the cabbage.

Sauté the chopped onions in the same skillet and add water to make 2 cups of stock. Chop the bacon that has covered the breasts and add this to the stock. Sprinkle the cabbage with pepper and nutmeg. Pour in the stock. Cover the casserole and put in a 350° F. oven for 2 hours.

Serve with boiled potatoes.

PÂTÉ OF PARTRIDGES
Patrijzen pâté

This is an old recipe, but very useful, as old partridges can be used. Turkey could be used too, although I have never tried that out myself. It is a very nice dish for a cold supper.

- 4 old partridges
- 1¼ cups butter
- ½ pound uncooked veal
- 4 tablespoons flour
- 6 egg yolks
- 3 ounces grated Parmesan cheese
- 1 teaspoon salt
- ½ teaspoon pepper

Roast the birds (as in the recipe for Roast Chicken) in ½ cup butter. Remove skin and bones and put them, with the veal, through a meat chopper twice. Melt 4 tablespoons butter, add the flour, stir in 2 cups of bouillon made with partridge gravy diluted with water, and make a smooth sauce. Whip ½ cup butter until creamy. Stir into the sauce one by one the egg yolks, cheese, meat, creamy butter, salt, and pepper. Mix well.

Press this mixture into a well-greased baking tin, the kind that is used to bake cakes in. Put the tin in a pan with boiling water and bake in a moderate oven (325° F.) for 2 hours. Cool and unmold the next day. Cut into slices and decorate with Aspic (see recipe for Aspic).

ROAST GOOSE
Gebraden gans

1 goose
10 sour apples, sliced
½ cup butter
Salt and pepper

8 SERVINGS

Pour boiling water over the inside and outside of the goose. Fill the body cavity with the sliced apples and secure with skewers, or sew it up. Melt the butter in a roasting pan and roast the goose in a moderate oven (325° F.), allowing 25 minutes to the pound. Baste every 15 minutes. When the goose is half done, sprinkle with salt and pepper. Should the breast get too brown, cover with a piece of greased wax paper or aluminum foil.

ROAST PHEASANT
Gebraden fazant

1 pheasant
6 tablespoons butter
Salt

3 SERVINGS

Pour boiling water over the pheasant, inside and outside. Sprinkle a little salt inside the bird and put in a lump of butter. Take a skillet as small as possible; the bird should just fit in it. Brown the butter, place the pheasant for a short time on the breast side, then turn it over. Cover and roast in 350° F. oven for ½ hour. Baste three or four times.

Serve the pheasant with the following sauce.

SAUCE FOR ROAST PHEASANT

2½ tablespoons flour
1½ cups heavy cream
½ teaspoon salt
2 tablespoons brandy
½ tablespoon Worcestershire sauce

Pour off all but 3 tablespoons of the drippings. Add the flour and let this get slightly brown. Stir well. Add the heavy cream and the salt. Cook and stir until sauce is creamy and smooth. Stir in the brandy and the Worcestershire sauce.

ROAST DUCK
Gebraden eend

1 wild duck
Salt and pepper
6 tablespoons butter
1 sour apple

2 SERVINGS

Pour boiling water over the duck, inside and outside. Rub the inside with salt and pepper and put in the apple. Take the smallest possible pan. Melt the butter and put in the duck with the apple inside. Cover and roast in a moderate over (325° F.) for 1½ hours, basting every 10 minutes. The duck is done when a fork goes in easily between the joints.

STUFFED DUCK
Gevulde eend

1 cup chestnuts
1 duck
6 tablespoons butter
Salt and pepper

2 SERVINGS

Make two cross-cut gashes over the flat side of each chestnut. Boil them for 5 minutes in water, drain, and peel. Cover them with water or stock and cook for 20 minutes. Prepare the duck as in recipe for Roast Duck. Put the chestnuts inside and roast the duck.

SALMI OF DUCKS
Salmi van eend

2 ducks
½ cup butter
4 cups stock
4 carrots
3 small onions
½ bay leaf
½ teaspoon salt
4 tablespoons flour
1 small can champignons
2 tablespoons Madeira

4 SERVINGS

Sauté the ducks in 6 tablespoons butter. Add stock, carrots, 2 onions, bay leaf, and salt. Bring to a boil and simmer for 2 hours. Take the duck out of the stock and cut the meat off the bones in equal pieces. Put the bones back in the stock, bring to a boil, and reduce stock to 2 cups. Chop the remaining onion and sauté in 2 tablespoons butter. Add flour and brown. Strain the stock and add to this mixture. Stir well, making a smooth sauce. Put the duck back into the sauce. Add champignons and simmer for 15 minutes. Add Madeira just before serving.

HARE OR RABBIT
Haas of konijn

Do not forget that hares and rabbits are a favorite dish in Holland and therefore there are many recipes to choose from. One does not see them on the menu in the United States very often, but I hope that these recipes may serve to make this dish more popular.

ROAST HARE
Gebraden haas

1 hare
1 bottle vinegar
Salt
Mustard
4 slices of fat, smoked bacon, ¼ inch thick, cut into strips
½ pound butter
1 cup sour cream
½ cup blood
½ cup red wine

6 SERVINGS

Marinate the hare in the vinegar for a couple of hours. Take it out and pour boiling water over it. Sprinkle with salt and rub with mustard. Lard (with a larding pin) the back of the hare by drawing one row of thin strips of fat, smoked bacon through it—2 rows through the hind legs. Melt the butter, but do not let it get brown, and roast the hare for 2–2½ hours in a 350° F. oven, basting every 10 minutes. If the butter gets too brown, baste with sour cream. The hare is done when the meat from the hind legs can be taken off with a spoon. An old hare takes more time, of course. In that case one covers the hare with a greased piece of wax paper or aluminum foil, because otherwise the back would get too dry. Take the hare out of the pan. Mix the blood with the wine and stir into the sauce, but do not heat the sauce again.

Serve with boiled potatoes, red cabbage and apple-sauce.

STEWED HARE OR RABBIT

Gestoofde haas of konijn

1 hare or 2 rabbits
½ pound and 2 tablespoons butter
Salt and pepper
6 slices fat, smoked bacon
2 cups sour cream
4 tablespoons flour
1 cup bouillon
1 teaspoon grated lemon rind

6 SERVINGS

Cut the legs in two, the rump in six, pieces. Sauté in butter for 20 minutes. Sprinkle with salt and pepper. Cover the bottom of a pot with bacon slices and cover these with the rabbit pieces and the drippings. Pour in the sour cream. Cover the pot well and steam in a 325° F. oven for 2½–3 hours. Take the game out. Mix 2 tablespoons butter and the flour with a fork on a plate and add to the sauce. Stir in the bouillon; you should have a cream sauce—and not too thin. Pour through a fine sieve. Add some extra pepper and the grated lemon rind.

HAZEPEPER

A spicy dish of hare

1 large hare
1 cup vinegar
3 cups red wine
1 cup and 2 tablespoons butter
2 onions, sliced
5 tablespoons flour
2 teaspoons sugar
1 teaspoon salt
½ teaspoon pepper
1 bay leaf
4 cloves
2 tablespoons soy sauce

Cut a large hare into ten or twelve pieces. Marinate these overnight in vinegar and wine. Drain and sauté in ½ cup butter for 15 minutes. Sauté the onions in the rest of the butter, add flour, and brown. Stir in the wine-and-vinegar mixture and make a smooth sauce. Add hare and onions with the butter they are sautéed in, add sugar and spices, and simmer for at least 3 hours.

PÂTÉ OF HARE OR RABBIT

Hazen-of konijnenpastei

1 hare or 2 rabbits
½ pound veal
½ pound fresh bacon
4 egg yolks
1 teaspoon ground mixed spices
½ teaspoon salt
12 slices fat, smoked bacon

Stew hare or rabbits as in recipe for Stewed Hare or Rabbit. Take all the meat off the bones, keeping aside the big pieces. Put the small pieces with the veal and fresh bacon through a meat chopper twice. Add egg yolks, mixed spice, salt and ¾ cup sauce from the stew. Mix well. Cover the sides and bottom of a pudding mold with bacon slices. Put in alternate layers of the mixture and the big pieces of game. The top layer should consist of the mixture. Cover and put into a pan with boiling water. Steam in a 325° F. oven for 2 hours. Cool for ½ hour and unmold. Chill before serving.

This is a nice dish to start a dinner, served with toast and butter.

SAUCES

It is impossible to give you recipes from Holland without mentioning the best known of all sauces: the Hollandaise sauce. The only trouble with this sauce is that there are so many different ways of preparing it. The original sauce is rather difficult to make and has to be served at once, which can create great difficulties without a "Cordon Bleu" in the kitchen.

HOLLANDAISE SAUCE

Hollandaise saus

Pinch of salt
2 egg yolks
8 tablespoons butter
½ teaspoon lemon juice
1 cup cold water

Put some water in the lower half of a double boiler—there should be a space of about ½ inch between the bottom of the top half and the surface of the water. Put this on the heat. Meanwhile mix together ½ tablespoon of cold water with a pinch of salt, the egg yolks, and 1 tablespoon butter. When the water in the bottom half is nearly, but not quite boiling, put the top half on and start stirring with a wire whisk until the mixture begins to thicken very slightly. Add another piece of butter and so on until all the butter is used up. Now, the point of the cup of cold water is this: if the sauce is thickening too much, add ¼ teaspoonful of water from the cup. This makes the sauce cook as slowly as possible and makes it lighter too. Add ½ teaspoon of lemon juice, or more, according to your taste. If you have to keep the sauce waiting for a few minutes, do so in the double boiler, but the water in the bottom half should not come too near the boiling point.

If the butter starts to clarify and the eggs to curdle during this process, immediately take the top half off the stove, add a tablespoon of very cold water, and stir vigorously until the sauce becomes smooth again.

MOCK HOLLANDAISE SAUCE
Namaak Hollandaise saus

1 teaspoon arrowroot
± 6 tablespoons milk
3 egg yolks
8 tablespoons butter
½ teaspoon lemon juice
Pinch of salt and pepper

4 SERVINGS

Mix the arrowroot with 3 tablespoons cold milk. Stir in the egg yolks and 1 tablespoon butter. Place the pan over a very low flame. Whisk with a wire whisk until the sauce looks like a very creamy scrambled egg. Take the pan off the heat and stir in another tablespoon butter. Keep on doing this, off and on the heat, until you have added 8 tablespoons butter in all. Toward the end, stir in some more milk; the sauce should not become too thick. Stir in the lemon juice and a pinch of salt and pepper.

MAYONNAISE

1 egg yolk
Pinch of salt
1 teaspoon vinegar or lemon juice
8 tablespoons oil

3 SERVINGS

To make a good (and quick) mayonnaise it is necessary that all ingredients have the same temperature, more or less.

Beat the egg yolk in a bowl with a pinch of salt; one gets the best results with a wire whisk. Add 1 teaspoon vinegar and stir well. The first tablespoon of oil should be added slowly, but as soon as the sauce thickens, one can put in a tablespoon at a time. Every time the sauce gets too thick, add a few drops of vinegar or lemon juice. For three persons, 8 tablespoons of oil is sufficient, but one can easily use more. With 2 egg yolks one can make mayonnaise for at least 6–8 servings.

To start with adding the vinegar is a much quicker method than to start with stirring in the oil drop by drop, and it gives the best results.

With mayonnaise as a base one can make the following sauces:

1. Add chopped herbs (parsley, celery, tarragon, etc.)
2. Add chopped dill pickles and capers
3. Add paprika
4. Add catchup and whipped cream

In addition to the above sauces, I have, throughout the book, given the recipes for other sauces. They follow directly the recipes for dishes that they may accompany.

Amsterdam vegetable market

VEGETABLES

Vegetables are an important part of the daily Dutch menu. Although all kinds can be obtained the year round, canned or frozen, vegetables are usually eaten fresh, in season.

Early every morning the vegetables are brought into town to be sold at the greengrocers' and in little stalls at the vegetable markets. These stalls make a pretty, colorful picture. The fresh, sparkling greens are mixed with the bright red of tomatoes and radishes in early spring and summer. Orange carrots brighten the darker hues of green and red cabbages in autumn and winter.

Every season is represented by its own special kinds of fruit and vegetables, and the greengrocer really is the "merchant of the four seasons," as he is called in France.

Vegetables are sometimes mixed with potatoes and meat or bacon and served as a one-pot meal.

SPINACH

Spinazie

6 pounds fresh spinach
1 tablespoon salt
6 tablespoons butter
3 slices white bread, cut into strips
3 hard-boiled eggs, quartered
Lemon quarters

6 SERVINGS

Clean the spinach thoroughly and cook with the salt for about 15 minutes. Drain and chop very finely. Add 4 tablespoons butter and reheat. Fry the strips of bread in 2 tablespoons butter; in Dutch they are called *soldaatjes*, or little soldiers, as one puts them upright on the spinach. Put the egg quarters in between the croutons on the dish. Serve lemon quarters separately.

SORREL

Zuring

2 pounds sorrel
3 tablespoons butter
3 tablespoons sugar

4 SERVINGS

Strip and wash the sorrel; cook without water. Drain, and simmer with the butter and sugar.

To make a very old-fashioned dish, add 2 tablespoons raisins.

ASPARAGUS

Asparagus is considered a great delicacy in Holland. Late spring–early summer is the season in which one can buy them. The all-white variety or the white asparagus with purple heads are grown here, but the following recipes can just as well be used for other kinds, such as the green ones.

Asparagus can be prepared and eaten in many different ways, but let us start with the typical Dutch one.

ASPARAGUS
Asperges

± 12 asparagus
2 hard-boiled eggs
¼ teaspoon grated nutmeg
Salt

1 SERVING

Scrape the asparagus with care and cut the stalky ends off. Boil in ample water till done, minimum 1 hour. When the cooked asparagus are served, one makes the following paste on one's plate: Mash the eggs very finely with a fork in the melted Butter Sauce (see below). Sprinkle with nutmeg and salt to taste. The asparagus is taken carefully in the left hand and—with the fork in the right hand—is lightly dipped in this paste. The ends, which may be a bit stalky, are left on the side of the plate.

The butter sauce that goes with it can be made in two ways:

MELTED BUTTER SAUCE I
Gewelde boter I

3 tablespoons butter

1 SERVING

This is the easier way. Melt 2 tablespoons butter slowly, so that the yellow color does not change. Never brown it. Remove from heat and add the third tablespoon; stir well until all has melted.

MELTED BUTTER SAUCE II
Gewelde boter II

6 tablespoons butter
Salt

4 SERVINGS

Stir the butter till it becomes creamy and add 1 tablespoon warm water very slowly, stirring all the time. It should be a creamy sauce. Salt to taste.

ASPARAGUS À LA CRÊME
Asperges in roomsaus

18 asparagus stalks
1 tablespoon salt
2 tablespoons butter
2 tablespoons flour
½ cup cream

4 SERVINGS

Scrape the asparagus with care, cut into 1½-inch lengths—leave out the stalky ends—and cook in boiling water with salt until done.

Mix the butter and the flour over low heat, add cream and ½ cup asparagus liquid. Stir well; keep at boiling point for 10 minutes. Simmer the asparagus in the sauce.

ASPARAGUS AU GRATIN

Asperges au gratin

18 asparagus stalks
1 teaspoon salt
1 tablespoon flour
1½ tablespoons butter
½ cup cream
½ cup broth
½ teaspoon grated nutmeg
¼ cup minced lean ham
2 tablespoons Parmesan cheese

4 SERVINGS

Cook the asparagus as in the recipe for Asparagus à la Crême.

Place the asparagus in a baking dish, cover with the sauce, made with the flour, 1 tablespoon butter, cream, broth, and nutmeg, minced ham, grated cheese, and dot with the remaining ½ tablespoon butter. Brown in moderate oven (350° F.) for about 20 minutes.

CAULIFLOWER
Bloemkool

1 medium-sized head cauliflower
1 tablespoon salt

4 SERVINGS

Cook in ample boiling water with salt for about ½ hour. To preserve the white color, cook with stem upward. After draining thoroughly, place the cauliflower on a platter and cover with Cauliflower Sauce (see below).

CAULIFLOWER SAUCE
Bloemkool saus

2 tablespoons butter
2 tablespoons flour
½ cup hot milk
Pinch of salt
Grated nutmeg

4 SERVINGS

Melt the butter. Stir in the flour until blended. Slowly stir in the milk and ½ cup cauliflower liquid. Cook and stir until the sauce is smooth and boiling. Add salt to taste and season with grated nutmeg.

CAULIFLOWER AU GRATIN

Bloemkool au gratin

1 large head cauliflower
3½ tablespoons butter
3 tablespoons flour
3 cups milk
¼ teaspoon salt
¼ teaspoon pepper
3 tablespoons grated Gruyère cheese
3 tablespoons grated Parmesan cheese
2 tablespoons bread crumbs

6 SERVINGS

Cook the cauliflower as in the recipe for Cauliflower.

Mix 2 tablespoons butter and the flour over low heat, add the milk, the salt and pepper. Keep the sauce at the boiling point for about 10 minutes. Remove from heat and stir in the 3 tablespoons Gruyère cheese. Place the cauliflower in a baking dish. Cover with the sauce and sprinkle with the 3 tablespoons Parmesan cheese. Cover with 1½ tablespoons melted butter and sprinkle with bread crumbs. Brown in moderate oven (350° F.) for 20 minutes.

RHUBARB

Rabarber

1½ pounds rhubarb stems
½ cup sugar (more if necessary)
1 teaspoon grated lemon rind
1 egg yolk
1 egg white

6 SERVINGS

Peel off the outer rind, cut the rhubarb into 1-inch pieces, and wash. Cook with ½ cup water to a mash, stirring frequently. When the mash is ready, add the sugar and the lemon rind. Stir in the yolk and the white of an egg, beaten separately.

BRAISED LETTUCE
Stoofsla

16 heads lettuce
1 tablespoon salt
1 cup meat gravy
3 tablespoons butter
2 tablespoons bread crumbs

6 SERVINGS

Remove the outer green leaves from the lettuce and wash the heads thoroughly. Cook in ample boiling water with salt for ¼ hour. Drain well and place in baking dish. Cover with the gravy, dot with butter, and sprinkle with the bread crumbs. Heat in moderate oven (350° F.) for about 15 minutes.

STUFFED LETTUCE
Gevulde stoofsla

12 heads lettuce
1 slice white bread
1 pound ground veal
¼ teaspoon grated nutmeg
1 teaspoon salt
2 cups stock
1 tablespoon butter
1 tablespoon bread crumbs

6 SERVINGS

Take off the outer leaves. Quickly boil the lettuce heads in water till tender. Drain. Soften the bread in a little water and mix with the ground veal, nutmeg, and salt. Divide the mixture into 12 little balls, open the lettuce heads, and put a ball inside each head. Arrange in a baking dish, pour in the stock (2 bouillon cubes dissolved in 2 cups of hot water will do instead of stock). Dot with butter and sprinkle with the bread crumbs. Brown in moderate oven (350° F.) for 20 minutes.

(BELGIAN) ENDIVE I
Brussels lof I

1½ pounds (8 pieces) endive
1 teaspoon salt
2 tablespoons melted butter
¼ teaspoon grated nutmeg

4 SERVINGS

Cook the endive (without cutting) in water and salt until tender, about ½ hour. Drain well. Arrange in a shallow baking dish, cover with butter, sprinkle with nutmeg, and put in a hot oven (450° F.) for 10 minutes.

(BELGIAN) ENDIVE II
Brussels lof II

1½ pounds (8 pieces) endive
1 teaspoon salt
4 tablespoons melted butter
4 hard-boiled eggs, cut in quarters

4 SERVINGS

Boil the endive (without cutting) in water and salt until tender, about ½ hour. Drain well. Melt the butter.

Garnish the endive with the hard-boiled eggs and serve the butter sauce separately.

(BELGIAN) ENDIVE III

Brussels lof III

1½ pounds endive
1 teaspoon salt
2 tablespoons butter
3 tablespoons flour
1 cup milk
2 tablespoons grated Parmesan cheese

4 SERVINGS

Cut the endive into pieces. Wash and boil in salted water until tender. Drain well. Make a sauce of the butter, flour, and milk. Stir in half of the cheese. When this is melted, add the endive. Put in baking dish and sprinkle with the rest of the cheese. Bake in a hot oven (450° F.) for 15 minutes.

BRUSSELS SPROUTS

Spruitjes

4 cups Brussels sprouts
1 teaspoon salt
3 tablespoons butter
½ teaspoon grated nutmeg

4 SERVINGS

Remove the outer leaves and cut off the stems. Wash thoroughly and cook the sprouts in ample salted water. Drain well and simmer with the butter and the nutmeg.

BRUSSELS SPROUTS WITH CHEESE
Spruitjes met kaas

4 cups Brussels sprouts
1 teaspoon salt
1 cup stock
2 tablespoons grated Parmesan cheese
½ teaspoon grated nutmeg
1 tablespoon butter

4 SERVINGS

Cook the sprouts as in the recipe for Brussels Sprouts. Drain well. Put in a shallow baking dish. Pour the stock (or 1 bouillon cube dissolved in water) over the sprouts and sprinkle with the cheese and the nutmeg. Dot with butter and bake in a hot oven (450° F.) until the cheese is melted.

PURÉE OF BRUSSELS SPROUTS
Spruiten purée

4 cups Brussels sprouts
1 teaspoon salt
1 teaspoon grated nutmeg
½ cup cream

4 SERVINGS

Cook the Brussels sprouts in the usual manner. Rub through a sieve. Add salt and nutmeg and stir in the cream. This purée goes very well with duck or pork.

WHITE CABBAGE
Witte kool

1 large head white cabbage
Salt
3 tablespoons butter
½ cup milk

6 SERVINGS

Remove outer leaves and core. Cut in pieces. Wash the cabbage thoroughly and cook in boiling water and salt for about ½ hour. Drain well. Chop very fine and simmer with the butter, milk, and 1 teaspoon salt.

WHITE CABBAGE WITH POTATOES
Stamppot witte kool

1 head white cabbage
4 cups peeled and quartered potatoes
Salt
4 ounces bacon fat or lard

4 SERVINGS

Cook the cabbage as in the recipe for White Cabbage. Cover the potatoes with 2 cups water; add salt and fat. Put the cooked cabbage on top of the potatoes as soon as they are done. Mix well.

This dish is eaten as a whole meal and is a typical "winter dish." Meat is not necessary, although frankfurters or pork chops go very well with it.

RED CABBAGE
Rode kool

1 medium-sized head red cabbage
¼ cup vinegar
4 tablespoons butter
4½ tablespoons brown sugar
1 teaspoon salt
4 sour apples, cut in quarters
1 teaspoon mixed spice

4 SERVINGS

Remove the outer leaves of the cabbage and shred it fine. Cook with all other ingredients and 1 cup water, but use only 2 tablespoons of the butter. Cook the cabbage for 1 hour, stirring now and then and adding water if necessary. Add the rest of the butter before serving.

STEWED ONIONS
Gestoofde uien

1 pound onions
½ tablespoon salt
2 tablespoons butter
2 tablespoons flour
Juice of ½ lemon
1 cup stock

2 SERVINGS

Clean and slice the onions. Cook in boiling water and salt till tender. Drain well. Make a sauce of the butter, flour, and lemon juice with the stock. Simmer the onions in this sauce for 10 minutes.

STUFFED ONIONS
Gevulde uien

4 large onions
1 slice white bread, softened in a little water
5 ounces ground beef
¼ teaspoon salt
2 tablespoons butter
1 cup stock
2 tablespoons bread crumbs

4 SERVINGS

Don't slice the onions for this recipe; cook them in boiling water till tender. Drain well.

Mix the softened bread with the meat and salt. Divide into four parts. Scoop out the onions; chop and reserve insides. Stuff onions with the meat. Arrange in a greased baking dish. Press a large dot of butter in each onion. Mix the stock with the insides of the onions and pour in the dish. Sprinkle with the bread crumbs and bake in a moderate oven (350° F.) for ½ hour.

BRAISED LEEKS
Gestoofde prei

2 pounds leeks
2½ tablespoons butter
2 tablespoons flour
1 cup milk
1 tablespoon vinegar
¼ teaspoon salt

4 SERVINGS

Clean the leeks by cutting off the roots and removing the outer leaves. Cut in 2-inch lengths. Cook in boiling water for about ½ hour. Drain well. Make a sauce of the butter, flour, and milk. Add the vinegar and salt. Simmer the leeks in the sauce for about 10 minutes.

RED BEETS
Bieten

6 Small beets
2 onions
2 tablespoons butter
2 tablespoons flour
½ cup milk
½ cup water
4 cloves
Pinch of salt
2 tablespoons vinegar

4 SERVINGS

Wash the beets and cook them in water till the skin can be pulled off easily. In the winter this takes 3 to 4 hours; in the summer, 2 to 2½ hours. In Holland they are usually sold cooked, which makes it much easier, of course. Chop the onions. Make a sauce of the butter and flour with milk and water. Peel the beets and cut them in thin slices. Add these, with the chopped onions, the cloves, and the salt, to the sauce and stew for 20 minutes. Stir in the vinegar and take the cloves out before serving.

BEET SALAD (Cold)
Bietensla

6 beets
6 boiled potatoes, cold
4 hard-boiled eggs
2 apples
3 large sour gherkins
Mayonnaise or oil and vinegar
Salt and pepper

4 SERVINGS

Cook the beets as in previous recipe. Peel and cut them in small dice. Chop all the other ingredients and mix with the beets. Mix with mayonnaise, or, if this is considered to be too nourishing, use oil and vinegar. Add salt and pepper to taste. The salad should be of a rather solid consistency.

This dish is a great favorite with cold meat.

WINTER DISHES

To end this chapter, I will give you the recipes for some typical winter dishes. They can all be prepared in advance, which makes the flavor even better. They are easy to prepare and taste very good when one has been in the open for a whole day.

NOTE 1 For these dishes one uses fat, lard, or, if these are not obtainable, fat bacon that one melts slowly.

NOTE 2 With these dishes we eat a kind of sausage called *rookworst.* It has a smoked and spicy taste and has to be cooked very slowly. Knockwurst or frankfurters would be the best equivalent.

KALE WITH POTATOES AND SAUSAGE

Stamppot van boerenkool met worst

4 pounds kale
4 pounds potatoes, peeled and quartered
1-pound can of frankfurters or other sausage (see NOTE 2)
5 tablespoons fat (see NOTE 1)
1 teaspoon salt

6 SERVINGS

Strip the kale, wash, and boil for about 1 hour. Drain and mince very fine. Take a big pot and first put in the potatoes, half covered with water. Put the kale on top of the potatoes with the fat and salt, and simmer. If necessary, add some of the liquid from the frankfurters. The result (after about ½ hour) must be rather dry. Mix thoroughly. Put in a dish with the hot frankfurters—or boiled knockwurst, if available—on top.

HODGEPODGE WITH BOILED MEAT

Hutspot met klapstuk

2 pounds of boiling beef (flank)
2 teaspoons salt
5 pounds carrots
3 pounds potatoes
9 big onions
Pepper

8 SERVINGS

Put the meat with the salt in 4 cups boiling water and let it cook slowly for about 1½ hours, depending on the quality of the meat.

Clean and dice the carrots and add them to the meat. Let cook ½ hour. Cut the potatoes and onions in pieces and add these to the meat and the carrots. Simmer until the liquid has nearly evaporated. Add water if necessary. When this dish is ready, take out the meat and serve separately. Stir the vegetables and potatoes with a wooden spoon till they have the consistency of a stew. Add pepper to taste.

HODGEPODGE WITH WHITE BEANS AND SALT PORK

Hutspot met witte bonen en spek

2 pounds salt pork
5 pounds carrots, diced
3 pounds potatoes, peeled and quartered
9 large onions, cut in pieces
1 large can white beans

8 SERVINGS

Boil the salt pork in 4 cups water. Taste, and if the water is too salty, add fresh water. Add the carrots, onions, and potatoes, and cook till nearly done. Take the salt pork out. Stir the vegetables and let them cook till they have the consistency of a stew. Add the beans and the salt pork, cut in thin slices. Reheat.

SAUERKRAUT WITH POTATOES, BACON, AND FRANKFURTERS

Stamppot van zuurkool met spek en worst

3 pounds sauerkraut
5 pounds potatoes, quartered
1½ pounds fresh salted bacon
1 large can frankfurters

8 SERVINGS

Rinse the sauerkraut with clear water. Put it in a big pot and add fresh water to cover. Let cook slowly for about ½ hour. Add the potatoes and the bacon and simmer for about 40 minutes. Take the bacon out and cook until the liquid has evaporated. Mix well. Serve on a plate with slices of bacon and top with heated frankfurters.

APPLES WITH POTATOES AND FRIED BACON

"Hete bliksem"

Meaning that this dish is hot as lightning. Eat carefully, otherwise you may burn your mouth!

4 pounds potatoes, peeled and quartered
2 pounds sweet apples, peeled and cut up
2 pounds sour apples, peeled and cut up
4 tablespoons lard
16 slices smoked bacon

8 SERVINGS

Half cover the potatoes with water. Start boiling. Add the apples and the lard. Boil slowly, stirring often, till the mixture has the consistency of a purée. Add water if necessary. Fry the bacon till crisp and serve on top.

BROWN BEANS
Bruine bonen

2 pounds dried brown beans
1 teaspoon salt
1 pound fat smoked bacon
6 onions, cut into rings

8 SERVINGS

Wash the brown beans and let them stand overnight in plenty of water. Cook the beans the next day in the same water for about 1 hour, making sure that there is always enough water to cover the beans. Add salt. Drain, keeping the water for soup. Dice the bacon fine. Fry it in a frying pan till very crisp. Mix through the beans. Fry the onions in the fat that is left in the frying pan. Serve these separately.

Sour dill pickles and mustard accompany this nourishing dish.

POTATOES

Potatoes are a national dish in Holland. This may sound strange to Americans, who—if they eat them at all—eat them as a side dish. But a meal eaten by the farmers and in the villages consists in the first and only place of an enormous dish of potatoes which is put in the middle of the table. All the members of the family gather around, armed with a cup and fork. In this cup is gravy, if they have recently butchered a pig and fried the meat; otherwise bacon fat is used.

Now everybody in turn (old grandfather starting) picks a potato out of the big pan in the middle with his own fork, dips it in the fat in his own cup, and eats. Two pounds per person is the usual portion, children included. No plates, no nothing—easy, what? Even van Gogh was inspired by this family scene and painted one of his most famous pictures.

But of course, since potatoes play such an important role in Dutch life, there are many other ways of preparing them.

PURÉE OF POTATOES I

Aardappel-purée I

1 pound boiled potatoes
¾ cup milk
2 tablespoons butter
½ teaspoon salt
⅛ teaspoon nutmeg
1 egg yolk, beaten
1 egg white, whipped stiff
1 tablespoon bread crumbs

3 SERVINGS

Rub the potatoes through a sieve. Blend in the milk, 1 tablespoon butter, the salt, nutmeg, and the beaten egg yolk; fold in the beaten egg white. Put the purée in a baking dish slightly greased with butter. Sprinkle with bread crumbs and dot with the remaining butter. Put in a moderate oven (350° F.) for 20 minutes.

PUREE OF POTATOES II

Aardappel-purée II

1 pound boiled potatoes
¾ cup milk
3 tablespoons butter
½ teaspoon salt
⅛ teaspoon grated nutmeg
Pinch of pepper
1 egg

3 SERVINGS

Rub the boiled potatoes through a sieve. Heat the milk with the butter, salt, nutmeg, and pepper and add to the potatoes. Keep on a slow fire for 15 minutes, stirring all the time. Beat the whole egg and stir in just before serving.

PURÉE OF POTATOES WITH CHEESE

Aardappel-purée met kaas

2 pounds boiled potatoes
2 eggs
1 cup sour cream
½ teaspoon salt
3 tablespoons grated Parmesan cheese
2 tablespoons butter
1 tablespoon bread crumbs

6 SERVINGS

Rub the boiled potatoes through a sieve. Beat the eggs with the sour cream and the salt. Add 2 tablespoons of the cheese and mix with the purée. Grease a baking dish with some of the butter. Put the purée inside and sprinkle with 1 tablespoon cheese mixed with 1 tablespoon bread crumbs. Dot with the rest of the butter and bake for ½ hour in a moderate oven (350° F.).

PURÉE OF POTATOES WITH HAM AND ONIONS

Aardappel-purée met ham en uien

2 pounds boiled potatoes
1 cup milk
½ teaspoon salt
2 medium-sized onions chopped fine
3 tablespoons butter
¼ pound diced ham
1 tablespoon bread crumbs

6 SERVINGS

Rub the boiled potatoes through a sieve. Stir in the milk and salt. Fry the onions in 2 tablespoons butter. Grease an ovenproof dish and put in alternate layers of potato purée, onions, and ham, ending with a layer of potato purée. Sprinkle with the bread crumbs, dot with the rest of the butter, and bake for ½ hour in a moderate oven (350° F.).

POTATO SOUFFLÉ

Aardappel-soufflé

2 pounds boiled potatoes
1 cup milk or cream
3 tablespoons butter
5 egg yolks
½ teaspoon salt

⅛ teaspoon grated nutmeg
5 egg whites

6 SERVINGS

Rub the boiled potatoes through a sieve. Heat the milk or cream with the butter and mix with the potatoes. Stir in the egg yolks, salt, and nutmeg. Whip the egg whites until stiff and fold into the mixture. Grease a rather deep ovenproof dish with butter. Put the mixture inside and bake in slow oven (325° F.) for 45 minutes. Do not open the oven to take a look, or your soufflé will collapse.

POTATO RISSOLÉS

Aardappel croquetten

1 pound boiled potatoes
2 tablespoons melted butter
½ teaspoon salt
⅛ teaspoon grated nutmeg
2 egg yolks
2 egg whites, whipped stiff
1 tablespoon bread crumbs
Fat for frying

3 SERVINGS

Rub the potatoes through a sieve, blend in the melted butter, the salt, the nutmeg, and beaten yolk of 1 egg. Fold in the 2 egg whites. Shape the purée into small balls of about 1 inch. Roll in a mixture of the yolk of the second egg diluted with 2 tablespoons water, then through the bread crumbs. Fry in deep fat until brown. Drain on absorbent paper.

SPEKKIE SLA

4 pounds purée of Potatoes
1 pound escarole
1 pound fat bacon
Vinegar
Pepper

4 SERVINGS

A dish from the province of Gelderland, consisting of three quarters potato purée and one quarter finely cut raw escarole (endive), washed and well drained. Heat the purée very well and mix in the escarole at the last moment, just before serving. With this dish goes a huge cupful of fried, diced, fat smoked bacon in its melted fat. Put the Spekkie Sla on your plate, pour the fat and bacon over it, and make a little hole in the middle to pour in some vinegar. Grind some pepper over it—and, "*Smakelijk eten*" or, "Eat well."

This dish is very easy to prepare in advance and to mix at the last moment. A soup plate full for each person will easily disappear.

SAUTÉED POTATOES
Gebakken aardappelen

1 pound cold boiled potatoes
3 tablespoons butter or oil
½ teaspoon salt
Chopped parsley

3 SERVINGS

Slice the *cold* boiled potatoes. Fry the slices in butter or oil and salt in a frying pan. Serve topped with chopped parsley. This dish is always on the menu, even in the smallest restaurant, usually served with *biefstuk—filet mignon*—and salad.

POTATOES SIMMERED IN PARSLEY SAUCE
Aardappelen, gestoofd in peterselie saus

1 pound cold boiled potatoes
3 tablespoons butter
3 tablespoons flour
2 cups stock or water and milk
½ teaspoon salt
1½ tablespoons chopped parsley

3 SERVINGS

Slice the potatoes. Melt 1½ tablespoons butter, add the flour, and stir in the liquid. Add the salt. Simmer for 10 minutes, stirring well. Stir in the other 1½ tablespoons butter, and after the sauce is ready, add the parsley. Heat the sliced potatoes in this sauce.

Staphorst pancakes

DESSERTS

As a dessert we always have a sweet. Although we start the day having cheese for breakfast and having cheese again for lunch, it is not customary to have it as a savory.

Ice cream is still a luxury, but simple sweets, having as a base stale bread, macaroni, rice, etc., are eaten in large quantities. Pancakes are a favorite too. Maybe some of these recipes may appeal to you as a breakfast dish, instead of cereal, and certainly most children will like them.

BREAD DISH WITH APPLES

Broodschoteltje met appelen

2 pounds apples
½ cup sugar
18 slices stale bread
6 tablespoons butter
3 teaspoons cinnamon

6 SERVINGS

Make applesauce in the usual manner: boil or steam apples, rub through a sieve, and add the sugar. Butter the slices of bread on both sides and put them in layers with the applesauce in a greased ovenproof dish. The top layer should consist of bread. Mix the cinnamon with a little sugar, sprinkle on top, and bake in a moderate oven (325° F.) for 20 minutes.

BREAD DISH WITH RAISINS

Broodschoteltje met rozijnen

18 slices stale bread
2 cups milk
2 egg yolks
⅓ cup sugar
3 ounces raisins
3 ounces candied orange peel
½ cup brandy
2 teaspoons cinnamon
2 egg whites, stiffly beaten
1 tablespoon butter

6 SERVINGS

Soften the bread in warm milk and mash it fine. Add the egg yolks, sugar, raisins, candied orange peel, brandy, and cinnamon. Mix well. Fold in 2 beaten egg whites. Pour into a buttered ovenproof dish, dot with butter, and let rise in a moderate oven (325° F.) for ½ hour.

BREAD DISH WITH ALMONDS
(for children)
Broodschoteltje met amandelen

18 slices stale bread
2 cups milk
6 ounces almonds, blanched and finely chopped
2 egg yolks
1 cup sugar
2 egg whites, stiffly beaten
1 tablespoon butter
¼ teaspoon cinnamon

6 SERVINGS

Soften the bread in warm milk and mash it fine. Mix with the almonds, egg yolks, and sugar. Fold in the beaten egg whites. Pour into a buttered ovenproof dish. Sprinkle with the cinnamon, dot with butter, and let rise in a moderate oven (325° F.) for ½ hour.

BREAD DISH WITH ORANGES

Broodschoteltje met sinaasappels

½ pound white bread without crusts
2 cups orange juice
½ cup butter
2 egg yolks
¾ cup sugar
½ teaspoon grated lemon rind
2 egg whites, stiffly beaten

6 SERVINGS

Mash the bread fine in warm orange juice. Stir the butter until soft and fold in the egg yolks, sugar, and lemon rind. Blend these ingredients till they are very light and creamy. Mix with the bread. Fold in egg whites. Pour in a greased baking dish and let rise in a slow oven (325° F.) for about ½ hour.

BREAD OMELETTE

Broodomelet

½ pound stale bread
1 cup milk
½ teaspoon vanilla
Grated rind of ½ lemon
¼ cup sugar
4 egg yolks
4 egg whites, beaten stiff
4 tablespoons butter
Orange marmalade
2 tablespoons confectioners' sugar

6 SERVINGS

Soften the bread in warm milk and mash fine. Add the vanilla, lemon rind, and the sugar. Mix well with the egg yolks and fold in the beaten whites. Brown half of the butter in a frying pan, pour in *half* of the dough, and bake an omelette. Turn it over and brown the other side. Place on a warm dish and cover with some orange marmalade. Bake the other half of the dough in the same way. Put the second omelette on top the first and sprinkle with confectioners' sugar. This dish may be eaten cold or warm.

BREAD WITH RASPBERRY SAUCE

Turfjes met bessensap

12 slices stale bread without crusts
5 tablespoons butter
Bottle of raspberry sauce
Cinnamon
4 tablespoons sugar
1 cup heavy cream, whipped

4 SERVINGS

Sauté the slices of bread in the butter. Take a bottle of raspberry sauce—if necessary, add water or sugar—and pour some of the sauce over a layer of baked bread. Sprinkle with cinnamon and sugar. Cover with another layer of the baked slices of bread, pour some sauce over, and so forth. Let stand for a couple of hours. Decorate with whipped cream on top.

FRIED SLICES OF BREAD
Wentelteefjes

2 eggs
½ cup sugar
½ teaspoon grated lemon rind
¼ teaspoon cinnamon
1 teaspoon vanilla
2 cups milk
16 slices stale bread
6 ounces butter
Confectioners' sugar

4 SERVINGS

Beat the eggs with the sugar, lemon rind, cinnamon, and vanilla. Add the milk, slightly warmed. Arrange the slices of bread in layers in a shallow dish and pour the milk over them. Let stand for ½ hour. Fry the slices in the butter, but be careful that they don't break. Sprinkle with confectioners' sugar.

ZWIEBACK WITH RHUBARB
Beschuit met rabarber

6 zwieback
2 cups cooked Rhubarb (see Vegetables chapter)
1 teaspoon cinnamon
2 tablespoons confectioners' sugar
1 cup heavy cream, whipped

6 SERVINGS

Cover the zwieback with the rhubarb. Sprinkle with cinnamon and confectioners' sugar. Decorate with whipped cream and serve immediately.

ZWIEBACK WITH APPLE IN THE OVEN

Appelschoteltje

1 cup milk
¼ teaspoon grated lemon rind
Pinch of salt
½ cup flour
½ cup butter
8 sour apples, peeled and sliced
10 tablespoons sugar
3 egg yolks
8 zwieback
3 egg whites, beaten stiff

6 SERVINGS

Bring the milk to the boil with the lemon rind and the salt. Mix the flour with 3 tablespoons butter and add to the milk. Stir well and blend into a thick sauce. Simmer the apples for 10 minutes with 1 tablespoon butter and 5 tablespoons sugar. Beat the rest of the butter until soft and stir in the remaining sugar. Blend into a creamy mixture. Add the egg yolks, the sauce, and the apples, and fold in the egg whites.

Crumble the zwieback. Take a greased ovenproof dish, put in a layer of the mixture, a layer of zwieback, etc., with the zwieback on top. Dot with a little butter and bake in a slow oven (325° F.) for about 45 minutes.

MACARONI WITH RAISINS

Macaroni met rozijnen

¼ pound macaroni
4 cups milk
3 tablespoons butter
Pinch of salt
¼ cup brown sugar
3 tablespoons raisins
1 tablespoon bread crumbs

4 SERVINGS

Boil the macaroni in the milk with the butter and salt for about 1 hour. Stir from time to time. Add the sugar and the raisins. Pour in a buttered dish, sprinkle with bread crumbs, and bake for ½ hour in a slow oven (325° F.).

RICE WITH RAISINS

Rijst met krenten of rozijnen

1 cup rice
3 ounces raisins
Pinch of salt

4 SERVINGS

Wash the rice, add the raisins, salt, and 3 cups water, bring to a boil, and simmer till dry.

Serve with butter and brown sugar.

MILK RICE

Rijstebrij

1 cup rice, washed and drained
6 cups milk
1 teaspoon salt
2 tablespoons butter
1 teaspoon vanilla

6 SERVINGS

Bring the rice to the boil in the milk with the salt and simmer till tender, about 40 minutes. Stir frequently. Add the butter and the vanilla and simmer for 5 minutes more.

This dish is eaten warm with sugar and cinnamon. When you eat it cold, combine it with fresh or stewed fruit or with a can of apricots.

RICE PUDDING

Rijstpudding

1 cup rice, washed and drained
2½ cups milk
Pinch of salt
4 tablespoons sugar
1 teaspoon vanilla
2 eggs, beaten
Grated rind of ½ lemon
⅓ cup raisins
1 tablespoon butter
Bread crumbs

6 SERVINGS

Bring the rice to a boil in the milk with the salt, sugar, and vanilla. Simmer till tender for about 40 minutes. Stir frequently. Take this mixture from the fire and stir in the beaten eggs, lemon rind, and raisins. Grease a baking dish and cover the bottom and sides with the bread crumbs. Pour in the rice mixture. Dot with butter and sprinkle with crumbs. Bake the pudding in a moderate oven (325° F.) for about ½ hour, until the pudding is set. Cool and unmold.

Serve with strawberry or raspberry sauce or stewed fruit.

RICE SOUP WITH FRUIT SAUCE

Rijstsoep met vruchtensaus

1 cup rice, washed and drained
Pinch of salt
¼ teaspoon finely grated lemon rind
3 ounces raisins
1½ cups strawberry or raspberry juice
¾ cup sugar

6 SERVINGS

Bring the rice to a boil in 4 cups water, salt, and lemon rind. Simmer for ½ hour. Add the raisins, fruit juice, and sugar. Simmer for 15 minutes more. May be eaten warm or cold.

BUTTERMILK CREAM

Hangop

This means "hang up," as one hangs up the buttermilk to let the superfluous liquid run off.

4 quarts buttermilk
½ cup heavy cream
Brown sugar
6 zwieback
Cinnamon

6 SERVINGS

Take a clean kitchen towel and knot the four corners together. Pour the buttermilk in this "sack" and hang this over a washbasin for 6 hours. It will then have the consistency of cream. Beat the heavy cream until stiff. Mix with the buttermilk and chill well. Eat this with lots of brown sugar, crumbled zwieback, and cinnamon to taste.

Another way is:

1½ cups sugar
1 can chopped pineapple

Mix the hangop with the sugar and add the pineapple. Chill well.

COCOA PUDDING
Chocolade pudding

3 tablespoons cocoa
⅓ cup sugar
¾ cup milk
1 teaspoon vanilla
1 tablespoon gelatine
½ cup heavy cream, whipped

4 SERVINGS

Mix the cocoa with the sugar and add a little milk. Boil the rest of the milk with the vanilla. Pour in the cocoa and stir until dissolved. Soak the gelatine in ¼ cup water. Add to the mixture, and stir until dissolved. Pour into a moist mold. Chill thoroughly. Unmold and decorate with whipped cream.

BUTTERMILK PUDDING
Karnemelk pudding

2 tablespoons gelatine
1 pound sugar
1 cup lemon juice
2½ cups buttermilk
1 cup heavy cream, whipped

8 SERVINGS

Soak the gelatine in ½ cup water and dissolve in as little hot water as possible. Dissolve the sugar in the hot lemon juice. Add these to the buttermilk. Stir well. Pour into a moist mold. Chill well. Unmold and decorate with whipped cream.

LEMON PUDDING
Citroen pudding

5 egg yolks
¾ cup brown sugar
Juice of 4 lemons
1 tablespoon gelatine
5 egg whites
Pinch of salt
1 cup heavy cream, whipped

6 SERVINGS

Beat the egg yolks with the sugar until light. Add the lemon juice and cook in a double boiler until creamy. Take this mixture from the fire. Dissolve the gelatine in 3 tablespoons warm water and stir into the mixture. Whip the egg whites with the salt until stiff and fold in the mixture. Pour into a moist mold. Chill well, unmold, and decorate with whipped cream.

BLANCMANGE
Roompudding

1 tablespoon gelatine
½ cup milk
2 cups cream
½ cup sugar
1½ teaspoons vanilla
1 cup heavy cream, whipped

8 SERVINGS

Soak and dissolve the gelatine in 3 tablespoons water. Bring the milk and the cream, the sugar and the vanilla to a boil. Stir the gelatine into this mixture. Cool. When this mixture starts to thicken, fold in the heavy cream, whipped stiff. Pour into a moist mold, chill, and unmold.

This is the basic recipe. The following ingredients may be added to the mixture before it starts to thicken.

6 broken macaroons
or ladyfingers soaked in brandy and crumbled
or ¼ cup ground almonds
or chopped candied fruits, (red and green)
or chopped dates or figs

RUM PUDDING
Rumpudding

4 eggs
½ cup sugar
½ teaspoon grated lemon rind
¾ cup rum
1 tablespoon gelatine
2 cups heavy cream

8 SERVINGS

Beat the eggs until light with the sugar and lemon rind. Thicken this mixture in a double boiler, and add the rum. Soak the gelatine in 3 tablespoons water, heat, and dissolve. Stir into the mixture and let cool. Whip the cream until stiff and fold into the mixture. Place the pudding in a moist mold, chill thoroughly, and unmold.

We'll conclude this chapter with Dutch pancakes and *flensjes*, very thin pancakes.

Pancakes are a national dish, usually baked with bacon and eaten with molasses. As they are very nourishing, they are considered a "meal in one." Use a large skillet, with a bottom approximately 9 inches wide.

PANCAKES

Pannekoeken

1½ cups bread flour
1 teapoon baking powder
½ teaspoon salt
2 eggs, beaten
1 cup milk
Oil or lard
Molasses or brown sugar

± 7 OR 8 THICK PANCAKES

Mix the flour with the baking powder and the salt. Make a hole in this mixture and pour in 2 beaten eggs. Mix well. Warm the milk and 1 cup water and add these slowly—stirring continually—to the mixture. No lumps are permitted in this batter. They are baked in oil or lard, not in butter. Pour a little oil in the skillet, and take care that the entire bottom is greased. Pour in the batter, tip the skillet, and let the batter spread out over the bottom. Bake brown on one side, turn over, and, adding a few drops of oil, bake the other side brown. Eat these with molasses or brown sugar.

With this same batter one can make "three in one" (*drie in de pan*), meaning bake 3 much smaller pancakes at the same time. Add 3 ounces of raisins to the batter and serve with sugar. Baking these goes much more quickly and they taste very well eaten cold.

PANCAKES WITH BACON

Spekpannekoeken

1¼ cups bread flour
2 eggs, beaten
2 cups milk
1 tablespoon oil
5-ounce slab smoked bacon
Molasses

6 PANCAKES

Make a hole in the flour and pour in the 2 beaten eggs. Mix well with a wooden spoon. Add the warm milk, stirring continually. Mix the oil through the batter. Cut the bacon in slices and put three or four pieces in a skillet to fry. Take care that the entire bottom of the pan is greased. Pour in the batter, tip the skillet, and let the batter spread over the bacon. Bake brown on one side, turn over, and brown the other side. These pancakes are eaten with molasses.

PANCAKES WITH APPLE

Appel pannekoeken

½ cup butter
3–4 sour apples

6 PANCAKES

Follow exactly the same procedure as in the recipe for Pancakes with Bacon, using sour apples cut in thin slices instead of bacon. Bake in butter instead of bacon fat.

FLENSJES (*very thin pancakes*)

¾ cup flour
3 eggs
Pinch of salt
2 cups milk
confectioners' sugar

24 PANCAKES

Make a hole in the flour, beat the eggs with the salt, and pour into the hole. Mix thoroughly with a wooden spoon. Add the milk in small quantities, stirring well. Heat a 6-inch skillet, put in a little lump of butter, and grease the bottom. Pour in a small quantity of batter. Tip the skillet and let the batter spread out. Brown on one side only. Sprinkle with sugar, roll up with two forks, and place on a warm dish.

There are various ways of eating these *flensjes*. If you bake them a day in advance, don't roll them up, but make layers with Custard Sauce (see below) in between. Chill well and cut before serving.

Of course *flensjes* can also be eaten with all kinds of jams and marmalade instead of sugar. With ginger they taste very well.

CUSTARD SAUCE

Custard saus

3 egg yolks
¼ cup sugar
Pinch of salt
1 cup milk
1 cup cream
1 teaspoon vanilla

ABOUT 2½ CUPFULS

Beat the egg yolks slightly. Add sugar and salt. Scald and stir in slowly the milk and cream. Place the custard over a very slow fire. Stir it constantly and take care that it does not boil. Or cook it in a double boiler. Strain and cool the custard. Add the vanilla.

As our food in the winter—such as bean soup or pancakes—is rather heavy, we like to end our meal with a fruit dish.

DRIED APPLES

Gedroogde appeltjes

1 pound dried apples, cut in slices or quartered
¾ cup raspberry sauce
Rind of ½ lemon
5 tablespoons sugar
Cornstarch

4 SERVINGS

Wash the apples the night before and cover well with water. Drain and add the raspberry sauce, lemon rind, sugar, and 2 cups water. Cook them gently until they are soft. Drain. Mix the cornstarch with some water (the quantity depends on the amount of juice). Add this to the juice and simmer until the syrup is thick. Remove the lemon rind. Pour over the apples and chill.

DRIED APRICOTS
Gedroogde abrikozen

1 pound dried apricots
4 cups white wine, or 2 cups wine and
  2 cups water
2 cups sugar

4 SERVINGS

Wash the apricots and soak them for 1 hour in water. Drain, add the wine and sugar, and simmer for about ½ hour. Chill.

Serve with whipped cream.

STEWED PEARS
Stoofperen

1 cup red wine
1 cup sugar
12 pears, peeled, cored, and quartered
2 sticks cinnamon
½ teaspoon grated lemon rind

8 SERVINGS

Boil 1 cup water, wine, and sugar. Drop in the fruit and cook until nearly tender. Add cinnamon and lemon rind and stew until tender.

STRAWBERRY COMPOTE
Aardbeien compote

1 pound strawberries
2 cups sugar

4 SERVINGS

Wash the strawberries and rub half the amount through a sieve. Bring the juice with the sugar to a boil. The sugar must be dissolved. Pour over the rest of the fruit and chill.

Serve with whipped cream or vanilla ice cream.

As there are so many different kinds of ice cream in America, it would be difficult to tell you something new about this subject. But I am sure that this old family recipe will amuse you.

SPICED ICE CREAM
Gekruid ijs

3 cups vanilla ice cream
3 slices stale black rye bread
2 tablespoons maraschino
½ teaspoon ground cloves
½ teaspoon cinnamon

6 SERVINGS

Let the ice cream get a little soft. Put the bread through a nut grinder. Add this with the maraschino and the spices to the ice cream. Mix well and freeze in the refrigerator.

"Koek en Zoopie"

BEVERAGES FOR PARTIES

Of course we have the ordinary beverages, such as tea, coffee, and cocoa. Drinking endless cups of tea and coffee keeps most people happy during the daytime. However, as their preparation is more or less the same all over the world, they do not call for special recipes. But on special occasions we have certain drinks that belong to that particular festivity and are part of the celebration. Maybe that is the reason why most of them are alcoholic to a certain degree. So it might be quite a good idea, when you are going to give a party and you want to do something special, to try out one of these.

ANISE MILK

This drink belongs to the festivity of skating, an occurrence that has not changed much through the ages. A little hut is built on the ice, usually of reeds, without a roof, but where one can find some shelter against the icy cold east wind. There is no floor either, as one keeps one's skates on, and the furniture consists of rough wooden benches round the walls. In the middle burns a little stove with a large pot of Anise Milk on top, and cups are handed round by a very old man all wrapped up in shawls, who tries to make a little money out of this enterprise. It is a lovely feeling to take off one's gloves and to warm your hands round the cup and feel this warming drink inside you. It gives you courage to go on skating for miles, or to the next "*Koek en Zoopie*"—meaning "Cook and Drink," because simple cookies are sold there too. There is no alcohol in this drink, as skating combined with liquor might lead to some very painful results.

ANISE MILK
Anijs melk

4 cups milk
1 tablespoon crushed anise seed
½ cup sugar
2 tablespoons cornstarch

4-6 SERVINGS

Scald the milk with the anise seed, add the sugar, and simmer for 5 minutes. Dissolve the cornstarch in a little water and add to the mixture. Stir and cook over a low fire until the cornstarch is cooked, about 5 minutes.

SLEMP

A spicy, non-alcoholic drink the children drink on the evening of the Sint Nicolaas Festival (see Sint Nicolaas chapter).

Pinch of saffron
8 cloves
1 stick cinnamon
Piece of mace
4 cups milk
½ cup sugar
2 tablespoons cornstarch

4-6 SERVINGS

Tie the herbs in a piece of cheesecloth and put in the milk. Scald and simmer for ½ hour. Add the sugar. Dissolve the cornstarch in a little water and add to the mixture. Stir and cook for 5 minutes more. Press the little bag with herbs between two spoons and remove.

CANDEEL

This drink belongs to a different type of festivity. It is a very old custom—although in the cities it has disappeared, it lives on among the farmers—that of showing a new baby to the friends of her (or his) mamma. It usually happens when the mother feels well enough to sit up in bed and enjoys wearing her most becoming bed jacket. The baby looks its very best in its christening robes, an old heirloom of handmade lace and bows. The friends admire the little newcomer, while eating various cakes, exchanging the latest gossip, and drinking Candeel out of special cups. Sometimes oblong in form, always highly decorated, they are now a cherished item of the antique shops. New ones are not made any more.

4 eggs
1 cup sugar
1 teaspoon grated lemon rind
Juice of 1 lemon
1 bottle white wine
1 stick cinnamon

Beat the eggs with the sugar until light, add the lemon rind and the lemon juice. Add the wine, and warm the mixture slightly, stirring well all the time with a wire whisk. The mixture is not allowed to boil. Add cinnamon.

CLARET CUP (warm)

This drink is called *Bisschop*, meaning Bishop, probably because of its red color. It is drunk on family gatherings in the winter. One must not forget that whisky is not our national drink, as it is in America and England. It is imported and very expensive. Only the upper classes drink it, and ninety per cent of the population has never tasted it. And as everybody wants to have a good time, one must invent another drink.

15 cloves
1 orange
1 lemon
1 cup sugar
1 stick cinnamon
2 bottles red wine

Stick the cloves in the orange and the lemon. Dissolve the sugar in 2 cups hot water and add these ingredients with the cinnamon to the wine. Put over a very slow fire for about ½ hour and strain.

PUNCH IMPERIAL

2 tablespoons tea
1 cup sugar
Juice of 3 lemons
Juice of 3 oranges
½ bottle rum or arrack
1 bottle white wine
½ bottle champagne

Prepare 1 cup very strong tea. Strain and dissolve the sugar, add the fruit juices and the arrack. Cool. Add the white wine, put on ice, and add the champagne just before serving.

Cold drinks are popular in the summer for garden parties, balls, and so on.

KALTE ENTE
"Cold Duck"

2 bottles Rhine wine
Rind of 1 lemon
¼ cup brandy
1 bottle champagne

Pour in a large bowl the wine, lemon rind, and the brandy. Cover and put on ice. Remove the lemon rind before serving and add the champagne. When this drink is made in large quantities, you may add a bottle of soda water.

Birthdays are celebrated more elaborately in Holland than in any other country in Europe, as we do not have name days. Family and friends come together to congratulate the unfortunate victim on having added another year to his or her age. Genever, or Dutch gin, is the popular favorite of all the drinks on those occasions, but as they are sold in bottles, I cannot give you the recipe. But another drink, very popular with the ladies, is the following one.

ADVOCATE
Advocaat

12 eggs
2 cups sugar
2 teaspoons vanilla
4 cups French brandy

Beat the eggs until light with the sugar and the vanilla. Put in a double boiler and add the brandy, but very slowly, stirring all the time with a wire whisk. Cool.

Serve in glasses with a little grated nutmeg on top, and with whipped cream. This "drink" is eaten with a spoon.

I will conclude this chapter by adding an old family recipe with the strange name of Hoppel-Poppel. What this means, I do not know—maybe it is a corruption of a French or English word—but for me it will always mean a souvenir of gay parties in bygone days.

HOPPEL-POPPEL

4 egg yolks
½ cup sugar
1 cup rum or arrack
¼ teaspoon grated nutmeg
1 cup heavy cream, whipped

Beat the egg yolks until light with the sugar, add, stirring well, the rum and the nutmeg, and fold in the whipped cream. Chill well. Like Advocate, this "drink" is eaten with a spoon. It could serve quite well as a dessert, accompanied by cakes or cookies. If you have an electric mixer, this is easy to make and worth while trying out.

A very simple version of a painting by Jan Steen. Saint Nicolas night, painted in the second half of the 17th century. Rijksmuseum, Amsterdam.

SINT NICOLAAS
A Festival for Children

The evening of Sinterklaas, as he is called in Dutch, is the children's party of the year. It is the evening which brings joy and merriment to all Dutch families. Sinterklaas is an entirely different person from the Santa Claus who frolics around America at Christmastime, with his sledge and reindeer. This is a stately bishop, who arrives from Spain by boat, accompanied by his faithful servant, Black Peter. As the patron of children and sailors he can be traced back in Spain to the time of the Moors. Peter wears the seventeenth-century Spanish costume, with beret and white ruff.

To be able to visit every family in Holland, rich and poor alike, he rides his famous white stallion over the rooftops and dispenses his presents through the chimney. Black Peter, or *Zwarte Piet*, carries on his back a huge sackful of presents for the children who were well behaved during the past year, but a birch for the naughty ones.

Preparations start at least ten days before the big evening, and in the meantime the tension mounts: who will receive presents and praise, or for the unlucky ones, birch strokes and punishment?

During these days the children put one of their shoes —filled with bread, hay, or a carrot for Sinterklaas's horse—in front of the fireplace. Before going to bed they sing special songs which are taught to them at school. Next morning the food has gone and a little present or some sweets has taken its place. On the way to school they will tell each other, bragging, what the good saint has brought them.

On the big evening the whole family with its closest friends and children gathers to receive Sinterklaas, singing Sinterklaas songs in anticipation of the Bishop's arrival. Suddenly a knock on the door is heard and there enters the stately saint in full bishop's garb with his staff and long white beard. He is a friend or relation of the family, who knows everybody very well, but in his make-up no child could recognize him. After being welcomed by the head of the family and being seated in the best armchair, he asks his Peter for the big "Golden Book" in which everybody's good and bad deeds of the

Saint Nicolas

past year are recorded. Distributing the presents, he praises or reprimands the children and grown-ups alike. After he has left, the presents, accompanied by an amusing little rhyme making fun of the receiver's good or not-so-good side of his character, are opened.

Now that the tension created has been relieved, drink and food are distributed. The children drink Slemp and the grown-ups Claret Cup (see Beverages for Parties chapter). The sweet and solid foods consumed on this occasion are of a bewildering number and variety. People present each other with letters of chocolate up to eight inches in size, corresponding to their initials. Or with puppets made of a special tough gingerbread dough (*taai-taai*) in male and female forms, roughly resembling the jacks and queens of a pack of cards. The female of the species is called *vrijster* and the male *vrijer* (the sweetheart and the suitor). Needless to say, all this is shared and consumed on the spot. In between, there is Speculaas (see below), or Spiced Cookies, marzipan, baked fondant, nuts, etc., until later in the evening the party settles down to real business. At that time large platters are brought in with heaps of apple fritters and—the most devastating of all—the national Oliebollen or Dutch Doughnuts.

I will start to give you the recipe for Hard Fondant, made of sugar to which an essence has been added, such as strawberry essence, etc. This fondant is made in special molds in the shape of hearts (all sizes!), stars, squares, etc. Or small round ones the size of a dollar are used. As these are not available in America, one can use lids of tins, such as cigarette tins or cooky tins. The following recipe is very easy to make, and a successful one.

HARD FONDANT
Borstplaat

½ pound sugar
4 tablespoons milk or water
Flavoring essence (vanilla, pineapple, raspberry, etc.)
5 drops glycerine

Put the sugar and the milk or water in a small pan and bring to a boil. Let this boil until a drop of the liquid falling from a spoon makes a thread. Remove from the fire. Add a few drops of essence and stir continually (especially round the sides of the pan). Keep stirring until the mixture has lost its transparency and starts getting more solid. Stir in the glycerine. Have greased lids of tins ready, about ⅓ inch high, pour the mixture into these, and let it become solid. Unmold by putting them for 1 second in hot water.

There are various kinds of this sweet.

If you are fond of ginger:

½ teaspoon ginger powder
½ pound sugar
1 tablespoon preserved ginger, finely chopped with its liquid

Mix the ginger powder with the sugar and boil with 4 tablespoons water for 10 minutes. Add the chopped ginger and cook for 2 minutes more. Remove from the fire, etc. (see Hard Fondant, above).

To prepare Cream Borstplaat, use cream instead of water.

To prepare Coffee Borstplaat, use half coffee, half cream.

SPICED COOKIES
Speculaas

¼ cup shelled almonds
1 pound flour
½ pound butter
1 tablespoon milk
½ pound brown sugar
4 teaspoons baking powder
1 teaspoon salt
1 tablespoon cinnamon
1 teaspoon powdered cloves
1 teaspoon grated nutmeg
½ teaspoon pepper
½ teaspoon powder anise

Pour boiling water over the shelled almonds. Let them stand for 5 minutes. Drain and pour cold water over them. Remove the skins. Knead the other ingredients into a supple ball. Add more milk if necessary. Roll the dough with a lightly floured rolling pin until it is ¾ inch thick. Place on a greased baking sheet and cut it into fairly large pieces. Press the almonds in the dough. Preheat a 425° F. oven for 7 minutes. Reduce the heat and bake in a 325° F. oven for about 25 minutes. It should be nicely brown.

DUTCH DOUGHNUTS

Oliebollen

1½ cakes yeast
1½ cups milk
3 cups bread flour
2 eggs
2 tablespoons sugar
2 tablespoons raisins
1 tablespoon chopped candied orange peel
½ tablespoon grated lemon rind
1 teaspoon salt
Oil or fat for frying
Confectioners' sugar

Dissolve the yeast in a deep bowl in 3 tablespoons lukewarm milk. Put in another bowl the bread flour. With a wooden spoon, stir in, one by one, the eggs. Slowly add the rest of the milk. Stir until all lumps have gone. Add sugar, raisins, orange peel, and grated lemon rind. Add this mixture to the yeast. Cover with a cloth and set to rise for about 1½ hours. Add the salt. Fry in deep oil or fat (370° F.), dropping in a tablespoon of the dough at a time. Drain on absorbent paper. Sprinkle with confectioners' sugar.

APPLE FRITTERS

Appelbeignets

12 apples, peeled and cored
½ pound bread flour
About 1½ cups beer
½ teaspoon salt
Oil or fat for frying

Cut the apples crosswise into ⅓-inch slices. To make

the fritter batter, combine the flour and the beer with a few quick strokes. Stir with a wooden spoon until there are no more lumps in this mixture. Add salt. Dip the apple slices in this batter and fry them in deep oil or fat, 370° F. Drain the fritters on absorbent paper and sprinkle with confectioners' sugar.

BANANA FRITTERS
Bananen beignets

Peel and cut bananas into halves lengthwise. Prepare them in the same way as in the recipe for Apple Fritters.

PINEAPPLE FRITTERS
Ananas beignets

1 can pineapple slices

Drain the pineapple slices and follow the recipe for Apple Fritters.

Indonesian dishes

INDONESIAN DISHES

Many Dutchmen have spent part of their lives in Indonesia, and when they returned to Holland they brought with them a taste for Indonesian food. This they have not kept to themselves. It has become customary, even among people who have never been to the Far East, to eat Indonesian or Chinese food regularly.

There are many Indonesian and Chinese restaurants in Holland, not only in the larger cities but also in the smaller provincial towns. There exist countless Indonesian dishes, some of which take hours to prepare; but a few easy ones have become so popular that they can be regarded as "national dishes."

The Indonesian Nassi Goreng (fried rice) and the Sateh (broiled meat on skewers) or the Chinese loempiah (rissolés) and Bahmi can even be bought at every snack bar and lunch counter.

A book on Dutch food therefore cannot be called complete without a few recipes for Indonesian food.

NASSI GORENG

Always use cold, cooked rice for this dish.

Foolproof way to cook rice:

1 cup rice, rinsed 4–5 times
2 cups water
Pinch of salt
4 SERVINGS

Bring the rice to a boil and simmer for 20 minutes. Never lift the lid of the pot, or stir. Wrap the pot in a thick layer of newspapers and put it between pillows. Let it stand for at least ½ hour. This will give you dry, crisp grains, and provide you with a handy way to keep the rice warm, if need be, for hours.

For Nassi Goreng always use *cold* rice. Cooking it the day before is the easiest and best way.

INDONESIAN FRIED RICE

Nassi goreng

2 medium-sized onions, chopped fine
2 cloves garlic, crushed
1 teaspoon red chili pepper, chopped fine
1 teaspoon salt
Oil
3 cups cooked, cold rice
½ pound roasted pork or ham
4 eggs
1 tablespoon butter

4 SERVINGS

Fry the onions with the garlic, red pepper, and salt in oil in a heavy skillet until the onions are brown. Add the rice and fry till golden brown, stirring frequently with a wooden spoon. Dice the pork or ham into small pieces and add to the rice. Fry for 5 more minutes.

Beat 4 eggs; add 1 tablespoon water. Heat the butter in a frying pan and bake an omelette. Cut into long strips. Serve the Nassi Goreng with these strips on top. Some people prefer a fried egg to the omelette.

This dish is eaten from a soup plate with a spoon and fork. A knife is never used. Beer is the drink that goes with it. Instead of pork or ham, roasted chicken or prawns/shrimps (1 cup) can be used.

As side dishes one should use:

2-inch pieces cucumber cut lengthwise
Roasted peanuts
Chutney
Baked Bananas

BAKED BANANAS
Pisang goreng

4 bananas
2 tablespoons butter
Pinch of salt
Lemon juice

4 SERVINGS

Peel the bananas and cut in half lengthwise. Place them in a well-greased baking dish. Dot with butter and sprinkle with salt and lemon juice. Bake in a hot oven (450° F.) for 6 minutes.

CHINESE RISSOLÉS
Loempiahs

3 eggs
½ cup flour
⅔ cup water
Pinch of salt

For the stuffing:

10 tablespoons *taugé* (bean sprouts)
8 tablespoons fried chicken, shredded
8 tablespoons roast pork, shredded
2 tablespoons chopped celery stalks and leaves
1 tablespoon chopped chives
1 tablespoon soy-bean sauce
Oil

12 RISSOLÉS

Make a light pancake batter with the eggs, flour, water, and salt. Fry twelve very thin pancakes.

For the stuffing: Mix all the ingredients together, divide into twelve parts, and put 2½ tablespoons of the mixture in the middle of each pancake. Roll the pancakes up, moisten the edges with egg white, fold, and led stand for a few minutes, till they stick together.

Fry in deep hot oil or fat until crisp and golden brown. Drain on absorbent paper.

CHINESE NOODLES

Bahmi

1½ pounds dry Chinese *mi* (noodles)
½ pound fried pork
6 tablespoons shredded leeks
4 tablespoons chopped celery stalks and leaves
2 tablespoons *taugé* (bean sprouts)
2 cups shredded Chinese cabbage
2 cloves minced garlic
1 cup shrimps or prawns
2 tablespoons soy-bean sauce
Oil

6 SERVINGS

Soak the *mi* in warm water and drain. Bring a pan of water to the boil and put in the soaked *mi*. Wait until the water is again on the boil, then turn off the heat! Leave the *mi* in the hot water until done, but don't let it get too soft. Drain.

In the meantime dice the fried pork. Fry the leeks, celery, and Chinese cabbage with the garlic in some oil.

Add a little water and the *taugé* and simmer till half done. The vegetables prepared this way taste at their best in the Bahmi. Mix the vegetables into the Bahmi, add the meat and shrimps, and season with 2 tablespoons soy-bean sauce. Reheat for a few minutes in the oven.

MEAT ON SKEWERS
Sateh

There are three different kinds of Sateh:

Chicken Sateh — Sateh ajam
Lamb Sateh — Sateh kambing
Pork Sateh — Sateh babi

Cut the meat or chicken in bite-size cubes, rub with salt and pepper, and let stand for 15 minutes. Thread five or six pieces onto a skewer. Baste with oil and roast in a slow oven (325° F.), turning frequently, or grill on a barbecue.

As the genuine sauces that go with the Satehs are very complicated, and require a great many Indonesian ingredients, I will give you a short-cut recipe for a sauce for the three of them.

SATEH SAUCE

4 tablespoons peanut butter
½ teaspoon crushed red chili pepper
2 teaspoons molasses
1 tablespoon soy-bean sauce
1 clove minced garlic
Few drops lemon juice

Mix the peanut butter with 8 tablespoons hot water, stir in all the other ingredients, and simmer for 5 minutes. Cover the Satehs with the hot sauce (sufficient for eight pieces) just before serving.

And last but not least:

SAMBAL OELEK

This is an Indonesian chili seasoning eaten with all Indonesian dishes to heighten their taste. Without Sambal, no dish is complete.

2 tablespoons red chili peppers, chopped very fine
½ teaspoon salt
½ tablespoon oil
½ teaspoon lemon juice
½ teaspoon grated lemon rind

Mix all the ingredients into a paste. This can be kept for some time in a tightly closed jar for further use.

INDEX